Marketing to the Affluent

Marketing to the Affluent

Thomas J. Stanley, Ph.D.

IRWIN
Professional Publishing®
Chicago • London • Singapore

© Thomas J. Stanley, Ph.D. 1988

This publication is designed to provide accurate and
authoritative information in regard to the subject matter
covered. It is sold with the understanding that neither the
author nor the publisher is engaged in rendering legal, accounting,
or other professional service. If legal advice or other expert
assistance is required, the services of a competent
professional person should be sought.

*From a Declaration of Principles jointly adopted by a Committee
of the American Bar Association and a Committee of Publishers.*

Acquisitions editor: Susan Glinert Stevens, Ph.D.
Project editor: Joan A. Hopkins
Production manager: Bette Ittersagen
Compositor: TC Systems, Inc.
Typeface: 11/13 Times Roman
Printer: Arcata Graphics/Kingsport

Library of Congress Cataloging-in-Publication Data

Stanley, Thomas J.
    Marketing to the affluent / Thomas J. Stanley.
        p.   cm.
    Includes index.
        ISBN 1-556-23105-9 : $49.95   ISBN 0-7863-0532-0 (paperback)
        1. Rich as consumers–United States.   2. Marketing–United States.
I. Title.
HF5415.3.S73 1988
656.8'348–dc19   88-2629

Printed in the United States of America

16 17 18 19 20 QK 0 9 8 7

For Janet, Sarah, and Brad

About the author . . .
Dr. Thomas J. Stanley is the head of the Affluent Market Institute, an organization that designs research-based marketing strategies and training programs for identifying, attracting, and retaining wealthy customers. The Institute was on *American Demographics'* list of the 100 best sources for marketing information. Dr. Stanley has developed affluent market strategies and sales training programs for many national and regional corporations. His work on the affluent market has been cited in many publications such as *The Wall Street Journal, The New York Times, Forbes, Fortune, Time, Reader's Digest, Working Woman, Advertising Age,* and on major network and cable news programs.

Dr. Stanley has been a main platform speaker at the Million Dollar Round Table's international convention. He was also a top-rated main platform speaker for many other important organizations.

He is the author of two other marketing classics, *Selling to the Affluent* and *Networking with the Affluent and Their Advisors. Marketing to the Affluent* was selected by the editors of *Best of Business Quarterly* as a finalist for the Benjamin Franklin Business Book of the Year award and as one of 10 outstanding business books in America.

PREFACE

In the mid-1950s, Fieldston was one of the wealthiest neighborhoods within the boundaries of New York City. When I was nine years old, I convinced my older sister to give up our practice of trick-or-treating in our own blue-collar neighborhood. That Halloween, we decided to get into the big time and walk one-half mile across three social classes into Fieldston. The trip took us through the woods into total darkness. The large, exclusive houses were well spaced from each other. We expected a lot of competition, but we encountered no other trick-or-treaters there.

The first house we approached was a very large, Spanish hacienda-type structure situated on several choice acres. No lights were on, but I knocked on the door anyway. Nothing happened, but I kept on knocking. Finally, James Mason, the actor, opened the door. He was startled, and I remember distinctly what he said: "No one ever trick-or-treated me, hit on me" during Halloween.

Often, marketers make the assumption that all of the affluent are heavily prospected. My finding on this occasion was just the opposite. James Mason, assuming that no other gremlins would visit, said, "Ladies and gentlemen, I will give you all the silver I have in my home." And he did—every nickel, dime, quarter, and half-dollar he could find.

The next house we visited had a sign posted on the front door: "My husband is ill; please do not ring the doorbell. I have placed coins in different packages for different group sizes in the milkbox outside." I opened the milkbox and found packages for groups of two, groups of three, groups of four and so on. There were four of us. Our integrity was being tested. This was our first experience with the concept of discretionary funds. We did, in fact, only take the "group of four" envelope and left. Even today, every time I visit New York City, I feel an urge to ask a cabdriver to take me up to Fieldston and stop at every milkbox!

This first experience with the affluent market is still vivid in my memory. Those two sales calls generated the same number of dollars that we normally expected from over 100 calls in our own neighborhood.

The basic ingredients of my success in Fieldston parallel those that have enabled many of the top sales professionals to penetrate the affluent market. These extraordinary sales professionals (ESPs) demonstrate exceptional courage, and they are relentless in asking the basic marketing question—"Will you do business with me?"—of prospects who, like James Mason, often have more wealth, more status, and more experience than they do.

Most ESPs have their own unique methods of identifying affluent prospects. The affluent, however, are not as easy to identify as some observers may think. Persons who have accumulated considerable wealth often do not demonstrate this fact via conspicuous symbols. If one were to knock at random on 100 doors in America, on average not even 2 in 100 of the people who answered would be affluent. On the other hand, most of the top marketers who target the affluent have had many Fieldston experiences of their own and have therefore come to realize that precise targeting of the affluent is essential.

ACKNOWLEDGMENTS

The cornerstone for this book was put in place during the fall of 1973. At that time, I undertook my first study of the affluent population. This book reflects the knowledge and insights that I gained from that initial study and from the dozens of studies of this segment that followed it. Along the road of gathering intelligence about the wealthy, I have been assisted by truly extraordinary people.

I am indebted to my wife, Janet, for her guidance, patience, and assistance in the development of the manuscript. I am also indebted to Dr. Bill Danko of SUNY, who sacrificed much of his "oceans of spare time" to help me with this project.

Special thanks are accorded to Howell Ann Bell and Susan McNair for their help in number and word crunching. I owe a deep debt of gratitude to Miss Sharon Weaver for typing the preliminary drafts of the manuscript and to Mr. Bill Moore for his sage editorial comments.

Finally, I wish to acknowledge the contribution of my father, Thomas J. Stanley, Sr., who stated on numerous occasions that the affluent are more concerned with selling than buying.

Thomas J. Stanley, Ph.D.

CONTENTS

CHAPTER 1

AN INTRODUCTION TO THE AFFLUENT MARKET: THE HARD FACTS

THE LETTER TO BRADFORD

Dear Brad:

Your request for advice concerning a career change is flattering. It appears from your letter that you have already made up your mind to become a sales professional. On balance, I am in favor of your decision.

I do not pretend to be an expert about the lifestyles of people who sell. Nevertheless, from my research findings I can give you many of the hard facts about this profession. I believe that the opportunities for you are excellent. However, you will have to really assert yourself if you plan to become a top producer. Also, if you are interested in generating a high income, you must be selective in what you sell. Three of the top-ranked areas are security sales, insurance sales, and real estate sales. The materials that you have requested are applicable to a wide variety of products and services ranging from asset management and financial planning to clothing for executives and gems and precious metals.

With your background, a security sales position may be an ideal choice. I estimate that there is a higher concentration of security/financial sales professionals than attorneys in the six-figure (affluent) income bracket. Some may argue that this is a temporary phenomenon related to the recent changes in the market. In reality, the security sales profession has often ranked near the top even during mediocre market conditions.

As a rookie selling investments, you may wonder why some of your new colleagues are top producers while others are only marginally productive at best. Those who are most successful are tougher mentally; rejection does not discourage them. I know of instances where millionaire prospects have said no to the same sales professional four times in six months. The fifth time the situation was right—the prospects became clients. Those who reject you should be debriefed about their future financial lifestyle. Time your next solicitation according to the prospect's situational needs—for example, bonus income, a windfall, the birth of a grandchild. The best sales professionals learn from their mistakes and capitalize on them. Do autopsies and catalog your setbacks.

There are only so many hours in even the longest day. You must learn to work smarter so that you receive the optimal return on your marketing efforts. Place your greatest efforts with prospects who have the greatest potential. Even some of your colleagues who are veterans have difficulty in distinguishing those who have money to invest from those who do not. My research suggests that far too many Americans have one goal in life: to look affluent. All too often, investing is given stepchild treatment. Only the money that remains after consumption is invested. This is an interesting decision calculus when the pro forma budget system is to spend all that is generated from employment.

Obviously, some people who look and live as if they are affluent do have considerable dollars to invest. Unfortunately, people who display wealth attract marketers in droves. I find, however, that for every household worth $10 million in a so-called affluent neighborhood, there are many more with net worths of under $500,000. Along these lines, I believe that a major objection to your solicitations will be *no money to invest*. But people who are supposed to be affluent have a difficult time admitting to you that this is the case. You must discipline yourself to recognize that symbols of wealth and dollars to invest are not complementary to each other; they are substitutes for each other.

To be successful in this industry, Brad, you must clear your memory banks of 26 years of indoctrination by the press, television, and motion pictures about the affluent in America. The reality is not "Dynasty" or "Dallas." A television show that depicts the lifestyle of a typical American millionaire would be a flop! The "real" American millionaire is John Doe, age 57, who has been married for 32 years to the same woman, owns a highly productive small or medium-sized business, has two children, and works 10–14 hours a day, six days a week.

This past summer, I read a book entitled *Memoirs: Ten Years and Twenty Days* by Karl Doenitz. Admiral Doenitz was in charge of the German U-boats during World War II. In his book, he spoke of his most famous captain, Otto Kretschmer of U99. Why was Kretschmer so successful while many others were not? Kretschmer stated that "my proclivity was to surface in the middle of the convoy; that's where the ammunition and other important ships were." Younger, less experienced captains attacked from outside the convoy, often encountering decoys and unimportant ships that contained nonessentials. To the unsophisticated eye, however, these ships looked as if they contained the important cargo.

Brad, don't waste your marketing torpedoes on decoys. Surface in the middle of the affluent convoy. In a recent interview, I discussed some of my favorite "blue-collar millionaire categories." I mentioned that a good number of the more productive construction contractors achieve millionaire status before retiring. These people are among the least prospected affluent investors. Last week, I met a millionaire contractor at his favorite "restaurant." Actually, it is a combination gas station, convenience market, and makeshift lunchroom. Five other millionaire contractors and several excavation/foundation contractors were also present. Interestingly, this heart of the convoy" has never been approached by a single security broker. Why? These people are hidden in the middle of the convoy. Brokers are too busy tracking decoys—that is, prospects who just look wealthy.

People who drive trucks with dents, wear muddy boots, and have lunch in the back room of a convenience market/gas station can't be wealthy! But—more than $10 million is represented at this strategic window, which is open every Thursday for about 50 minutes. Here is a great opportunity to reach these people, because they are loose and not in the middle of giving instructions to their crews. A clever broker could enter this convoy and capture the fleet. No broker ever calls on these self-designated "good old country boys." Make this month your month for targeting construction contractors and excavation/foundation contractors.

Selling investments to the affluent is a lot like fishing. To be successful in either area, you must understand who the "catch" or prospects are, what their habits are, when they are ready to be caught, what turns them on, and what turns them off. The best sales professionals in your industry are flexible. They will change marketing methods when conditions and prospects change.

Last June, I took a fishing trip to the top trout stream in the East, the Ausable River in northern New York. On the second day there, I approached a large pool in the trophy section. Two expensively equipped fly fisherman were just moving downstream. They told me I was wasting my time fishing in the pool. They had fished there all day and had caught nothing. I asked them how they were fishing, and they replied, "Surface fishing with dry flies." I mentioned that deep-running lures might be more successful because the fish might be in the deep pools. One of the fishermen stated that if the fish weren't attracted by surface lures, then he was not interested in catching them. In the same pool that day and during the next two days, using deep-running lures, I caught eight of the largest trout of my career; all were over 23 inches long. Even after seeing my success that day, one of the fly fishermen said disgustedly, "I think it's a disgrace to catch trout with ultralight equipment." My reply was, "When I travel 1,000 miles, I want to catch fish. One must use the techniques that are most productive given the water conditions."

This analogy holds true for the securities industry. All over this country, brokers are using the same stale techniques on the same target markets. Hardly a week passes by without a broker calling me and requesting a list of millionaires. When I ask such brokers what they will do with the list, they reply, "Telemarketing." Telemarketing 9 A.M. to 5 P.M.! The very best sales professionals learn to fish by developing their own proprietary lists of affluent prospects. Lists that are widely available have no strategic advantage.

Most affluent prospects are different from other people. They typically work harder and longer hours. If you insist on calling them on the telephone, try calling before 8 A.M. at their office. They are often the first in the office and the last to go home. But before you call them, attempt to find out as much about them as you possibly can. Always have some common ground beyond investments. When you have identified and qualified a really affluent prospect, try to make an appointment to meet him in person. There is no substitute for a face-to-face meeting with a prospect.

What should you discuss with a prospect? Of all the questions I ask the affluent, none is more revealing than the question regarding the traits they look for when selecting a financial adviser. The most desirable trait is "empathy for my goals." Affluent prospects will be favorably impressed with you if you take the time to develop an understanding of their needs, desires, risk-taking propensities, and so on.

Never attempt to shove an investment down a prospect's throat when he resists. The affluent market is situation-driven, and gestapo tactics are unproductive in the long run. If the prospect is not in the right situation, if his personal timing is not right, he will not buy. Thus, you must try to stay in contact. You must present your offer at the proper time. I often find that an affluent consumer has money to invest only once during the entire year. This period of sensitivity may last for only two weeks. Thus, you can cold-call 25 affluent people and find only one who happens to be susceptible to your message. Don't be shy about asking prospects when they think situations conducive to investing, such as bonuses, will take place.

Business owners are not the only prospects with dollars to invest. One of the trends in the affluent market is the growth of incentive compensation for employees. More and more businesses are giving substantial extra compensation to employees who perform. This bonus compensation is often distributed at only one time period of the year. This system is actually good for your business because people who receive a predictable payment each period tend to spend all or most of it. A single, large payment is less likely to be spent so quickly. The prospect is much more likely to be sensitive to your ideas about investment opportunities concerning this windfall. Thus, place a priority on prospects who will probably receive large bonus payments. Take Edith, for example, a sales professional in high-tech country. I spoke to her sales manager at a recent dinner party. She had just closed a $3 million deal. Her commission was 8 percent, or $240,000 for one sale. Edith, who is in her early 30s, has no financial adviser, no brokerage relationship. What will happen to her windfall bonus? Her window will not be open for too much longer.

The Edith scenario will be played out many times during the next 10 years. For it is likely that by 1995 the age group 35–44 will have the greatest number of households earning six-figure incomes. More babies were born in this country in 1957 than in any other year. Those babies born within 10 years of this date represent the so-called pig passing through the boa constrictor or baby boomers moving through the age distribution. Obviously, you will often find prospects who appear to be "too young to have a six-figure income." In these cases, you need to remind yourself about the case of Edith and other top sales professionals.

In spite of the baby boom, do not overlook the traditional millionaire market. The large majority of millionaires (those with a net worth of $1 million or more) are over 50 years of age. Also, only about 1 in 10 of them are under 40 years of age. The millionaire designation is the standard definition of affluence in terms of wealth accumulations.

Another opportunity is the growth of small and medium-sized businesses, especially those that sell services and/or intellect. Such firms often generate substantial amounts of profits for their owners. Unlike other types of traditional businesses, they have minimum fixed investments and lower operating costs overall. Thus, the owners have the constant problem of "a too high realized income." In addition to needing your advice with regard to their personal investment problems, they will also need your advice about pension and profit sharing programs and investment opportunities for corporate cash.

I know what you're thinking: "Dr. Stanley would make a great client." Someone recently referred to me as an *expert on wealth.* Does being an expert on the affluent translate into one's personal net worth? On December 20, 1984, Jackie Judd of CBS interviewed me about my research on millionaires. During the course of the interview, she had the nerve to ask me if I was a millionaire. She seemed shocked when I said no.

I'm not feeling guilty about not being a millionaire. And I'm not too worried either. Most millionaires do not become so until they are over 50 years of age. In fact, I judge my own economic position according to the wealth equation that I developed with Dr. Bill Danko of SUNY. Simply stated, your net worth should equal 10 percent of your age times your annual realized household income ($0.10 \times \text{Age} \times \text{Income} = \text{Expected net worth}$). If your actual net worth is above this expected figure, I consider you affluent, given your age and income characteristics.

Hopefully, with this information you will be able to transform some prospects into serious clients. Many high-income producers are unaware that they are well below normal in accumulated wealth. Be certain not to show them your personal position on the wealth equation until you are on the other side of the norm. Eventually, you may want to demonstrate how well some of your current affluent clients are positioned on the wealth vector. By the way, Brad, there are many ways to improve your own position. These methods include (a) increasing your net worth faster than your age or income—put yourself on a restricted consumption diet and simultaneously develop a viable investment strategy for yourself; (b) decreasing your realized income without decreasing your net worth; and (c) decreasing your age! Obviously, the younger you become, the less likely you are to be far along on the wealth vector. Unfortunately, I cannot help you become younger. However, several of our top research scholars are developing a new youth serum that will enable people to reverse the aging process. I am looking for the right company to help me go public with this new venture. Do you have any suggestions?

I wish you well in your new profession. Given the opportunities in the market, if you don't succeed, you have only yourself to blame. I have enclosed some information that should help you become an extraordinary sales professional (ESP). ESPs are sales professionals who generate incomes of six figures or more from sales commissions. A profile of these top producers is also enclosed.

Best wishes,

Thomas J. Stanley, Ph.D.
Chairman
Affluent Market Institute

TJS:sw

COURAGE: CHARACTERISTIC ONE OF THE ESP

The trait most often found among ESPs is courage. That trait is expressed in many ways. Certainly, it takes courage to earn one's income purely from sales commissions. Sales cannot be inventoried. Thus, there are few, if any, income guarantees in the business called selling.

Compensation by commission only suggests that the sales professional operates almost independently of a sales manager's mandates. The commission sales professional often sets his own sales standards, office hours, call plan, and prospecting efforts. In this regard, the sales professional operates almost like an entrepreneur. But most entrepreneurs, as well as most sales professionals, never become truly successful. Most fail within a few years or remain marginal at best.

There are many reasons why most sales professionals never achieve ESP status. However, the most fundamental reason relates to courage. Courage is especially necessary in selling to the affluent. Sales professionals with considerable courage demonstrate this characteristic in their prospecting. Stated simply, most ESPs will tell you that they are more successful than other sales professionals because they ask more people the really important question: "Will you do business with me?" Courage also means being able to call yet another prospect after having been turned down by the last 100 prospects.

Few ESPs inherit a group of clients or even a Rolodex. Few have been so popular before entering sales that prospects pursue them once they enter the sales profession. No, the vast majority of the people who market to the affluent are completely self-made successes. Countless sales professionals have achieved ESP status before their 30th birthday. It is important for aspiring ESPs to recognize the age issue in relationship to courage. Most of the people who have accumulated even modest amounts of wealth are at least 40 years of age or older. Millionaires in America, on average, are in their middle to late 50s. It takes a special type of courage for young sales professionals to ask affluent prospects, who in many cases are old enough to be their parents, "Will you do business with me?" Why would someone who is significantly more affluent, older, and worldly deal with an aspiring ESP? Part of the explanation lies in the matching of personality traits. Most of the affluent people in America are either business owners or employees who are compensated according to their performance. In fact, one category of the affluent that aspiring ESPs often overlook comprises those who have themselves achieved affluent status. Most successful people have considerable courage and admire courage in others. Remember that most of the affluent in America acquired their own wealth. They had the courage to undertake entrepreneurial and other business opportunities that were associated with considerable risk.

Many of the present American millionaires will not produce children who will repeat as winners in the economic game. The children of these millionaires are often at odds with their successful parents. In fact, there is a direct relationship between the number of years that a "child" lives in its parents' home and the level of a household's affluence. It is not at all unusual for the sons and daughters of the affluent to remain in their parents' home and be supported by them even after their 30th birthday. This, of course, does not include "outpatient care." Therefore, it is not surprising that the affluent parent will respond positively to a young, aspiring ESP who demonstrates significantly more courage and independence than his own children do.

One of the greatest ESPs of all time, Ray Kroc, used the courage dimension in selecting potential McDonald's franchise owners and executives. He sold his first franchise outside California for $950 to Sanford and Betty Agate (see John Love, *McDonald's: Behind the Arches,* [Toronto: Bantam Books, 1986], pp. 78–79, 96–97). Kroc first encountered Betty Agate while she was cold-calling people in Chicago's financial district. Kroc's secretary asked her, "What the hell is a Jew doing selling Catholic Bibles?" "Making a living," was her reply. Kroc reasoned that anyone courageous enough to do what Betty Agate was doing would be a prime prospect for purchasing one of his franchises. He found, as many others have, that sales professionals are often the easiest prospects to close.

Cold callers who prospected Kroc and his executives included some of "the most important hires McDonald's made . . . Robert Ryan, McDonald's treasurer, and Richard Boylan, senior executive vice president and chief financial officer . . . two life insurance salesmen [who] walked into McDonald's, to sell executive life insurance." But instead of selling life insurance and estate planning, they bought the McDonald's concept.

I am still waiting for a wire from an ESP that states: "Today, just before receiving communion from the Holy Father at St. Peter's Cathedral in Rome, I asked him if I could help him manage his company's cash accounts." I would be just as thrilled to receive a call from an aspiring ESP who states: "Yesterday, in person, I cold-called Lee Iacocca while he was presiding over a board of directors meeting. I asked Lee and his colleagues for their business. They all seemed to be impressed by my request."

KNOWLEDGE: CHARACTERISTIC TWO OF THE ESP

Analyze the career development of ESPs who target the affluent, and what will you find? Most of them first established a beachhead in this market by positioning themselves as specialists. Many remain specialists throughout their careers. Generally, a market segment can be penetrated more rapidly and more deeply by concentrating one's firepower. Superior knowledge of a narrowly defined set of offerings and particular subsegments of the affluent market is an ESP hallmark. Conversely, those who fail to reach ESP status often spread themselves too thin. They attempt to master multiple offerings and multiple target segments.

The strategy of the deep and narrow is played out every day in the marketing arena. Emerging marketing organizations as well as aspiring ESPs can benefit from the deep and narrow strategies that launched the Banana Republic, the Gap, the Limited, and so on. It is unlikely that any of these retail firms would have survived their first year if they had begun by offering a wide variety of products to all market segments.

The deep and narrow strategy has been adopted by most of the ESPs who target the affluent. Tom Cloud, a former student of mine and the founder/head of Cloud and Associates, provides a perfect example of how the deep and narrow strategy was successfully implemented. Not long after graduating from college, Tom decided to become a financial planner. Like most ESPs, he instinctively realized that there were far too many "me too" generalists in his chosen profession. After carefully analyzing the current service offerings and various affluent market segments, he concluded that few, if any, financial planners focused on providing investment advice and tangible products in the areas of investment-grade gems and precious metals. Once he decided to go deep and narrow in terms of offerings, Tom applied the rule of marginal analysis in targeting an affluent subsegment. What segment of the affluent market would be most accessible, most responsive to his solicitations? Tom gave me the answer to this question by simply stating: "I went to high school with a fellow who became an All-Pro football player, and I was a classmate of the star running back for the same pro team. . . . I was also the football team manager for a Southeastern conference powerhouse."

Tom's initial success stemmed from focusing his energies in a service area that most others had completely ignored. In so doing, he insulated himself from competition. Each day, his insulation, his proactive barrier became stronger because he developed more and more product knowledge.

What about the other side of the equation, namely the market? Once Tom picked a narrowly defined affluent target with which he had been affiliated previously, he aggressively expanded and exploited his knowledge and his client base. His first two clients made many referrals in his behalf to other affluent athletes and their investment managers. Tom's interaction in high school and college laid the foundation for his success in target marketing.

Tom's insight in this regard parallels that of one of the most successful ESPs in America. Nick DiBari retired from the sales profession at the age of 38. The year before he retired, his compensation exceeded $1.5 million. DiBari recently stated, "College life is a more sophisticated form of interaction than high school—the main difference really is that the *contacts* made follow you throughout your career" (Nick DiBari, "Your Business Success Can Be Planned," *Sales and Marketing Management,* December 3, 1984, p. 53).

Sales and marketing managers will be particularly interested in DiBari's recommendations to aspiring ESPs. Managers, be on the lookout for young sales recruits who exploited their college experience in some of the ways that Nick recommends:

- Choose a respected school.
- Live in the dorm your first two years. You'll meet 100 times as many people that way than you will if you live off campus.
- Play every sport you are capable of playing competitively.
- Keep a relatively light academic schedule. (So what if it takes a little longer to graduate.)

- Socialize in a diverse manner—which includes partying with the so-called nerds once in a while. High school and college nerds have developed into some of the most influential and solid businessmen this world has ever seen. Marketing people must sell to them throughout their careers.
- Plan to take at least 15 credit hours of postgraduate work at night. You'll be sure to meet businessmen with all types of credentials and contacts.
- Keep in touch with all of your college and postcollege friends through the school's newsletter or alumni bulletin. You never know when you might be of help to one another. (ibid.)

Tom still targets the affluent athletic market, but he has also broadened his market horizon. He supplies both products and consultation to advisers of the affluent as well as the affluent themselves. His current strategy is much broader than the strategy he used when he founded his organization. But it is unlikely that this strategy would have enabled him to succeed initially.

The Tom Cloud case is an important means of grasping the realities of the affluent market in America. It is a myth to consider *the affluent market* as *one market*. In reality, it is many markets, a highly fragmented market. Hundreds of segments and subsegments can be defined along many dimensions, such as physical location, occupation, business ownership, life cycle, lifestyles, and patronage habits. How else can one explain why thousands of ESPs flourish by marketing to the affluent? Most of these ESPs know instinctively that they cannot thrive if other ESPs do exactly the same thing, targeting exactly the same segments, and occupy exactly the same space at the same time. Chapter 3 contains 11 case studies of ESPs who followed or will follow the deep and narrow road to success.

TECHNIQUE: CHARACTERISTIC THREE OF THE ESP

Not all ESPs have developed a unique brand of sales and marketing techniques. However, most of the ESPs I have surveyed do have one or more unique methods of relating to their target population. Interestingly, most of these methods are completely original. They are not typically found in any salesmanship textbook or even in any related literature. Most often, these sales techniques are a product of trial and error and/or instinct on the part of the ESP.

Chapter 4 contains many examples of innovative techniques that selected ESPs have developed and aggressively exploited. It is appropriate at this juncture to point out that *no one told them how to:*

- Relate to affluent widows.
- Succeed in selling qualified investors via the underdog image.
- Start a breakfast club for ESPs and millionaires.
- Ensure that affluent physicians would listen to sales proposals.
- Precipitate the prospect's need for the products and services offered.
- Surface in the middle of an affluent convoy.

Innovation in marketing is more art than science. The techniques discussed in this book are just a sampling of the unique contributions that have been made by the ESPs of this country.

SOURCES OF INFORMATION: CHARACTERISTIC FOUR OF THE ESP

Many of the ESPs I have interviewed have the instincts of a naval intelligence officer when it comes to developing accurate sources of information on the identities of persons with significant wealth. Some of these ESPs have even tapped sources that indicate when the affluent prospect is likely to have a major positive change in his cash flow.

On the other side of the coin, many marginal producers find it very difficult to identify persons with significant wealth. One problem that young sales professionals have to deal with is that much of the marketing literature produced in this country focuses on describing the consumer, the buyer, the spender, the very heavy user. Those who seek prospects with high net worth will be better served by focusing on information sources that are not part of the traditional basic marketing textbook variety.

Chapter 5 discusses several important sources of information that can be used to distinguish the affluent from the pseudoaffluent. Some of these sources also provide insights about the time in which affluent prospects will encounter favorable changes in their economic position. Much of the information presented in these sources is based on methods developed by selected ESPs and British naval intelligence. Almost all of the market intelligence sources mentioned in Chapter 5 are readily available and in the public domain.

BIG-LEAGUE ORIENTATION: CHARACTERSTIC FIVE OF THE ESP

Why are so many marketers interested in the affluent market? One reason is that the wealthiest 1 percent of U.S. families account for approximately 11 percent of the total income of U.S. families. The use of financial services and the amount of money spent on them, it is theorized, are highly related to income. The affluent often use a wide variety of financial services ranging from investment management to large lines of credit.

Another reason is that the number of affluent households in the $100,000 and over annual income category has grown 10 times as fast as the total number of households. Affluence is very often expressed in terms of net worth. Someone with a net worth in excess of $1 million is popularly regarded as affluent. The millionaire population was estimated to contain 832,602 households in 1985 and over 1.2 million in 1987. This unprecedented growth provides tremendous opportunities for those who seek to market to the very wealthy. In terms of the wealth held by individuals, two tenths of 1 percent own more than 10 percent of the net worth in America.

While it is intuitively appealing to discuss the affluent market in terms of individuals and households, there is an inherent problem with this approach, that is, the myth of the affluent consumer. When most people think of the affluent, they are likely to perceive them as consumers of homes, automobiles, clothing, and, of course, personal types of investments, insurance products, and so on. However, this is only one side of the affluent market. My research points out that the relationship between wealth and the ownership of privately held or closely held businesses is highly significant. With the exception of inherited wealth, fortunes are most often made by the founders of successful business organizations. Thus, these affluent are an important target for extraordinary sales professionals. The affluent often have significant and wide-ranging investment needs that relate to both their personal and business situations—for example, asset management financial planning, major league whole life insurance, deferred compensation, employee benefits, estate planning, keyman insurance, and buy-sell agreement products.

The ESPs with the really big-league orientation are those whose focus is not necessarily on affluent individuals, affluent neighborhoods, or affluent individuals who own businesses. The really big-league orientation is to focus on high concentrations of affluent business owners. In reality, the process described above reflects the developmental process of some ESPs. They initially start with only *courage* and aggressively prospect anyone whom they perceive to be wealthy. Those who survive tend to develop a posture of the deep and narrow. However, the deep and narrow target is often greatly limited by the ESP's self-designated trade area and other self-imposed success parameters. Innovative *techniques* and proprietary *sources* then emerge.

Despite the possession of considerable *courage,* superior *knowledge,* innovative *techniques,* and excellent *proprietary sources*, most sales professionals, including ESPs, never reach their full potential. The need to develop a *big-league orientation* and to implement a strategy based on that orientation is so obvious that it is often overlooked. Targeting individuals as opposed to high concentrations of affluent business owners is the equivalent of targeting individual sailors and ships instead of the Pacific fleet at Pearl Harbor. The fundamental theorem of marketing is to allocate one's resources where they will be most productive. On three or four days each year, some of the highest concentrations of the affluent can be found at the American Bar Association national conference; the national conference of plumbing, heating and air conditioning contractors; and the national conference of beverage wholesalers. Using conventional prospecting methods, it would probably take the ordinary sales professional years to reach the number of affluent that can be marketed at one major trade conference. Thus, enlightened ESPs are currently developing innovative methods for penetrating such "industrial strength" segments of the affluent.

For one reason or another, some sales professionals do not relate comfortably to industries that contain affluent business owners. Chapter 6 details alternative affluent targets.

EXPERTISE: CHARACTERISTIC SIX OF THE ESP

The ultimate goal of an aspiring ESP should be to develop an image of expertise in his chosen field. Expertise in this context typically relates to the traditionally defined product or service being marketed. However, expertise in areas outside one's core element can sometimes be leveraged in terms of a broader marketing strategy. Too often, ESPs are guilty of promoting themselves as sales experts and not as experts in their product and/or service. They communicate their sales achievements by placing such designations as president's council member, million dollar round table, and million dollar club on their business cards and stationery. Designations of this kind are usually more important to the ESP and his competitors than they are to most affluent prospects except in the cases where the affluent prospects want to sell something, such as real estate, a business, jewels, and so on. In these cases, they often seek a sales expert.

An affluent prospect who is interested in having someone provide him with a financial plan seeks knowledge and expert advice. He is not looking for someone who can give him advice on how to improve his personality, handshake, and prospecting technique.

Being very knowledgeable in a chosen field, whether it be pension planning for an affluent business owner or direct investment for decamillionaires, does not mean that one is perceived as an expert.

What is the difference between being very knowledgeable and being an expert? An expert is someone who is very knowledgeable in his discipline and communicates this fact aggressively and effectively. Those with knowledge who are unknown are not experts. More often than not, prospects view with skepticism claims on your part that you are an expert. One-sided, self-serving messages lack credibility.

Experts gain their status because credible sources of information directly or indirectly endorse them. Today a growing number of sales professionals who target the affluent are positioning themselves as experts. Some even hire public relations firms to enhance their exposure and their credibility. Others write articles on the affluent and their needs. A minority of ESPs target members of the press in order to publicize their activities.

Some truly enlightened ESPs are giving speeches, holding seminars, and writing papers and articles for publications read by professionals who influence the patronage decisions of the affluent. Because of these communications activities, such ESPs are perceived as experts by the affluent and their attorneys and CPAs.

What are the benefits of enhancing one's credibility via the press? Why should a sales professional take time and other resources away from prospecting to get favorable press? The benefits of positioning oneself as an expert are many. One benefit is that it makes cold calling become warm calling and eventually hot calling. For example, an ESP in his early 30s recently told me of his first experience in getting press. He had chosen several affluent targets. One of these targets was affluent retirees from a particular industry. He initially attempted to market to this group by telephone cold calling and was moderately successful in generating new business in this way. However, some prospects would not allow him 30 seconds of telephone time and others were rude, unimpressed, or generally unsellable. This cold calling became warm calling after he wrote his first article in the newsletter of the industry's trade association, which most of the targeted prospects read. The article discussed their investing needs. The young ESP soon discovered that publishing articles in key vehicles made his prospects more receptive to his solicitations. He learned that for many affluent prospects "talkers are hawkers, writers are experts."

The benefits of getting good press are not limited to the warming of the cold call. The ESP in this case also discovered another advantage of becoming a recognized expert. There are two ways to fish for the affluent. The traditional method dictates finding, chas ing, and landing the prospect. But some of the very best ESPs have discovered a different method—the chumming method. This method is based on the principle that the affluent find, chase, and land the ESP!

The very day that the young ESP published his first article in the trade association newsletter, he received a phone call from an affluent prospect who had read the article and *sought* his advice. A growing number of prospects are seeking his advice. The ultimate marketing achievement for an ESP is to have the affluent do the chasing. A small but growing number of ESPs in this country are generating more new clients from chumming than from traditional marketing methods. A very select few have developed and maintained such a strong image of expertise that they no longer *have* to solicit business in the conventional way. Nevertheless, some of these ESPs still knock on doors and still cold-call by telephone. They do this because of the challenge and thrill and not necessarily because they need more clients.

Apart from the advantages discussed above, chumming is an important marketing method because even within a narrowly defined market segment, not all of the affluent prospects can be identified by the traditional method. What alternative method is there for finding these prospects? The answer is chumming. The prospects contact the ESP and designate themselves as members of the "affluent with need" category.

Some might argue that all or most affluent prospects can be identified by examining lists of professionals and business owners. I counter this argument, that is, the occupational myth, with an argument of my own. During an address to a group of top producers in the insurance industry, I stated:

"I would estimate that the bulk of the households that have incomes in the six-figure range in this country are headed by an entrepreneur, a sales professional/marketing professional, a physician, or an attorney. Did he say sales professional? Yes, I did. In fact, the insurance sales/marketing category ranks in the top 10 in number of high-income workers among the hundreds and hundreds of occupations studied."

I would estimate that in this country there are more sales/marketing professionals in the six-figure income category than there are affluent physicians. The sales area, though highly fragmented, is one of the most affluent areas and also one of the most overlooked areas. The typical high-performance sales professional has a real poverty-of-time problem. Thus, many sales professionals could benefit greatly from both financial planning and estate planning. In addition, sales professionals often have a "too high realized income problem" and could benefit from deferred-compensation products.

The sales professional is not the only undersold affluent category. Remember that there are more affluent blue-collar workers in America than there are affluent dentists. One of my favorite blue-collar occupations is that of the materials handler. Recently, the *New York Times* published an article that discussed the affluent crane operators of New York City. "The employees obtained the six-figure wages through collective bargaining agreements that allowed their unions to designate them as supervisors with the titles of master mechanic or working foreman" (Selwyn Raab, "84 Pay for New York Construction Job: $308,651," *New York Times,* June 12, 1985, p. 1). The article stated that the top-ranked crane operator would probably earn over $400,000. When a reporter attempted to telephone this crane operator for details, he found out that this materials handler was "in the field." Where would you be if you made $400,000 last year for operating a crane?

Crane operators are not on most people's list of affluent prospects. This is exactly why they should be targeted. But not all crane operators make $400,000 per year. Prospecting all of them may be counterproductive. An alternative is to write articles for the trade publications that they read. An article or speech directed to crane operators that addresses investment needs, tax-advantaged investments for the high-income individual, pension planning, or insurance alternatives will probably generate inquiries from those who are not only affluent but have not yet been discovered by the competition. You do not have to be a nationally recognized expert to become an ESP. Being an expert in the eyes of materials handlers with six-figure incomes or of the members of the American Bar Association, the United Fresh Fruits and Vegetables Association, the International Fabricare Institute, and the Associated General Contractors of America would be an excellent foundation for your sales success.

CHAPTER 2

COURAGE: THE BASIC CHARACTERISTIC OF THE EXTRAORDINARY SALES PROFESSIONAL

COURAGE

Extraordinary sales professionals (ESPs) are defined as sales professionals who generate incomes of $100,000 to over $1 million per year from commissions. I would estimate that the average sales professional in America makes less than $40,000 a year. How is it possible for some individuals to make 3, 4, or even 20 times more than the average? They are able to do this because they have developed a style and character of marketing that are not found in any marketing textbook. If this information were widely diffused in the marketing and sales training literature, would there be an improvement in the quality of sales professionals? Actually, if this information were readily available, there might not be a significant increase in the number of sales professionals in the ESP category. ESPs do not succeed only because their proprietary marketing methods, knowledge, and behaviors provide them with a significant relative advantage over the rest of the field; they also succeed because they aggressively utilize these precious elements every day.

In the last few years, I have interviewed and surveyed several hundred ESPs. These superachievers came from diverse marketing areas, including real estate, securities, insurance, industrial products and services, and apparel. I have always been of the opinion that sales professionals should study the marketing methods of ESPs in fields of endeavor other than their own. Very often, a particular field has parochial ideas about marketing methods. Frequently, too much inbreeding and not enough innovative marketing ideas and sales techniques are found in any single marketing area. This is not to suggest that the aspiring sales professional should ignore the fundamentals of his own marketing area.

I have identified several characteristics that tend to discriminate ESPs from others in their profession. Often, individual ESPs do not have a high score on all of these characteristics. However, a large majority of ESPs rank high on at least half of them. Of the characteristics that I have identified, courage is the most pervasive among ESPs. Courage is particular to one's field of endeavor. Usually, it reveals itself early in one's career; however, many people have been able to develop, nurture, and enhance their courage later in life. *Webster's* defines courage as mental or moral strength to venture, persevere, and withstand danger, fear, or difficulty. ESPs will often tell you that they achieved their status by demonstrating more courage than other sales professionals. How is courage demonstrated in selling? What element of the selling equation conjures up the greatest fear or difficulty? Asking for the business—asking the toughest prospects, the biggest prospects, the most affluent prospects for their business. ESPs achieved their star status because they more frequently asked more prospects and clients for their business than did other sales professionals. Other sales professionals tend to delude themselves into thinking that they are truly in the marketing business. Often, they dress to appear as if they are selling. They sit at desks that appear to be occupied by sales professionals. They converse with their colleagues about future victories on the battlefield of sales. They familiarize themselves with "important" worldwide news stories by reading the newspaper intently. In short, they do everything but the hardest thing—the thing that requires courage. They fail to ask and ask again, no matter how many times the response is negative, "Can I have your business?"

Some people delude themselves into thinking that they are asking for the business. I recently debriefed a young insurance sales professional. He complained that his direct mail campaign had not been very successful. Of the 5,000 letters he mailed out to prospects, only 113 letters were answered and of these only about a dozen had some real probability of making this young man a commission. The letter asked that prospects call him if they needed insurance. This is not aggressively asking for the business. This young man seemed to be in the direct mail business and not in the marketing business.

I asked him about how he spent his time during a typical workday. Not surprisingly, he rarely came into face-to-face contact with a prospect. This method of marketing reduces the probability of personal rejection, but it also reduces the probability of ever making a sale. This insurance sales professional still had to learn what real marketing is and what it is not.

Marketing is getting as close as possible to the target. Third-class mail is not getting close to the target. Major Erich Hartmann, the ace of fighter pilot aces in World War II, attributed his success to the aggressive way in which he engaged his target. He believed in getting as close to the target as possible before firing—so close that the target's image completely darkened his canopy and cockpit!

Those sales professionals who are on their way to becoming ESPs spend significantly more time asking for the business than do sales professionals who will never achieve this status. One example is an ESP whom I recently interviewed in California. In the marketing business for 16 years, he made nearly 20,000 cold calls and 8,000 contacts in his first year. Out of 20,000 times at bat, he made fewer than 100 hits. But he never gave up asking for the business. He learned something from each contact. Each year since his first, he has improved his batting average.

Some would suggest that anyone can ask the important question. This is not true. Most people have a great fear of rejection. ESPs regularly demonstrate their ability to overcome this fear. But they are only a small part of the sales population. Can their ability to overcome fear be transmitted to the marginal producers? The courage characteristic is not readily diffused from ESPs to other salespeople, and the single most important reason for this relates to the image that the marginal producers have of their high-performing counterparts. The marginal producers often assume that one is born with courage. They think that ESPs have ice water in their veins. They think that their own status is preordained, and this pessimistic outlook perpetuates their mediocre performance. Some of them even believe that ESPs never encounter rejection. Yet nothing could be further from the truth. ESPs across this nation will tell you that their success can be directly related to the fact that they broke the hard crust of rejection in the marketplace. Abraham Lincoln lost most of his campaigns for political office, but he never stopped asking for people's votes until he became president. Major Hartmann, history's top fighter pilot, was shot down during his first combat mission and 15 times after that, but he was also credited with shooting down 352 planes!

Sales professionals who hope to achieve ESP status should understand fear and how their role models handle it. Most ESPs will tell you that they are always frightened just before they ask for the business. In fact, in asking the important question, most encounter the same level of fear today as they did much earlier in their career. What often separates the ESPs from the marginal producers is not their level of fear but the fact that at the same level of fear, the ESPs have enough courage to ask for the business, whereas the marginal producers do not. As one top producer recently said to me, "If more of my colleagues knew how frightened I am just before asking for the business from a big-league prospect, there would be a much greater number of top guns in my office." Yes, ESPs are often just as frightened as other sales professionals, but they are more seasoned and have more experience in overcoming their fright. They are experts at disguising their fear when they are about to ask the question. They practice thousands of times how to look composed when their heartbeat quickens just before they make the proposition. They often transform their fear into excitement and enthusiasm for the product and the prospect they are selling.

David the Lecturer

David is one of the best teaching professors in America. He has lectured for over 30 years and given thousands of speeches. Yet he is always frightened just before he speaks. "It's never been easy from the first time I lectured." But David always overcomes his fear. Although speeches are an extremely effective marketing tool, most people, even sales professionals, are too frightened to give them. But being an ESP often requires giving speeches. The difference between many ESPs and mediocre producers is that the former, despite considerable fear, will give speeches to the most critical audiences and ask those audiences for the business.

No one should be ashamed of encountering fear in the practice of his profession. Top producers in any field are top producers because they regularly do things that others will not do. I have taught nearly 10,000 students during my career as a professor, and I am considered one of the more "hard-nosed" graders at my university. How many students have ever made a personal cold call to my home to ask the toughest question in college: "Dr. Stanley, will you change my grade?" In my entire teaching career, only one student ever did this. Many years later, he told me that he "sweat bullets" before making his proposal. But he overcame his fear. I am sure that many others who received an F on their midterm considered the same bold move but were unable to deal with their fear.

I will wager that a certain young man in my first marketing class is now an ESP. He missed his first exam, and he also missed his case presentation. One day, he appeared at my office and asked if he could make his case presentation to the class. "If you don't like it," he said, "you can still give me an F. No problem—we'll shake hands." I agreed but had little confidence that he would complete the assignment. His case assignment dealt with fashion— for example, the marketing of swimsuits. What did this fellow do that demonstrated courage? He had seven models in bikinis give a fashion show to the class. I was almost asleep in the back of the room when all of a sudden the room was filled with handsome models wearing bikinis made during a severe "shortage of material." As soon as the class was over, I walked out of the room. The chairman of the department approached me and said, "The dean wants to talk to you." I thought, "There goes my career in teaching." I walked down to the dean's office. The dean stood up and said, "Stanley, I understand there were seven women in bikinis in your classroom today." I told him that I didn't know anything about it. "An overzealous student was behind the fashion show." "Forget it, Stanley," he said. "I hope you gave that student an A. I want him to put the show on at 3 P.M.; I'm going to be there."

William D. Caller

I first encountered William, the cold caller, in my fall 1971 class at the University of Georgia. On the first essay exam, he received the lowest grade in the class. His paper was so bad that I placed an F on the top of it and raised the F to the third power. I noted, "This is the worst paper I have ever reviewed in my entire teaching career." What did William do about his F?

At 5:30 that afternoon, there was a knock at the front door of my home. Since I was in my study at the time, my wife answered the door. William, the cold caller, appeared. "Mrs. Stanley, I received an F on your husband's exam. You know I *was* an orphan [he was near tears now]. I'm thinking about quitting school, but I just wanted to stop by and talk to your husband about my options." He had a case of beer under his arm. Yes, courage can be enhanced by carrying artifacts that hostile forces may enjoy consuming.

My wife came to my study and said, "Tom, there's a young man out there who says that you were awfully mean to him in class." I asked her who it was. "It's William, the cold caller." I told her to get rid of him, that he was just trying to get me to change his grade. "But, Tom, I've invited him to stay for dinner. Did you know that he was an orphan? Tom, this is not New York! In the South, we do not embarrass students in front of their classmates."

Well, what do we call it? We call it guts, brass, courage.

"Professor Stanley, I wanted to come over here and get to know you better. I want to learn what you expect from me in your class and anything else. You mentioned in class that you enjoy Lowenbrau Dark. I have a case for you."

William did stay for dinner, and I gave him a five-hour tour of marketing.

At age 19, he was working his way through school. He was a full-time student, and he also sold real estate part-time. One day, he showed up at my house with a brand-new vacuum cleaner. He opened the door and started vacuuming my living room. I said, "William, what are you doing here?" He said that the vacuum cleaner was for my wife. I responded that I did not want a vacuum cleaner if this meant that I had to compromise my grading system. William assured me that he had studied very hard for the second exam and was confident that he had made an A anyway. "Next week, what would you like? How about a rotisserie? You can have it. I get one of these appliances every time I sell a house. I have an entire room full of them!"

How is William doing today at the age of 35? He is the number one, by far, salesperson for a modest-sized U.S. producer of apparel. He goes head-to-head every day against foreign competitors that often have better material and lower prices. But he's got courage.

And what is courage? William goes into anybody's office and asks for the business. If he does not get the business, he goes somewhere else. But he keeps asking for the business. He does not hesitate to call on the top executives of the firms he prospects. At the age of 19, he could make sales presentations. He had enough of what we will call brass to go to professors' homes—not only to my home but to the homes of other professors as well. "I do it all the time. About half the time, they throw me out; half the time, I come in and we have dinner. You can't win if you don't show up for the game. You will never get what you want if you don't ask the question."

I recall running into William on a flight from New York City to Atlanta. After persuading a handsome airline stewardess to change his seat to one next to mine, he pulled out a letter he had just received from a buyer. "This is one of the nicer communications I have received this week. I want you to read it."

Dear Mr. Caller:
    I have just received your shipment. This apparel is of the worst quality I have ever encountered. I have contacted my attorney. You should know that we are seriously considering legal action if you don't take back all of your shipment.

The letter gave me a chill. I advised William never to call on that buyer again. He just laughed at my comment. "Professor Stanley, I have already called on the buyer. He was surprised to see me. In fact, we had lunch. You'd be surprised what a first-class lunch will do for someone who now regrets sending such a nasty note to an orphan and the father of two small children!"

Charles the Painter

In the spring of 1976, a student in one of my classes told me that he was a painting contractor. I then asked, "Charles, how can you be a painting contractor? You're only 21 years old." He said that age was not a problem. You merely needed to have good help and to find people with painting needs. He hired fellow students so that they could earn enough money to pay their rent in the apartment house he co-owned. I said, "Good, Charles. I'm getting ready to sell my house and move to Georgia. Why don't you and your crew come and paint?"

One day, while painting my garage, Charles said, "I've got to leave now for a job interview with IBM." With paint in his hair and under his fingernails and without a tie, Charles got on his motorcycle and went to the interview. The interviewer said, "Charles, you have a lot of brass showing up for an interview without a tie." And what was Charles's response? "No problem. I would have to take a significant cut in salary to work for you. I would have to shut down my paint contracting company and give up my *New York Times* paper route of over 1,000 sales per day. But I would like to work for IBM. How about giving me a chance?" Only one of our students was hired by IBM that year. Whom did IBM hire? Charles, of course.

Why would a prestigious corporation want to hire this fellow? Obviously, because he had many fine traits, but also because one of those traits was courage. Within three years after Charles graduated, he was given a major role in encouraging a Fortune 500 company to change computer systems. He had enough courage to ask for the job of selling computers in the very big league to the officers very high up.

Move Over, Mel Tillis

After giving a presentation to a group of ESPs, I was approached by a sales manager from the audience. He had a speech impediment that at times sounded more severe than Mel Tillis'. He told me that, wanting to be a veterinarian, he had started his college career as a zoology major. He didn't do very well in some of the courses, so he changed his major to business—first accounting, then marketing. Upon graduating with a degree in marketing, he applied for sales positions in securities, direct investment, and real estate. He stuttered quite a bit during his employment interviews, and 18 interviews translated into 18 rejections. But he kept picking himself up, and in his 19th interview the interviewer was so impressed with his courage that he hired him. Despite his speech impediment, he excelled in both telephone prospecting and personal selling. In short, he achieved ESP status. Eventually, he was made a sales manager. He was an inspiration to recruits. He had courage.

Despite his impediment, he called on prospects and constantly asked for the business. Prospects cannot help but be impressed with marketers who demonstrate courage. Often, people with handicaps display greater courage than do other people. They often feel that this is the only way they can win out despite the odds against them. This ESP attributed much of his initial selling success to his choice of target market. During the early years of his career, sales managers accounted for much of his client base. I asked him why he thought sales managers were interested in dealing with him. He replied that it was probably because they liked the product being offered and because sales managers, though often affluent, were underprospected. I would hypothesize that he was successful in penetrating this market for reasons other than the wealth of his target or the product he promoted.

This ESP was appreciated by the sales managers. Most sales managers have to deal with the problems of motivating their sales force. They are constantly being given excuses for failures to meet sales objectives or make sales calls. What is puzzling to many of them is why potentially outstanding sales professionals fail to meet quotas. When a young sales professional with a speech impediment makes a cold call on such sales managers, they have to be favorably impressed. They are being confronted with a person who asks for the business despite his obvious impediment. Many sales managers achieved their position because they excelled as sales professionals. They had courage; they admire it; and they empathize and are likely to invest with those who demonstrate it. This ESP's handicap was a badge of courage with which sales managers could identify. Too few sales professionals seek ways of transforming problems into opportunities and weaknesses into strengths. The demonstration of courage translates into admiration. Admiration, in turn, translates into new business.

CHAPTER 3

KNOWLEDGE: A BASIC CHARACTERISTIC OF THE EXTRAORDINARY SALES PROFESSIONAL

KNOWLEDGE

Most ESPs are more knowledgeable than other sales professionals about the products or services that they market. ESPs are also more likely to have superior knowledge of the market segments that they target. This superior knowledge of offerings and targets results not only from dedication in learning but from the proclivity of ESPs to focus on a relatively narrow product line and on a well-defined target base.

Many ESPs have told me that their initial success in selling was a direct function of developing superior knowledge of a limited variety of products that addressed the needs of a rather narrowly defined target segment. Many top ESPs have spent years in non-selling positions where they developed significant amounts of intelligence about the product or service they would eventually market. This type of informal "apprenticeship" is often given credit by ESPs as a major factor in their selling success.

Table 3–1 illustrates the specialized knowledge that 11 ESPs have developed. These ESPs are from several product and service areas, including real estate, investments, building materials, insurance, and apparel. This table is not intended to suggest that ESPs are all specialists. They are not. Many, but certainly a minority, are generalists in both product knowledge and market knowledge.

TABLE 3-1 (continued)

Extraordinary Sales Professional	Specialized Product/Service Knowledge	Source of Product/Service Knowledge	Specific Market Targets
Dennis M.	Asset management	Intensive training and experience in sales career before entering the securities business	Privately held/closely held high-tech companies throughout America
Holly Boyett	Affluent residential housing market in north Atlanta, selected affluent neighborhoods	Initial knowledge generated from observation of market changes within her own affluent neighborhood; constantly and intensely studies listings of homes, proposed construction, and sales by owner classifieds	Affluent buyers/sellers of homes in selected neighborhoods in north Atlanta; also views her market as including other aggressive and successful brokers who have an interest in cooperating
William D. Caller	Private label ladies' bottom wear, including jeans, skirts, and related apparel	Began career as supervisor of apparel production; constantly studies changes in designs, production methods, production costs, materials, and character and quality of apparel	Large and medium-sized national and regional retail chains

TABLE 3-1 (continued)

Extraordinary Sales Professional	Specialized Product/Service Knowledge	Source of Product/Service Knowledge	Specific Market Targets
Richard D. Caller	Securities of emerging growth companies	Researched and wrote detailed reports on emerging growth companies; interviewed the chief executive officer and the chief financial officer of many of these firms	Local area investors and other investors who have a strong interest in area-based emerging growth firms
Connie G.	Residential real estate	Established reputation as the agent to call when others were unable to sell the property	Sellers with homes that needed extraordinary marketing effort
John Smith	Life insurance	Intensive study of offerings and characteristics of selected insurance companies	Selected affluent suburban neighborhoods within or near major midwestern city
Robert M.	Building materials for single-family residential homes	Began career at minimum wage as a framer, worked his way up to foreman and then to sales professional of building materials; also studies new product offerings, current offerings, and architectural changes and price variations	Large and medium-sized residential contractors who build within 50 miles of his home

Roger Thomas	Mutual funds and government/municipal securities	Intensive study of selected group of low-risk, high-quality mutual funds and government/municipal securities	Affluent farmers, other business owners, and widows who reside within an isolated community of 14,000
Lewis N.	Asset management and municipal bonds	Intensive study and course training in asset management service offerings and municipal bonds	Affluent fruit growers located within a specific region
Jack and Gene	Utilities stock	Intensive reading and training on selected gas and electric utilities and their security offerings; also researched utility organizations in preparing seminars for retail brokers and their prospects	Affluent "blue-collar entrepreneurs," such as plumbing, heating/air-conditioning, painting contractors, wholesalers, and retailers
Joel R.	Direct investments, private placements	Experience gained while employed by a leading firm specializing in private placements to qualified investors	Qualified investors, including very affluent contractors and other entrepreneurs, selected medical specialists, and senior corporate executives

Dennis M.

Most marketers, even many ESPs, perceive their target audience in terms of geographic territory. Most marketers never venture outside a real or imagined market area boundary. Dennis M. is successful because he views the world differently than most other sales professionals. While there are often compelling reasons for marketing intensely in one's "hometown," location is only one of several dimensions that define the affluent market. Why do most sales professionals limit their activities to a local trade area? Obvious reasons include convenience and referrals from local clients and patronage opinion leaders.

Dennis M. suggests, however, that the dimensions of common financial need and knowledge of industries that often produce affluent entrepreneurs are also important. When I asked Dennis how he defined his market area, he replied, "I define my market area as earth." He will market in any geographic area as long as he knows that an important prospect is present.

Why does Dennis view his territory in such an innovative manner? Prior to marketing investment products, he was a top-producing sales professional in the high-tech field. Once he mastered the marketing of high-tech products, he took a position as a security broker. He now markets asset management services to small and medium-sized high-tech firms that are privately held or closely held.

Dennis is becoming an ESP of asset management services primarily because of his superior knowledge of asset management services and because of his intense focus on the fringe benefit needs of entrepreneurially oriented high-tech firms. He beats out competitors who are generalists, even those with a "local presence" advantage, because he (1) focuses on marketing and not on a variety of investment decisions, (2) possesses superior product knowledge, (3) has superior intelligence about the special investment needs of firms in a very profitable high-tech industry, and (4) possesses a reputation within this industry as "the source" for asset management services.

Dennis is certainly not the only ESP who has employed a penetration strategy that is almost independent of physical distance. Other innovative ESPs have employed similar strategies. They sought and found a method of penetrating affiliation groups. Some penetrated ethnic groups, such as wealthy Italians, Poles, or Russians. Others penetrated industry groups, such as unions and their affluent members in skilled trades. Most of the ESPs who have succeeded in marketing to affiliation groups leveraged their knowledge of the needs of the members of these groups.

Why do so few sales professionals employ strategies similar to those used by Dennis and his special breed of ESPs? One major reason is that few sales professionals understand their own qualities and characteristics. On the other hand, ESPs recognize that they are the product that is being marketed. ESPs tend to be excellent judges of their own strengths and weaknesses. Dennis M., for example, fully understands that his main strength is his knowledge of and ability to relate to high-tech entrepreneurs. Just about everyone has something to offer, something in common with some segment or subsegment of the affluent population. A large part of successful marketing is based on allocating one's most important resources where they will generate the greatest return. This is the "deep and narrow" strategy.

Holly Boyett

Holly has been the top residential real estate sales professional in the biggest new home residential market in America. One of her most amazing marketing achievements was the speed with which she became an ESP. Her rapid success can certainly be attributed in part to her hard work, competitiveness, and intelligence. However, it resulted to a greater extent from her strategy of the "deep and narrow."

Holly recently told me about her initial listings.

> The owner of a company asked me if I would like to list a house, and everybody [fellow brokers] laughed because the house was way overpriced, but I didn't know it.

Immediately after Holly obtained her first listing, she decided to reward herself. She went into her favorite dress shop "walking and talking real estate."

> And then I went and bought a dress. . . . I was so excited about
> real estate (talking while trying on dresses) that the owner of the
> shop and the lady working there . . . listed their houses with me.

From her first experience in the business, Holly demonstrated an instinct for focusing on the most accessible targets—people with whom she conducted business on a continual basis. Unlike many marketers, Holly did not overlook reciprocal relationships.

Holly's first sales came from an area she knew quite well, her own neighborhood. While many other aspiring real estate agents attempted to list and sell real estate all over Atlanta, Holly directed her fire at one specific part of the most affluent neighborhoods in the metropolitan area. While others waited for business to walk in the door, Holly knocked on every door within her narrowly defined target area. She introduced herself in a businesslike fashion to affluent homeowners.

> I knocked on doors in my neighborhood . . . in northwest Atlanta.
> One of the gentlemen said that he was looking for a house, but he did
> not want to leave the neighborhood. When I went to the house next
> door, the lady told me she was thinking about selling, but she wasn't
> ready yet. I kept calling on her, but all of a sudden she listed with
> another company. It broke my heart, but you have to have a lot of
> rejection in this business. But I figured I could still get the person
> next door to look at it, which he did, and he bought it right on the
> spot. And then he said, "Come on, you can list my house." That
> was my fourth house, and then it just snowballed.

Holly established a strong position in her own neighborhood before she ventured into other market segments. This position was greatly enhanced by her high intensity in prospecting and delivering personal service in a narrowly defined market area.

> Originally, I would tell people I could be there every time their
> house was shown because I didn't have anything else to do. And
> now I can tell them that I have . . . the network, that I have the
> ability to speak with the appraisers and the mortgage people listen to
> me. I'm more professional with what I can do now. In the beginning,
> there were some people (clients) that loved the idea that I could be
> there *every* time.

Rarely do real estate brokers, security brokers, insurance agents, or even luxury automobile sales professionals in this country knock on the doors of affluent households. Holly will tell you that the most effective way to market oneself is by face-to-face contact with prospects. Within one week of initial prospecting, Holly obtained four major listings. Over a short period of time, she established the reputation of being "the person to deal with" if one had a home to sell or an interest in buying within her self-designated trade area. During her career, Holly did venture beyond her initial trade area. But she is wiser today.

> If someone calls me and wants me to evaluate their home and it's way out, I suggest that they get another agent. It's just not fair to the clients I'm serving now . . . in northwest Atlanta, the Riverside area, both in Cobb and Dunwoody, but Dunwoody is not that big anymore. . . . I have a man in Dunwoody who wants me to list his house, and it's very important to this man, my friend told me, socially, that he have me for his agent. Isn't that funny? Status. But it's in Dunwoody. He is a top stockbroker. So I told him what I would do is get the top Dunwoody agent at our local office and we would do it together.

What can aspiring ESPs learn from Holly Boyett? They should not attempt to master too many targets at one time. They should not be distracted by other market segments until the one at hand has been penetrated. Holly's methodology accounts for much of her success. She now has a considerable amount of market penetration in three affluent neighborhoods in Atlanta, yet she does not attempt to list real estate that is too far outside her trade area. Doing so would spread her service delivery too thin. Intensity of market, knowledge, and effort should never be jeopardized because of an occasional opportunity in a "foreign" territory.

William D. Caller

William D. Caller believes that his ESP status was achieved in large part because of his superior knowledge of a narrow line of women's apparel. Immediately after completing his undergraduate studies, he was confronted with two very different employment opportunities. His first employment offer came from Procter & Gamble. P&G wanted him to sell coffee to retailers in Florida. His second employment opportunity came from a small family-owned apparel manufacturer. This offer was not for a sales position but for a position as production manager.

Why did Caller decide to become a production manager for an apparel manufacturer? "I liked the people there. . . . Many of my friends lived in town. . . . We would not have to move. . . . Besides, my wife wanted to live in her hometown." Caller's decision to become a production manager was the base for a successful selling career.

For several years, Caller learned the details of producing women's apparel. He became conversant with the costs of materials, labor costs, scheduling, production economies, and the quality of materials and with the manufacturing problems associated with style and fashion changes.

After several years as production manager, Caller moved into a sales position for the apparel manufacturer. He was an almost instant success because he could respond almost immediately to a buyer who asked him how much it would cost to produce 25,000 or 50,000 pairs of the blue jeans she held in her hand. He could look at the styling, the fabric, the cut, and the workmanship and within minutes give the buyer a quote. Often, he could estimate how long it would take to produce and deliver merchandise.

Rapid response time is Caller's hallmark. This characteristic separates him from many other apparel sales professionals. It is often the reason why buyers, especially those with a poverty of time, give him the sale. Caller believes that to be successful in the apparel business, the seller must get the buyer out of the market immediately. Give the buyer an immediate quote, he says, "to get the money off the table and stop the buyer from searching for a source."

But knowledge of the production side of the business is not the entire story. Caller's focus is not only on detailed knowledge of a narrow line of merchandise but also on retailers who have a specialized need for a narrow line of women's apparel. Caller once told a graduate marketing class about an actual case that reflected the value of specializing.

Caller and a competing apparel sales professional arrived at a buyer's office at almost the same time. Caller left with an order nearly 10 times as large as that of his competitor. Why? Caller explained it this way:

The fellow shows up with over 200 different samples and proceeds to spread them all over the buyer's desk, tables, and floor. He confused the hell out of the buyer. Then, when my competitor attempted to answer questions about costs and delivery dates, he demonstrated ignorance or lack of authority to make such estimates. I showed the buyer only six items, . . . the ones I knew she was most interested in having in her stores.

Caller's suggestions are important to aspiring ESPs. The buyer in the example given above worked for a specialty retailer. This retailer's business strategy was based on selling millions of dollars of a very narrow line of apparel. Also, its success was attributed in part to its ability to train retail salesclerks easily and quickly because it offered a limited line of almost standardized apparel. Caller's competitor, armed with 200 different items, frightened and confused the buyer. Often, sales professionals fail to achieve ESP status because they attempt to market hundreds of different products to prospects with specialty needs. Such sales professionals, no matter how intelligent, will never be able to learn all there is to know about all of these products. Also, they will never be able to learn all there is to know about all the different needs of all the unique segments in the marketplace.

Richard D. Caller

Richard D. Caller became an ESP by using a market strategy similar to that of his older brother, William D. Caller. The strategy is one that can be defined as "deep and narrow." Shortly after graduating with a degree in finance, Richard took a position as a security broker for a regional firm. He recognized early in his career that to establish a beachhead for himself quickly, he would have to develop a market specialist strategy. All too often, security brokers fail to become ESPs because they attempt to market too many different products to too many different segments. Richard's initial success was predicated on his choice of a product offering and a target market.

Richard theorized that many investors within his local trade area had a keen interest in the emerging growth companies located within the same area. He took it upon himself to conduct interviews with the senior officers of several of these firms. These interviews, along with other data, provided a base for the reports he developed on these emerging growth companies. He also had videotapes produced of his interviews with the chief executive officers and chief financial officers of these firms. Richard's written reports and videotape interviews provided evidence to interested investors that he was well informed about these firms.

Richard became an ESP while still in his mid-20s primarily because he had a deep knowledge of a narrowly defined investment area. His targeting of prospective clients also adhered to the "deep and narrow" rule. He aggressively pursued local investors with a proclivity toward investing in local emerging growth firms.

Only after Richard established a solid base in product and client knowledge did he attempt to branch out into other offerings directed at varied targets. In most instances, as Richard found, a specialist will succeed much faster than a generalist in achieving the status of an extraordinary sales professional.

I Will Always Recommend Connie G.

Not everyone can sell real estate. Only a small number of real estate sales professionals achieve ESP status and maintain that status during downturns in the real estate market. Connie G. is one of them.

I was once in the unenviable position of having to sell a house when the mortgage rate was near 20 percent. What there was of a real estate market in Atlanta at that time was a buyer's market. Like millions of other homeowners, I made the mistake of asking the first person who came to mind—a friend, neighbor, and part-time real estate agent—to sell the property. This was the easy thing to do. After more than two months, the only results were no offers, no nibbles, and very little traffic.

It became apparent that a change had to be made. I called the manager of the largest real estate agency in Atlanta. "I want the name of your very, very best agent. . . . No, not the best in Dunwoody or Roswell. I want the best horse in your stable."

Connie and her assistant appeared at my home soon after I called her. She agreed to accept my case. Traffic increased overnight. Within a month, the house sold for 95 percent of the asking price. I was amazed at her success. Not only was the market difficult, but the home was cedar. Cedar is not my first choice for siding in Georgia. It discolors and mildews. Periodic cleaning is necessary. Who would pay 95 percent of the asking price? Connie found an executive from the lumber industry who loved cedar! "After all, Tom, what would you expect a lumber expert to live in—a brick colonial? It would be bad for his reputation and the image of the lumber company."

My experience with Connie taught me something about marketing. If you want to avoid losing money on your real estate dealings, call an ESP.

John Smith

John Smith is traditional in his lifestyle and his approach to marketing. This ESP penetrated the affluent market for life insurance by knocking on doors. He developed a considerable amount of knowledge about the whole life policies offered by a variety of companies. He memorized in minute detail the premiums and features of a selected group of policies with six- and seven-figure face values.

In addition to specializing in the products he marketed, John had a focused approach to the market. He intuitively recognized early in his career that residential neighborhoods varied considerably in terms of the character of their homeowners. Within the metropolitan area that he initially covered, he identified emerging affluent neighborhoods. Such neighborhoods contained a disproportionate share of relatively young, fast-track attorneys, physicians, sales professionals, entrepreneurs, and executives.

John noticed that these younger, fast-track affluent prospects were continually reaching new levels of insurance needs. He was amazed that so few of these targeted prospects had ever been approached by competing life insurance sales professionals. In fact, his prospects often told him that they had never been contacted on a face-to-face basis. John's approach to these prospects was to canvass neighborhoods door to door. He would cold-call the prospects at their homes in the evening and on weekends. During his initial visit, he never attempted to make a sale. He dealt with each prospect in a very professional manner. He always wore a suit and tie and carried a leather, coffee-colored briefcase. He presented each prospect with a brochure detailing the insurance needs of aspiring affluent individuals. The brochure also contained a biographical sketch that highlighted John's educational experience, family background, and other indicators of stability. During this visit, John spent "90 percent of his time listening to the prospect speak about his or her family, occupation, career path, and current insurance coverage."

After the initial visit, John would always write a thank-you note to the prospect. Such notes were always handwritten in black ink. Within two weeks of his visit, John would telephone the prospect to solidify a future meeting. Prior to the meeting, John would review his notes detailing the estimated insurance needs of the prospect and other family members.

John's rapid ascent to ESP status is another textbook example of the "deep and narrow" method. He says that mastering a limited number of insurance offerings was a major factor in his success. Equally important, however, was his ability to focus on a narrowly defined target segment of the affluent population. Cold calling in emerging affluent neighborhoods seemed so obvious to John that he thinks most sales professionals must have simply overlooked this highly productive method of marketing.

Henry Pro Forma Jones

Henry Jones is a financial planner who has decided to redefine his market. In the past, he has prospected what he defines as affluent individuals who live within his hometown of approximately 600,000 households. Having come to realize that the concentration of affluent prospects is much greater within selected trade associations than within his self-defined, geographic hometown territory, he has decided to prospect by a different set of dimensions.

After examining the profitability figures for various types of businesses and examining the financial statements of current clients, Henry decides to focus on the International Fabricare Institute. One of Henry's most affluent clients owns a chain of dry cleaning stores and laundries. In addition, this self-made millionaire is an active participant in several associations that represent specialists in fabric care.

Henry must now decide what level of involvement and commitment he will choose in his efforts to penetrate the fabric cleaning industry. At a very basic level, he could rent a booth at the annual international convention. Such a commitment would take a modest amount of money and time. However, it would enable Henry to come into contact with potentially thousands of affluent prospects for financial planning. At this level of commitment, Henry would be able to appear at other conventions, such as those of vegetable and melon farmers, construction contractors, accountants, and attorneys.

However, Henry reasons that just placing a booth at a convention will not provide him with a long-run strategic advantage over his competition. In other words, he is concerned about protecting the market that he has decided to target. His concern is reflected in his commitment to a specific industry. Henry's objective is to penetrate the fabric cleaning industry deeply and to develop long-term relationships with clients in that industry. Operating a booth at the annual international convention is just a small part of his plan. Other important parts of his plan are:

1. Developing a system of market intelligence. This system will provide Henry with information about trends in the industry and about the most profitable and well-thought-of cleaners in the industry. Henry's objective, in this case, is to know more about every aspect of the industry than do most of his prospects. As a by-product of reading the key journals of the industry, Henry will have access to a list of plants and stores that are for sale. A single monthly issue of *American Drycleaner* typically lists a dozen businesses for sale. Henry discovered long ago that his most profitable clients were those who were in the process of selling their businesses or had just sold them.

2. Being quoted by and writing articles for important publications read by owners of fabric cleaning businesses, including the *American Drycleaner*. The obvious theme of these communications will be Henry's views on financial planning for the owners of cleaning businesses and on what sellers of cleaning businesses should do with the proceeds of the sale.

3. Speaking at international, national, and important state conferences and conventions at which high concentrations of affluent fabric cleaners are present.

4. Gaining endorsements from the trade associations of fabric cleaners and from influential members of these trade associations.

Henry's aim is to be considered the foremost source of financial planning for owners of fabric cleaning businesses. He will find that carrying out his plan will generate substantial business from both solicited and unsolicited sources. He will also find that most of the prospects he calls on will have been preconditioned to respond favorably to his messages about enhancing the productivity of their investments. Essentially, he will be the endorsed financial planner of an industry and its members, and competitors will be unable to penetrate his market. Although it will take Henry years to develop this image and considerable energy to maintain it, the image will serve as a very strong protective barrier of a kind that is rare in the financial services industry.

Robert M.

Robert M. is an extraordinary sales professional who markets building materials. He achieved this status after only three years. His earnings of approximately $120,000 from commissions were generated from sales of over $4 million worth of materials. He is the top-rated sales professional among a sales force of 20 representatives. How did Robert achieve his number one ranking when many of the other sales professionals within his discipline had more years of selling experience?

Part of the answer to this question lies in Robert's focused approach to marketing. Another part of the answer lies in his experience in the construction business. Robert sells building materials to a specific type of customer—contractors who build single-family homes. All of these contractors are building homes within a 50-mile radius of Robert's home and office. Robert has found it much easier to succeed in selling by focusing his marketing resources on a specific segment within a defined geographic area.

Perhaps more important than Robert's focused market strategy is his background in the construction business. Many marketers of construction materials have little or no experience in actually constructing homes. Because of this, they lack Robert's sensitivity with respect to the problems and objectives of materials buyers. Robert did not develop these skills while he was a student of ancient Chinese history in college or while he was a diver for the U.S. Navy. He spent several years in the construction business working his way up from a minimum wage position as a framer to the position of construction foreman, in which he worked 80 hours a week for less than $40,000 a year. During his internship as a framer and then as a foreman, he acquired firsthand knowledge of all the problems associated with home construction. These included late deliveries of materials, incorrect specifications, and materials of inferior quality and design. As a foreman, he often had to deal with sellers of building materials who offered little or no advice about product offerings and few or no suggestions about ways to increase productivity. However, he saw that most of these sellers were making considerably more money than he was making as a foreman. He also felt that sellers of building materials had significantly more opportunity for income growth than he did.

Robert attributes much of his success as an ESP to the fact that he knows a great deal about the problems encountered by every framer, carpenter, and construction foreman. He is well informed about how each of the materials he offers matches the specific needs of his target market. During the evening and early morning, he spends a considerable amount of time studying architectural changes, product offerings, and variations in the prices offered by producers of materials. Like many of his ESP counterparts, Robert knows much more about the needs of his contractors and their workers than they do themselves. His apprenticeship as a framer and as a construction foreman provided him with an educational foundation that greatly enhanced his credibility with buyers.

Roger Thomas

Roger Thomas achieved ESP status within 18 months of starting his career as a security broker in the late 1970s. This in itself is quite an accomplishment. More significant is the fact that he reached this plateau by selling securities in an isolated rural community with a population of less than 14,000. When Roger opened his office in this community, no one had ever heard of him or the regional firm that employed him.

Roger says that at first he was not well received by the people in the community. This, however, did not deter him. His "deep and narrow" market strategy was highly productive. He focused on marketing a limited line of high-quality mutual funds and government and municipal securities. He quickly developed a comprehensive knowledge of these products and of the rural community in which he operated. How did Roger select his geographic target?

> I studied the map. I looked for a town that had no other towns around it for a 20-mile radius, that had enough population to be a trade center. I looked for a town that had good agricultural sales in one of the biggest agricultural counties in the state. I asked for a town that had bank deposits in excess of $100 million. And I looked for a town that was close enough to an airport so that if I could eventually start winning some of these trips, I could get to an airport without driving three to four hours. This town fit the bill for all of those criteria. So I went there sight unseen.

Roger was deep and narrow in his market orientation. He aggressively marketed to the affluent farmers, business owners, and widows of his area. He told me that he was successful because he never tried to be both an investment analyst and a marketer of securities. "You can either pick stocks or market them." Most marketers of securities who fail to reach ESP status are guilty of what Roger considers "a major issue in the securities business. Let the experts manage the money, and let the marketing professionals market the experts' services." Roger succeeded because he fully understood that he was in the marketing business.

Roger's initial marketing strategy embodied the classic components of the "deep and narrow." He focused his marketing resources in terms of product offerings, geography, and customer characteristics. He says that most generalists do not become extraordinary sales professionals. They become frustrated because they never feel comfortable dealing with the ambiguities associated with a wide range of offerings and targets.

Lewis N.

Lewis N. specializes in marketing asset management services and municipal bonds. After intensive training in and study of these offerings, he was able to penetrate a very narrowly defined affluent segment. He marketed these offerings to one of the most affluent and distinguished fruit growers in America. Once he was able to develop a client relationship with this fruit grower, Lewis fully exploited this advantage. He found that other fruit growers within his self-designated trade area often emulated the behavior of his client.

All too often, marketers fail to see the potential in penetrating deeply and narrowly within industries that produce a significant number of affluent business owners. Lewis, however, was wise enough to pursue aggressively other affluent fruit growers. During his initial visit to these fruit growers, he would always find some way to make them aware that he was the financial adviser and security broker of the most respected person in their industry. Not all of Lewis' business is generated from fruit growers. However, his best clients are fruit growers. Within his trade area, he is regarded as the financial expert when it comes to managing the money of successful fruit growers.

Throughout his career, Lewis has spent much of his time improving his selling skills. Like Roger Thomas and many other ESPs in the securities industry, he has never tried to do someone else's job. He was drawn to the concept of marketing asset management services because they fitted his marketing style. He believes that investment experts should manage investments, while brokers should manage the marketing function.

A Lesson in Economic Geography
It was almost by accident that Lewis N. uncovered an industrial infrastructure, an area where clusters of top fruit growers gravitated. His case history is an important one for marketers to remember. Many college students take courses in economic geography and never understand how very practical economic geography can be for the marketing practitioner. Most students probably throw away their economic geography notes and sell their textbook as soon as they have completed the course. However, economic geography is one of the most valuable courses that a marketing student can take. It is most significant for those who aspire to market to the affluent.

Analyze the areas where products and services are produced in high concentrations. What are you likely to find? Affluent wine producers in the Napa Valley of California; affluent cattle ranchers in Colorado, Nebraska, and Florida; affluent coal producers in Kentucky; affluent science professors in and around Boston; affluent timberland owners in Georgia; affluent apparel producers and printers in New York City; and affluent attorneys and lobbyists in Washington, D.C.

Knowledge of the industries that create wealth within various market areas is a critical foundation stone for the sales professional. Interestingly, economic geography is overlooked not only by many sales professionals who target the affluent but even by many strategic planners at the largest financial institutions. Few marketers in this industry have an accurate assessment of the various industries of the affluent even within their trade area. Lewis N. is an exceptional marketer because he understands the fundamentals of Economic Geography 101.

Jack and Gene

Both Jack and Gene developed considerable knowledge of a specific investment category before they ever attempted to market their offerings. Almost all of their career experience has been in the electric and gas utilities industry.

Jack has served as a utility analyst, participated in numerous utility underwritings, and testified in several rate cases as an expert witness before four state regulatory commissions and before the House Committee on Energy. He holds a B.A. degree in accounting and an M.B.A. in finance.

Gene also possesses a great deal of knowledge about utility offerings. Immediately after graduating from college, he became a utility security analyst for a major mutual fund. Four years later, he became the fund's director of financial research. Two years after that, he accepted a similar position with a gas utility company. Before his 30th birthday, he was hired as director of research by a securities firm.

Gene has testified on investor requirements in well over 200 rate cases and before 54 regulatory bodies. He is the point man for his firm when it comes to the utilities business. His task is to convince utilities to be represented by his firm. On the other side, he lends support to the marketing people in his firm who make presentations to affluent investors interested in utilities. Gene told me during an interview how he became interested in marketing.

> I don't know the extent to which it has been copied elsewhere, but after the first year or two in investment banking here, I realized that we were being successful in bringing [in] more and more clients but that the firm itself seemed to be unable to market the securities very well. So we were laying them off, which is the time-honored Wall Street tradition for firms like ours.
>
> So Jack and I decided what we would do was try to hold seminars if we could get some interest and explain directly to investors—if at all possible, individuals—exactly how utility regulation worked. That, of course, ensured that the salesmen would all come because either their clients or their prospects were not going to have an opportunity to be talked to without them being here.
>
> So that meant that our salesmen were becoming educated as to the basic fundamentals of utility investments as well. The approach was one that was very, very well received by investors, and therefore by salesmen. Anything their clients like, they like.

Jack is a strong believer in the importance for marketing of disseminating product knowledge. The nationwide seminars he and his partner conducted were effective because they were led by two or more highly knowledgeable experts in the utility field. The affluent have respect for knowledge and are attracted to people who possess it. Jack described the investor interest created by the seminars.

> We started in California. . . . We went to the Pacific Northwest, Southern California. We did parts of New England, the Middle Atlantic states, Pennsylvania and Maryland, the deep South, especially Florida. We did Texas in a week. We did the Midwest— Chicago, Milwaukee, Minneapolis, Cleveland, Detroit, Troy, just about every major city out there.
>
> "It took us at least six months to do our system. And then every year we had to do it again because people asked us to come back. The brokers got a lot out of it. We targeted the individual market. We talked to 50,000 to 60,000 people a year . . . in the first couple of years, and then that grew up to a couple of hundred thousand in a 12-year period. We still do them.

I'm not sure everyone in the seminar completely understood everything we were trying to teach them. It is difficult to do it in that short a period of time. Most people said they understood it. More importantly, those people, most of whom were extremely affluent, thought that we fully understood what we were talking about and had confidence in us. We built our credibility that way. Our brokers started selling new shares on offerings based on the experience of the seminar. They would use my name as a reference. . . . We built up a following by keeping the sales force current in the aftermarket for these new stocks. To the point where anyone could call in and get an opinion at any time of the day on any one of those names or any name in the utility industry. We also recommended to people that had problem companies that they sell out.

When I asked Jack about the types of prospects and clients (the extremely affluent) that attended the seminars, he had some interesting observations.

I met the people that you [are] interviewing. Not all of the people in the seminars in Spokane, Washington, or Atlanta, Georgia, were multimillionaires. But they were affluent. Many of them owned or had a net worth of $10–$20 million. You wouldn't know it to look at them. They didn't drive there in their Rolls-Royces, but when they came up to you after the seminar was over and showed you their portfolios, your eyes just bugged out of your head. They owned 20, 30, 50 different names. And big positions—more than 2,000 to 3,000 shares in each one.

Many of them were widows, as I think you pointed out, who had the responsibility after their husbands' death of managing the portfolios originally structured by their husbands in different economic times. They were concerned. They didn't trust brokers who just sold them anything. They had no one to go to to get a full follow-up story on some of these stocks. They were discouraged. I got to know a lot of them personally because I'd do five years in a row in Palo Alto or in Providence, Rhode Island, or San Jose, California.

I also found out where their money came from. Many of them were blue-collar millionaires. People who had started businesses after World War II. Many of them had [already] paid for the education of children, were looking forward to retirement somewhere where the sun shines all the time.

I think my experience kind of dovetailed with some of the things that you did through your research focus groups and survey interviews.

A deep understanding of a specific category of investments, sales force needs, and the characteristics of target clients was the cornerstone of Jack and Gene's market success. Their superior product knowledge not only helped sell affluent investors but also convinced many members of the sales force that they should align themselves with a specific variety of the "deep and narrow." Sales professionals on full commission often have complete discretion about the products they will push. In this respect, they are much like the ultimate consumer.

Jack and Gene succeeded on two important marketing battle-grounds—the channel target and the investor target. Rallying the troops is rewarded both in war and in business.

JOEL, FOLLOW THE DEEP AND NARROW ROAD TO QUALIFIED INVESTORS

Dear Joel,

Thank you for sharing your experiences regarding the affluent market during our telephone conversation. I am writing to follow up and to elaborate on the suggestions that were discussed. Do not be discouraged because your application to rent a booth at the medical association conference being held this fall here in Atlanta was rejected. Remember that this conference is not the only major event that will draw affluent prospects to conventions in your hometown.

Joining the conference bureau will pay large dividends for you in the future. You will be able to determine months, even years, in advance what major trade associations will be holding conventions in Atlanta. However, before you attempt to contact any of the trade associations that are scheduled, let me reemphasize some important ground rules. Your productivity will greatly increase if you follow what I consider the "deep and narrow" posture. This relates both to penetrating into selected trade conferences that contain high concentrations of affluent prospects and to focusing on the strengths that you have already developed.

You appear to have a natural aptitude for reaching

particular types of affluent prospects. Also, you have considerable knowledge of the direct invest- ments in which qualified investors are most inter- ested. However, you are likely to wear yourself out before you reach middle age if you do not begin to lev- erage these qualities in specific segments of the af- fluent market.

Most of your current clients are successful busi- ness owners or owners/partners of professional prac- tices. The hundreds and hundreds of clients that you have may appear from time to time to have no definitive similarities. I will wager, however, that you will be able to categorize more than half of your quality cli- ents into fewer than one dozen industrial classifica- tions. You probably do not realize it, but as a natural process, given your personality and interests, you have already begun to develop a deep and narrow strat- egy.

Many brokers in your industry have a large number of clients in a relatively small number of industries. Surprisingly, they ignore the inherent knowledge they have of the people in these industries, and cor- respondingly, their product needs. Each day, they fight a never-ending battle. They have to convince yet another new prospect of their identity. This is one of the major reasons why middle-aged brokers reach a pla- teau in their productivity. They often complain that prospecting never gets any easier. It will be easier for you if you take the time to analyze your current customer base thoroughly. It is more than likely that several of your current clients are major opinion leaders within their respective industries. Herein lies the key to penetrating trade association confer- ences and trade associations in general.

You have stated on several occasions that your cli- ent base contains several wealthy contractors and medical specialists. Contact these clients today. Ask them if they are active in one or more trade associ- ations that represent their industry and that will have future conventions in Atlanta. Some of your cli- ents will probably be officers of such associations. Let them know that you would like to participate in one or more of their future conferences.

Whenever you wish to make a speech, write a paper, or even rent a booth at a trade association, always remember who is in charge of such groups. You were probably unable to rent a booth at the medical association conference because you asked the wrong person for permission. Asking a staff associate of a trade association if you can participate is akin to asking a security guard outside a private party if you can join the celebration without an invitation! The job of staff associates is to keep the peace, not select the guests. Always focus on authority figures, i.e., the important members of such groups. A trade association is controlled by its members and not by hired staff assistants.

Even clients who are not currently officers in their respective trade associations will be able to direct you to those members who are currently in power. There are several steps that you need to take if you would like to exploit future convention opportunities in your hometown. The steps are as follows:

1. Purchase a copy of the latest Standard Industrial Classification Manual at the U.S. government bookstore.

2. Classify all of your current and future clients by the standard industrial taxonomy contained in the manual. Store all of this type of dossier data on your personal computer.

3. Correlate the industrial classifications of the associations that will be holding conferences in Atlanta with those of your clients.

4. Contact "quality" clients who are classified in the industries of the organizations that will be holding conferences in town in the future.

5. Identify those clients who are active in these organizations or those who can direct you to the leaders of such trade groups.

6. Ask these contacts for their advice and endorsement regarding your participation in future conventions.

7. At a minimum level of involvement, rent a booth at selected conventions. Even renting a booth is not a certainty. Increase your odds of being able to do so by gaining the support of key members. Initially, your

odds of being "invited" to speak at a major conference will be small. But do not be afraid to ask. Your odds will improve as you become familiar with selected industries.

8. Ask your firm for financial support in regard to the fees, rental costs, and expenses you incur in developing graphics and visuals.

9. Purchase a membership directory from each targeted trade association. Also, ask each association for a list of the members who have preregistered for upcoming conventions. Preregistration information should be made available to anyone who pays a registration fee. Precontact (before the targeted conventions) current clients and prime prospects who will probably attend. Ask them to stop by your booth or visit your hospitality suite. Promise them a copy of your booklet An Atlanta Native's Guide to Quality Dining if they will view your video program at your booth.

10. Prepare a statement on the products you offer that relate to the needs of industry members. Highlight the depth of your understanding of those needs by providing case studies of your clients in the targeted industry.

11. Focus on a narrowly defined set of product offerings for each targeted industry. For example, many affluent contractors are interested in direct investment opportunities in major construction ventures, such as large hotels and prestigious office buildings.

12. Prepare a videotape for presentation at conventions that includes interviews with (1) current satisfied clients of your direct investment offerings, (2) analysts who estimate the return characteristics of current and future direct investments, and (3) the general partners of these ventures.

I hope that these suggestions will help you reach your deep and narrow objectives. The basic goal of the deep and narrow is to penetrate selected industries more deeply than any of your competitors and to have greater knowledge both of the investment needs of these industries' members and of a narrow line of high-quality direct investments for qualified investors. It will take years to achieve these objectives. Even then, you will have to constantly enhance your position. However, once your deep and narrow strategy is in place, you will be well insulated from the competition. Also, you will find that a growing number of affluent prospects will be predisposed to deal with you even before you contact them.

To be successful with the deep and narrow, you do not have to market more than a few high-quality direct investments to qualified investors from as few as three or four classifications. Marketing specialists are able to capture markets much more effectively than marketing generalists. This applies both to your business and to retailing. Look at the spectacular success of The Limited, for example.

You have a natural affinity for marketing to contractors in the construction and building trades. Capitalize on that ability. Read what contractors read, attend the conferences they attend, understand their industry, and empathize with their investment needs. Ultimately, you will be considered the foremost investment authority among affluent contractors. But do not forget to hedge against downturns in the construction business. Penetrate two or three industries whose performances are independent of each other.

Your income will be more than the $250,000 you made last year if I see you at the next contractors convention.

Regards,

Thomas J. Stanley, Ph.D.
Chairman
Affluent Market Institute

TJS:sw

CHAPTER 4

TECHNIQUE: A BASIC CHARACTERISTIC OF THE EXTRAORDINARY SALES PROFESSIONAL

TECHNIQUE

Technique is a very broad concept. *Webster's* defines technique as the manner in which technical details are treated and the method of accomplishing a desired aim. The techniques employed by many ESPs are varied and often unique. One way in which to define the character of the techniques employed by ESPs is in terms of the hypersensitiveness of ESPs to certain details of the sales equation. Also, all of the ESPs that I have interviewed have some technical idiosyncrasy that differentiates the way in which they relate to the affluent prospect.

Most great hunters, fishermen, military strategists, and ESPs have unique techniques that distinguish them from others in their respective fields. The technique construct covers a great many unusual tactics that ESPs employ. Proactive marketing is a common subset of the domain comprised by technique. In such marketing, the marketer takes an active role in making something happen that enhances sales. In reactive marketing, on the other hand, just the opposite takes place—i.e., the marketer merely responds to happenings.

Some of the best real estate sales professionals create a market for themselves by sensitizing owners to become sellers and sellers to become buyers. Retail clothing ESPs who market to the affluent are also proactive. They often precipitate the sale of expensive clothing and accessories by calling their customers. Many have a dossier for each of the customers they serve. The dossier includes the customer's sizes, style preferences, seasonal buying habits, and anticipated cash flow changes. When the clothing ESP is reviewing upcoming merchandise, he always has his clients' needs in mind. He then informs his clients of the availability of suitable items. His goal is to precipitate action on the part of the customer.

I recently gave some advice to the marketing manager of a luxury automobile dealership about proactive marketing techniques. This manager was concerned about increasing the productivity of his sales force. I asked him what most of his sales professionals did during the workday. He said that they were all assigned to sell cars. But when I visited the dealership's showroom on several occasions, I found that reactive selling was most often taking place. During each of my visits, most of the sales professionals were in or near the showroom, waiting for prospects to arrive. They waited and waited for prospects who would be ready, willing, and able to purchase. This is not proactive selling. In fact, it is more closely related to order taking than to marketing. Although some of the waiting sales professionals were making follow-up telephone calls, most were just waiting.

The best automobile sales professionals are never idle. They will tell you that they would have never achieved ESP status just waiting for the business to walk into the showroom.

Within two square miles of the dealership discussed above, there are hundreds of owners of small but rapidly growing corporations and many six-figure sales and marketing professionals, physicians, attorneys, lawyers, and so on.

I suggested to the marketing manager that he require every sales professional who worked for him to generate calls, visits, and letters to the affluent population and that these contacts be timed according to the cash flow patterns of the target. Many of the six-figure sales professionals who are employed near the dealership receive more than half of their total compensation in a lump-sum bonus payment.

These prospects may be in the economic mood to buy a luxury automobile for only three or four weeks out of a purchase cycle of

100 or more weeks. Reactive sales professionals consistently miss
out on the opportunity to sell because they assume that the prospect will seek them out during the so-called buying mood. Although it is true that some affluent prospects will find their way to
the dealership at the right time, many others will exhaust their
additional economic resources or be intercepted by competitive
offers before they even consider patronizing the dealership.

Personal selling is most effective during the upswing in the
prospect's cash flow. Marketers to the affluent should therefore
determine the cash flow patterns, the important income-related
events of the target market and then allocate their marketing efforts according to these patterns. They should direct a large portion of their marketing dollars to programs that target those prospects who are in the economic mood to purchase.

Can a Middle-Aged ESP Learn New Tricks?

When Jack decided to reenter the business of marketing securities,
he changed his prospecting strategy. I had many conversations with
him before he made this recent career change. Much of my input
centered on the concept of money in transition. "Jack, always look
for money on the move. Target people who have just received or will
receive large numbers of dollars. Look for people who are selling
their businesses, going public, and retiring with large lump-sum payments and for authors who will receive large royalties. When you
capture the business of an affluent entrepreneur, ask for referrals to
his top suppliers and to sales professionals who sell on behalf of
those suppliers."

It was not long after Jack returned to "production" that he
realized the value of capitalizing on transition money. Early one
morning, he called on me and related a recent success scenario.
Several months before this conversation, Jack's firm had helped a
highly profitable manufacturing company go public. Jack called the
chief executive officer, a major stockholder of the firm, and congratulated him on a successful public offering. He informed the CEO
that he was a security broker employed by the same firm that did the
corporate underwriting. Jack was not the only sales professional
who called on this CEO.

Jack told his prospect that he had recently helped other CEOs
with significant transition dollars meet their personal investing ob-

jectives. The CEO replied that he had been so inundated with the corporate side of his financial lifestyle that he had been unable to give any consideration to investing a sum of money in the low eight-figure range. Jack was successful in capturing a significant portion of those transition dollars. Why did he succeed while others failed? Was this a direct consequence of Jack's timing of his solicitation? Timing was not the entire answer. Several other enlightened brokers attempted to capitalize on the CEO's transition game; their timing was also excellent. But those brokers focused more on their own needs than on the needs of the prospect.

Jack gained the respect of the CEO by asking him for endorsements and referrals to a particular group of affluent prospects. No, Jack did not ask for the names of the CEO's tennis or golfing co-horts. He followed the suggestions I had made to him concerning suppliers of corporations. "The owners of businesses that supply large corporations are often more affluent than any individual who works for the firm that is buying. Jack, focus on sellers, not buyers."

The CEO gave Jack endorsements and the names of several business owners who were important suppliers for his firm. Jack immediately called on these prospects. He wasted little time in asking them whether they would be interested in purchasing shares in the corporation that was one of their largest customers. He sold 16,000 shares during his initial contact.

I congratulated Jack on his fine performance in the game of "transition dollars." Then I raised this question: "Jack, when you spoke to the suppliers whom you just closed, did you ask them for the name of the commission sales professional who consummated all of those million-dollar deals? Most of the ESPs in this country are employed by small and medium-sized privately owned firms—just like the supply firms you spoke about. It is not unusual for an ESP to have a higher income than his employer/owner. Always ask for the names of the supplier's top sales professionals and when those sales professionals are about to receive their 3 percent commission on a $10 million sale. Money in transition does not stay in transition long."

But how can marketers efficiently allocate their resources if it is difficult or impossible to predict when major cash flow changes will take place among the affluent prospects? In such cases, a proactive marketing stance is still important. Many ESPs have devised clever methods of conditioning prospects. These methods include sending public relations–type articles and other communications to prospects. Prospects often retain such highly credible pieces of information. Then, having been conditioned by the ESP, when an unexpected upswing in cash flow occurs, they will communicate this situation to the ESP.

Some affluent prospects may experience major economic changes so infrequently and so unpredictably that even the most patient marketer can become frustrated. Moreover, the most important economic events may take place only once in the affluent prospect's lifetime. The most important economic event in the lifetime of many affluent prospects is the sale of their business. Such a sale often takes place only once in a generation. However, focusing on the affluent sellers of businesses is a worthwhile activity. For many ESPs in investment products and services, this activity is very worthwhile. Moreover, its value can be enhanced by adopting the "precipitation orientation." In situations where the marketer cannot predict when an affluent prospect will sell a business, he should consider precipitating the sale. In other words, when a marketer cannot predict the future, he should attempt to influence the future via proactive marketing.

How can a marketer of financial services sensitize the affluent prospect so as to precipitate the sale of the prospect's business?

A Precipitation Lesson from Procter & Gamble

Marketers interested in penetrating the affluent market can learn a great deal from Procter & Gamble. The great success of Procter & Gamble's Head and Shoulders shampoo can be attributed to a simple but powerful marketing technique. Procter & Gamble realized that marketing its shampoo as a hair cleanser would give Head and Shoulders no relative advantage in competing with dozens of other shampoos on the market. It realized that for Head and Shoulders to succeed, more had to be promised than clean hair. It therefore focused on the need of young adults to be attractive.

In a 30-second commercial, Procter & Gamble sensitized millions of impressionable young adults to the inverse relationship between dandruff flakes and attractiveness. "Bob is so handsome," suggests one attractive female to another, "but he has dandruff." The Bobs, Harrys, Toms, and Bills all over America saw themselves as being talked about disparagingly by members of the opposite sex. "Who wants to date someone with flakes?" But the commercial not only sensitized millions to the problem of dandruff; it also suggested a way of solving the problem. After the viewers spent 15 seconds becoming sensitive to their dandruff problem, Procter & Gamble provided a solution in the next 15 seconds. After shampooing with Head and Shoulders, Bob is surrounded by beautiful and admiring women. He attributes his attractiveness directly to the fact that Head and Shoulders removed his flakes.

How can the Procter & Gamble technique be applied to marketing to the affluent?

Precipitating the Need for an Investment Expert

Being the first to know about major changes in an affluent prospect's financial lifestyle is the key ingredient in obtaining his business. One of the most difficult changes to predict is when the affluent business owner will sell his business. It is important to remember that most millionaires in America own a business and will sell it at some time. Reactive marketers wait for businesses to be sold and then attempt to solicit the former owners. Proactive marketers, such as Procter & Gamble, precipitate a need. Procter & Gamble decided that it could not wait for young adults in America to sensitize themselves to the need for Head and Shoulders. Instead, it adopted a proactive posture by encouraging them to recognize the need to remove embarrassing flakes.

Marketers of investment services can follow the basic elements of Procter & Gamble's technique. Why not encourage affluent business owners to sell their businesses? In order to do this, these prospects must be sensitized to the opportunities that are available.

Often, affluent business owners do not recognize that they are affluent. Many of these business owners, in their 50s and 60s, would like to be able to retire comfortably. However, they are concerned that selling their businesses will not yield proceeds sufficient to maintain an adequate standard of living for them and their families. So they keep on working. The marketer of investment products and services can readily capitalize on these facts. He can create a need for his services by employing the technique of precipitating the sale of a business. Along these lines, I would like to consider a suggestion that I recently gave to a young woman who was employed as a registered representative.

This young woman entered the securities field several years ago. She had apparently been reasonably successful during her short career. However, her success had been largely a function of the wealth possessed by her father and his relatives and friends. In short, she became the security trader for several large accounts. More than likely, she never had to make many cold calls. I was not sure why her business had fallen off. However, even friends and relatives make objective trade-offs when it comes to blood or money.

This woman said that if she did not find new affluent clients, she would become an airline stewardess. I suggested that she closely examine her neighborhood, city, and regional newspapers for leads and opportunities. One of the neighborhood newspapers had a classified advertisement for a noncredit course on how to appraise the market value of small businesses. I suggested that she think about the opportunities presented by this advertisement. Her initial response was that she had little interest in becoming an appraiser. However, my objective was not to have her become a professional appraiser but to provide her with two opportunities. The immediate opportunity was that she would be in a class with people who had an interest in determining the value of small and medium-sized businesses. A good number of these people would be business owners who were interested in marketing their businesses. Could there be a better environment for an aggressive marketer of investment services? Where could one find a higher concentration of affluent prospects who were about to need investment information and products?

The other opportunity was that she would be able to learn how to value businesses, who the experts in this field were, and how to market and conduct business valuation seminars. With this knowledge, she could not only attract a high concentration of affluent business owners but also control the market environment by precipitating sales of business assets. Like Procter & Gamble, this young registered representative could distinguish herself by going beyond the traditional product offering. Most business owners will tell you that there are thousands of registered representatives who can market securities. Few, if any, can name one such marketer of securities who is also an expert in valuing and marketing small and medium-sized businesses.

The technique of precipitating the sale of a business will assure this marketer that she will be the first to know of the impending transaction. Also, in cases where she has accurately estimated the value of a business to be several times greater than the owner thought it was, she will be held in high esteem and perceived as having significant credibility. One of the greatest marketing weapons in the securities industry is an image of being more knowledgeable about the value of privately held businesses than the owners of these businesses. The registered representatives who adopt this technique will find the following axiom valuable: *If I can't predict when critical economic events will take place, I will precipitate those events.*

A Proactive Technique for Engineers

In the spring of 1979, the chairman of our marketing department received a telephone call from the marketing manager of an engineering design firm. The marketing manager asked him to recommend someone on the marketing faculty who could develop sales training seminars for engineers. The chairman recommended me because, I suspect, of my experience with professional services marketing.

After putting on the training seminars, the firm asked me to help it in developing a strategic marketing plan. I spent several months analyzing its market opportunities as well as the strengths and weaknesses of its product and service offerings. During this analysis, I uncovered two main problems facing the firm. First, several of its current service offerings were in the very late stage of their product life cycle. Second, the firm was reactive, not proactive, in its approach to the market.

One service offering of the firm provides a good example of both of these problems. The firm's environmental engineering division enjoyed an excellent reputation for its innovative designs and had captured a significant portion of the municipal treatment design business. The reputation of this division was so strong that business often gravitated to the firm. Sometimes, a favorable image creates a reactive marketing orientation. In this case, since business went almost naturally to the firm, which offered the best designs, the firm did not develop an aggressive marketing style.

The firm's lack of a proactive marketing philosophy coupled with a declining market dictated some major changes. Along these lines, I looked for new opportunities upon which the firm could capitalize. The best opportunity for the firm's environmental engineering division appeared to be in the area of industrial water treatment facilities. The need for design and consultation services in this area would increase significantly in the future. Also, the firm's innovative technology could readily be transferred to industrial water treatment products. But selling innovative technology to an unfamiliar market was not compatible with the firm's reactive marketing orientation. Also, I found that many corporate prospects were uninformed as to the possible negative effects that recently enacted environmental statutes would have on their production forecasts.

I told the firm's managers that they had two choices concerning the market for industrial environmental engineering. They could either wait until industrial water polluters recognized the need for the firm's offerings, or they could adopt a proactive strategy.

The firm took my advice and adopted a proactive strategy. The market's ignorance about the effects of water pollution control could be viewed as a golden opportunity. I suggested that the ultimate marketing tactic would be to position the firm as "the source" for intelligence concerning water pollution control.

What effect will a representative of "the source" firm have on a prospective client when he suggests the possibility of a plant shutdown due to water pollution? In all likelihood, the prospect will become very sensitive to its pollution problems. Since "the source" firm was the first to inform the prospect of its problem, this firm is also likely to be the first to be asked to suggest a solution. Being the first to sensitize a prospect translates into being the first in line to gain the business.

However, one key element was still missing from this equation. There were thousands of industrial prospects within the firm's self-designated trade area. Obviously, some of these prospects were more likely than others to have serious future problems with environmental statutes.

I reasoned that if the firm's marketing professionals were just given carte blanche to call on "prospects" randomly, their closing rate would be very small. To avoid this, I had to find a way to rank the prospects. How could I determine which organizations were most likely to be fined or shut down by the government and therefore most likely to spend money on the firm's consultation and design services.

I have always believed that if one looks long enough, he is bound to find information about any topic. After several weeks of examining secondary research reports, I found the missing link.

The federal government had contracted with a major research think tank to determine what types of plants would have the most serious pollution problems in the future. This little-publicized research probably cost the government at least several hundred thousand dollars. I suggested that the firm purchase a copy of the report from the federal government. The sales price was $10.95 plus postage! The report ranked several thousand products according to the future pollution problems that were likely to be associated with their production. It also specified the numerical code standard industrial classification (SIC) of each product. This information provided the foundation for the technique that was developed for marketing the firm's services.

I was able to classify each production plant in my client's trade area according to the plant's potential pollution problems. The plants with the greatest forecast pollution problems were selected as primary targets for prospecting. A list of the names and addresses of the top decision makers in each of the pertinent companies and plants was developed from various manufacturing directories.

A dossier was developed for each potential client specifying the names of its major decision makers, the types and amounts of the products it produced, estimates of its potential pollution problems, and estimates of the benefits it would obtain from adopting the firm's pollution control system.

In addition to the dossier, I developed a step-by-step procedure for the firm's marketing personnel to follow. These steps included:

1. Review dossier material and pollution control statutes.
2. Obtain an appointment with key decision makers at the targeted organizations.
3. Armed with significant amounts of highly credible information about the prospect's pollution problems, the firm's expertise, and the prospect's options, enter into discussions with the key decision makers.
4. Firmly establish the credibility of the firm by being the first to introduce data on forecast pollution problems and related intelligence about the details of the prospect's operation.
5. Present the firm's proposal as being the most productive solution.

The proactive technique employed by this engineering firm is directly analogous to the ones that I have suggested for those interested in marketing to the affluent. The engineering firm developed superior intelligence about the problems and identities of targets in its trade area. It was the first to recognize these problems and the first to identify the targets most likely to be desirous of solving these problems. In addition, the firm established significant credibility by demonstrating its superior understanding of the changes in pollution control statutes and of the individual prospect's problems and by offering innovative pollution control systems. The intelligence system enabled the firm's sales professionals to precipitate a need on the part of prospects and at the same time enabled them to be the first to present a method of meeting that need.

Roger of Henry

One of the most successful sales professionals in the securities industry operated in a market that most other brokers would ignore. In his first year of production, during the mid-1970s, Roger Thomas of Edward D. Jones had an income from commissions of nearly $100,000. This extraordinary level of production was developed in a rural town of around 14,000 that was located in northern Illinois.

Roger became an extraordinary sales professional because he designed and applied a customized set of sales techniques. His remarkable sales achievement translated into his current position as partner in charge of marketing training for Edward D. Jones, one of the most profitable security firms in America. This firm owes much of its success to a strategy of marketing in places that the competition often overlooks, namely small towns.

Like so many other extraordinary sales professionals, Roger recognized that the secret of selling securities was to offer more than a product or service. By researching his trade area, he developed an understanding of its social structure and network system. His research suggested that farmers who were middle-aged and older constituted one of the most affluent groups in the area. He also noted that many of these farmers were members of grange associations. Thus, he concluded that it would be advantageous to relate his security offerings to grange association activities.

Roger offered to conduct seminars for the members of various grange associations. These seminars were put on in cooperation with both the grange associations and feed companies. The feed company sales professional was delighted to pick up the complete cost of such seminars since they gave him an opportunity to market to groups of farmers. Roger told me that farmers came to the seminars primarily for the information they received from the feed sales professional and for the free refreshments, not to hear him talk about securities. However, he did speak at many of the seminars, and he found them extremely effective in marketing to wealthy farmers.

Roger also volunteered to speak at various church functions. These functions included refreshments and the opportunity to visit with friends. Roger had found that affluent farmers had a close affinity for their house of worship. He capitalized on this relationship and was very successful in gaining the endorsements of church groups.

While many mediocre sales professionals wasted countless hours every week taking unproductive coffee breaks, Roger generated considerable production even when he took a break from his formal duties. His closest friend in the town in which he became an ESP owned the home and farm store. Constantly, during any weekday, farmers could be found in this store. Roger took most of

reaks at the store. Meeting with prospects in this infor-
...... environment often prevented their defense mechanisms from
appearing. Even though U.S. farm communities have suffered
some economic reversals, Roger maintains that farmers are still
among the most affluent segment in America.

Widows were another affluent segment that Roger prospected.
He was known as the broker for widows in Henry County, Illinois.
"I went to all their birthday parties, gave talks to the garden clubs,
bought them cakes on their birthdays. I had a special relationship
with the local bakery, where I could call in the morning and pick up
a customized cake in the afternoon. I personally delivered each
cake to each widow. One of the great stories that my wife tells my
friends is about the day she saw me escorting two elderly widows
(clients) across the street." Roger also gave speeches at nursing
homes to people interested in setting up perpetual care funds. "I
would invest it so that they would get a monthly check to pay their
monthly bills."

During the off-season for farmers, Roger regularly invited affluent farmers and their wives to have lunch at his house. This
enabled him to demonstrate to these prospects and clients that he
had a stable family situation—that he was married and had children. Roger considers it very important for sales professionals to
demonstrate stability and permanence. He maintains that sales
professionals enhance their credibility and trustworthiness by letting their prospects and clients know that they are married and
have children. According to Roger, his affluent prospects and clients did not want to deal with "some bachelor guy who was breez-
ing through town."

Roger's automobile also demonstrated to the affluent population of his rural trade area that he was stable, conservative, and
down-to-earth. His five-year-old compact Oldsmobile sedan was
an ideal means of communicating economic discipline. Roger made
his first cold call in Henry County while still driving an eight-year-
old Volkswagen bus. When he knocked on the prospect's door, the
affluent farmer pointed out that the bus was sliding backward down
the steep driveway. "There goes your car, boy." The farmer was
so amused that he invited Roger inside the house. The farmer had
only one piece of furniture in his living room—a barber chair that
he used for midday snoozes. I asked Roger, "Could anyone with

only a barber chair in his living room have any money to invest?''
He answered, "You bet your life he has a lot of money. He's
loaded. And he became one of my best customers.''

The Underdog

If you ask Joel R. how, at the age of 29, he was able to generate
over $200,000 in income from the sale of securities, he will proba-
bly respond with two comments. First, "I'm the lowest-rated registered representative in the top group—there is a lot of room for
improvement." Second, "I don't know why people invest money
with me, but I can tell you what some seasoned pros say. They say
I'm a natural underdog.''

Joel's underdog technique is not unusual among young ESPs.
During a recent telephone conversation with a Connecticut-based
millionaire, Joel spoke about himself before discussing investment
offerings. "I'm just a kid—29 years old. I was born and raised in
the South—majored in Agronomy at the University of Georgia.
I've been in this business for three years. Not long enough to be
considered an expert—but I know a great deal about this particular
investment opportunity.''

Joel's human approach and his views on marketing investments to the affluent are reflected in his technique. He does not feel
a need to be pompous or competitive with clients. "I'm just myself. When I make a presentation to a group of wealthy prospects, I
tell them the truth—my age, my fear of standing up and addressing
a large group of very successful people who were winners before I
was born.''

According to Joel, the affluent do not want to deal with a
security broker who brags about how superior he is and whom they
perceive to be competing with them. In fact, Joel told me that he
had been most successful when telephone cold-calling the very
affluent in northern states. "People in the North think that 29-year-
old brokers with southern accents are harmless. Wealthy clients
don't want to think that you are interested in dominating the relationship.''

Joel's underdog approach is also employed by Bill Vanderford. Bill is a successful ESP in guided fishing trips for the affluent.
Every time a patron catches a fish in Bill's presence, he gets genu-

inely excited and praises the patron. He always makes his patrons feel that they are the experts, the finest sportsmen of the moment. In sharp contrast, one of the most talented younger fishing guides in the South (in terms of catching fish) will never reach Bill Vanderford's status. Typically, when a patron catches even a good-sized largemouth, this young guide says, "That's nothing. You should have seen the lunkers I took out of this lake last Friday. They make your catch look like bait fish."

William D. Caller, an ESP in the apparel industry, also uses the underdog technique. "I never give the buyer the impression that I'm making her decision, and I never flaunt my superior knowledge of the market, materials, styles. Buyers, especially the most important ones, have very tender egos. My job is to provide information. But the buyer must always believe that she is in charge—in control. This is especially true when I'm dealing with a buyer who recently took over for one of my previous contacts. I live by what my mother taught me long ago: 'Me, me, me is boring, boring, boring.' I added, 'Ex, ex, ex is death, death, death in my business.' " Caller always asks his prospects and patrons about their ideas, needs, families and so on. "I'm not important; they are." He pointed out that many sales professionals lose their current accounts when the buying responsibility changes. Why? "Because they keep telling the current buyer this is the way your predecessor did it, and she was really smart. The last thing a new buyer wants to hear is that some other buyer is a lot more perceptive than she is."

Many sales professionals in the investment area lose current business because they keep telling the pension manager of a privately held corporation, the new trustee of a foundation, or the "new attorney for the estate" that the person they dealt with before was "really smart, and this is what he would have done if he were still in charge."

David H. and His Breakfast Club

David H. is a young ESP in the insurance industry. He has developed several interesting sales techniques. One of them is a modified version of the chumming technique. David has used this technique to become acquainted with many multimillion-aires.

David belongs to what can be called an ESPs' breakfast club. Its members are noncompeting professionals who meet regularly at 7 A.M. to exchange ideas about marketing to the affluent and to share referrals. These members include several ESPs. One member specializes in insurance, another in accounting, a third in real estate, and so on.

At each meeting of the club, an invited guest makes a presentation. The invited guests are all multimillionaires. Even multimillionaires often feel that they are unappreciated and unrecognized, so the club has had little difficulty in attracting a steady stream of very wealthy "speakers" who are willing to share their experiences with its young members.

David and his fellow members understand a good deal about the ego needs of the affluent. Some of the most successful business owners, sales professionals, and senior executives have a great need to tell their story. Not many millionaires will visit a security broker's office for an hour-long sales pitch. On the other hand, successful people will go out of their way if they are given the opportunity to spotlight themselves.

People have often asked me how difficult it is to secure an interview with an affluent respondent. Why would a millionaire want to be interviewed? Why would he wish to be candid? My response to such questions is quite straightforward. "The real problem is to stop them from talking so that I can ask another question. There have been many occasions when I have had to turn the lights out to convince a group of millionaire respondents that the interview was over."

Most self-made affluent people are constantly taking care of other people and constantly listening to other people's problems and success stories. Often, the affluent feel that they bore even their own family members when they discuss business and financial success. Many ESPs who focus on the affluent always ask them to tell their story. When the affluent are allowed to do this, they often develop an affection for the listener. The development of affection has a great deal to do with success in selling. As a top ESP in the apparel business once told me, "If I can get them to like me, then I know they will love my products."

Ms. Reciprocity

I once asked a marketing student a simple question about reciprocity. "Philip, if you were an ESP in the insurance, real estate, or securities industry, from whom would you purchase your automobiles?" Philip thought for a moment and then said, "A Cadillac dealer."

Philip's answer was different from the answers given by some ESPs to the same question. But even many ESPs overlook the importance of exploiting reciprocal relationships. Most of the ESPs that I have interviewed are heavy spenders. ESPs are likely purchasers of expensive primary homes and vacation homes, luxury automobiles, expensive watches and jewelry, quality clothing, gourmet foods, expensive brands of liquor, and a variety of other high-priced items. They are also among the heaviest users of services—dry cleaning, accounting, automobile repair, decorating, grooming, landscaping, travel, and so on.

If Philip had been enlightened, he would not have merely answered "a Cadillac dealer" when asked about his future automobile purchases. However, even seasoned sales professionals answer this question incorrectly.

Recently, I interviewed an ESP in her mid-30s. During the debriefing, she told me of her excitement about her impending purchase of a Porsche. I asked her how she was going to decide where and from whom she would purchase her next automobile. She mentioned quality of service, the dealer's location, price, and the personality of the automobile sales professional. Not once, however, did she mention reciprocity.

This ESP was about to spend over $30,000 after having made an almost random choice of sales professionals. In two instances, she had merely walked into the dealership and let the sales professionals intercept her. In the third instance, she had been referred to the sales professional by a business associate.

My advice to her was to call the sales manager at each dealership and ask him for the name of his top-producing sales professional; to make appointments with each of these top producers; if possible, to introduce herself to the sales manager and owner at each dealership; and to tell each owner, sales manager, and top producer that she sold securities and strongly believed in reciprocal relationships.

There are several reasons why you want to deal with the top producer at your chosen dealership. First, many top producers who sell big-ticket automobiles are affluent. They can become quality clients. Second, their clout with the management of the dealership increases your chances of having your low price bid accepted. Third, they have a Rolodex filled with the names of other affluent ESPs and other high-income patrons who may benefit from a disciplined approach to investing. Remember, however, that most ESPs are more likely to be spenders than investors and that they often feel guilty about spending and not investing. Many of them would welcome a firm helping hand in getting their consumption/investment lifestyle under control. You can capitalize on this by selling them a structured, disciplined financial plan. Fourth, every ESP has a pool of valuable information on how you can market your services more effectively. Associate with ESPs. If you want to be a mediocre marketer, hang around mediocre marketers, but if you want to be a great marketer, associate with great marketers. And if you want to be affluent, associate with the affluent.

One word of caution is in order. Ownership of a luxury automobile is often a better predictor of heavy consumption than of significant amounts of real wealth!

Where Does Harry Go So Early in the Morning?

Harry achieved ESP status in the securities industry after only three years in the field by creating a method of surfacing in the middle of the affluent convoy. Harry realized that business owners are often very affluent and that some of the more affluent business owners in his self-designated trade area were apparel manufacturers. But he did not know any of these manufacturers. He determined that cold-calling them via telephone was not very productive since many of them had several layers of "interceptors of telephone solicitations" in their offices. Interceptors were also very effective in removing those who attempted to make cold calls in person.

Harry analyzed the activities of these apparel manufacturers in more detail. During this analysis, he discovered that before 6:00 A.M. every day many of them had breakfast together in a diner in a low-rent industrial area. Harry therefore began each workday by having breakfast at this diner. Eventually, he became acquainted with a majority of the "breakfast club" and captured a large share of their investment business. In all the time that he spent at the diner, he never encountered a single competitor. While at the diner, Harry did not have to compete with interceptors, phone calls, production schedules, and the like. What Harry instinctively understood was that some business owners start their business day before the sun rises and that such business owners prefer to deal with sales professionals who also begin their business day before most people wake up.

Marty of Nebraska

Marty J. had always wanted to pursue an acting career, so he set out for California immediately after graduating from the University of Nebraska. He found that there was very little chance of landing a major acting role in Hollywood, but he did succeed in becoming a stuntman. His work as a stuntman was often dangerous and difficult, and he never made much money at it.

Realizing that he could not become a high-paid actor, Marty pondered the question of what else he could do in Hollywood to generate a large income. He learned that a selling career provided some potential for making a big-league income and that some areas of selling were much more lucrative than others. The area he chose was the securities industry. But most security brokers never attain ESP status. Those that do have assets that set them apart from the pack. Marty had such assets. One of the most significant was his technique, which enabled him to become an ESP in almost record time.

Marty realized that the area of California in which he lived had a high number of older affluent prospects and that some of the wealthiest of these prospects were active members of the lawn bowling association. He reasoned that if he could surface in the middle of the affluent convoy (the lawn bowling club), he would have an excellent opportunity to capture several very large accounts.

With letters of reference from the "Nebraska Chapter of the Lawn Bowling Club," Marty applied for membership in the California lawn bowling club, whose members represented one of the highest levels of concentrated wealth anywhere in America. The California club accepted his application, though some of its members did think that a young man in his mid-20s would appear a bit odd lawn bowling with the other members, none of whom were under 55 years of age and many of whom were over 65. Some of the members had retired after selling their privately held corporations, and others were in the process of selling their businesses.

Marty's success inside the affluent convoy exceeded his expectations. He found that many of his club's members were eager to move their money out of low-yielding CDs and into something more productive. In time, he became the number one provider of investment services for most of the club's members. Eventually, he tapped into other pockets of very affluent segments outside the club as a consequence of referrals from members.

Sam L.

Sam L. has been one of the premier private banking officers in this country for over two decades. His clients include some of our most successful athletes, entrepreneurs, and professionals. When I asked him to explain his success, he said that my question was very timely. He had just brought in a $30 million asset management account. He told me that this account was a direct result of a very simple technique that he had developed over the years. "I just do everything I can do for my current customers. If more people would *knock themselves out over their current customers,* they would have more new business from new clients than they could handle." Sam treats all of his customers with the same devotion to service. He believes that all too often sales professionals neglect their current customers by spending a disproportionate part of their time and energy prospecting for new business.

Peter C. and Capital Vessels

Peter C. is one of the nation's leading authorities on fixed income investments. One of his major means for achieving ESP status was a modified version of the "surface in the middle of the affluent convoy" technique. Peter surfaced next to a very large battleship.

Even before Peter became a security broker, he knew that he wanted to market to very affluent prospects. But he was not personally acquainted with any. However, Peter had always loved to sail. He therefore read with great interest several news stories and articles about the interest of many wealthy people in sailing. This was the common thread that he felt would bring him into contact with his target. After a more detailed review of the sailing literature, he selected his first affluent target, a fellow sailor who was also the CEO of one of the largest and most prestigious corporations in America. This CEO was also a major stockholder of the corporation he headed. Peter would become his first broker!

When Peter read that this affluent prospect was planning to sail his yacht from New York to Europe during the summer, he wrote the prospect a letter in which he described his sailing experience and offered to work as a mate on the yacht. The offer was accepted. Peter was able to spend several weeks in close quarters with the CEO, who was very impressed both with Peter's seamanship and with his knowledge of investments. As a result of Peter's initial interaction with the CEO during the summer cruise to Europe, he became the CEO's number one supplier of investments.

Peter's innovative technique and his patience in marketing to the very rich are in sharp contrast with the more traditional lightning bolt cold calls and mass mailings of standard solicitations. Like many other ESPs, Peter recognized early in his career that it might take months, even years, to gain the confidence and respect of the very affluent.

Of Human Bonding

How did a security broker in his early 40s become one of the biggest producers in the industry? During my interview with this fellow, he suggested that bonding had a great deal to do with his success. What is this technique called bonding? To this ESP, it suggests that the more he can share his personal and family experiences with influencers, gatekeepers, prospects, or clients, the more likely he is to encourage them to behave in a manner advantageous to him.

This human bonding ESP is a master of the cold call. He often enters unannounced a business office or factory in which he suspects that the owner may be present. Once inside, he attempts to develop a bond with the owner's secretary. Secretaries are often gatekeepers and interceptors of their employers as well as important sources of information on their employers.

How does this ESP get the secretaries of targeted prospects to act in a manner advantageous to him? He said,

> I put on my dog face and beg her to tell me when her boss will have time to see me. I also show her pictures of my children. Afterward, I write her a card thanking her for her support. The card is often accompanied by a box of candy. I feel I must spend $1,500 on candy a year just for this purpose. Last year, I spent days on the phone telling secretaries that my wife was pregnant. Developing a human bond with secretaries is a very big part of my business. They have a great deal to do with whether or not their boss will ever take the time to talk with me. Secretaries will do a lot more for a cold caller when they realize that he has children for whom he must provide.

How does Tom C. establish a bond with affluent business

> d in my life—everybody has a picture of ... 1em to talk about [commission] discounts ... s is your livelihood. It's hard for them to ... I can't wait till my little girl gets big ... king her on appointments. By God, I will ... used to do it with me. Every time he ... ny father would take me out to the farm ... eady to fire him. I would come out and ... have got to get the human element. ... our mouth but not out of the mouths of ... s much in the office as I used to, and I ... in the office. But I think what is really ... ver to my house. I'm over to their ... it. I have breakfast with them. On my ... day), I go around with an open shirt, ... " but I stop and we just talk about ... s very important.

BIG 5 SPORTING GOODS
3935 STATE ST., SANTA BARBRA, CALIF.
4447   10   3764   00064   003

NIKE CALDERA II BA 1T   28.99 SALE
040001508365
SUBTOTAL   28.99
7.75% SALES TAX   2.25
TOTAL   31.24

CHECK/TRV CHK   31.24
CHANGE   .00

THANK YOU AND PLEASE REMEMBER BIG 5
FOR ALL YOUR SPORTING GOODS NEEDS !
MARCH 22, 1998   12:09 PM

When I interviewed this ESP, I was a bit skeptical about the bonding concept. Soon afterward, however, I began shopping for a new automobile for my wife. My automobile-buying philosophy is simply, "Always deal with the top sales professional at the selected dealer." This sales professional has more leverage with the sales manager than do the others.

At the first dealership I visited, I encountered the top-ranked automobile ESP of the entire Southeast. Before we began to discuss the possible purchase, he insisted that my wife and children come into his office. After providing us with soft drinks, he took out his wallet and said, "I have a family too—a big family. Look at these pictures. These are my two oldest sons. One is in medical school; the other will start medical school in the fall. And this is my youngest son. He is in a top-rated but very expensive private school. And these are my lovely daughters. Gee, Jamie just had braces put on her teeth. I love them all, but they are very expensive these days. How much do you want for your trade-in, Mr. Stanley?"

At this point, we retreated to the safety of our old station wagon and quickly removed ourselves from the premises. Why the withdrawal? I was not going to pay top dollar for any new car, but I could not be aggressive in negotiating price with a man who had all those mouths to feed and all those children to educate. I also felt very uncomfortable about negotiating to the bone in the presence of my children since this ESP had already bonded himself to them. They would regard being a hard bargainer in this situation as taking the food out of children's mouths and preventing two young men from completing medical school. It is noteworthy that this ESP closes more physicians than anyone else in the area. Physicians recognize the money needs of a person with two sons who want to be physicians.

Tommy of the Point and to the Point

Many people find it very difficult to market insurance products to affluent prospects because these prospects often set up barriers to "protect" themselves from aggressive marketers of such offerings. Many extraordinary sales professionals have told me that it is more difficult to gain an audience with some affluent prospects than it is to close the sale. However, Tommy, an ESP in the insurance field, has developed a technique that is effective in securing a personal visit with target affluent prospects.

Tommy is a West Point graduate who retired from the army when he was in his early 50s. At the time of his retirement, he gave no thought to the idea of sitting in a rocking chair all day or of being confined to an office. He wanted active employment. A service colleague told Tommy of the fun he was having marketing insurance. Tommy bought the story and signed up for career insurance training.

Like most of the people who start out in sales, Tommy made his share of mistakes early in his new career. But he also learned a great deal about how to secure an audience with affluent business owners and executives, even without making appointments. He became a master of the cold call.

Tommy found out early in the game that even with scheduled appointments, there were many situations where the prospect could not or would not be available. In other situations, the prospect would "be unavailable" until an hour or two past the scheduled meeting. To make up for the lost or delayed opportunities, Tommy began to cold-call. His success was based on the concept that "if you can get past the secretary, you can get the business from her boss."

Even secretaries who warded off some of the most aggressive sales professionals were no match for Tommy. He would first note and list the names of executives in an office building of his choosing. Then, he would enter the outer office of his target. Finally, with his 6-foot 3-inch frame at military attention, he would boom out this order to the secretary: **"Tell Mr. Smythe I am here."** At the same time, he would hand his card to her. After delivering his command, he would turn his back on the secretary and walk to the opposite end of the office. This reconfirmed the secretary's perception of who was in charge.

Tommy's method of penetration also had a positive influence on the prospects he reached in this way. When the secretary told her boss of Tommy's command and demeanor, he would react, according to Tommy, "as if he had forgotten an important meeting." Tommy's military technique differs greatly from the "finesse" methods of penetration used by many ESPs. However, given his military experience and his leadership qualities, it works very well for him.

Mutual Benefit

A few years ago, a gentleman called me in regard to some of the research I was doing for a mutual friend. He asked me to spend a day with him to discuss the opportunities in the affluent market. During the course of that day, he told me how he became head of marketing for a major mutual fund. He said that being the fund's top sales professional had helped him a great deal. How did he become an extraordinary sales professional?

My own research shows that mutual funds are hard to sell in situations if they are not major funds with tremendous advertising dollars. This ESP attained stardom by having to sell Three Great Unknowns: his firm, his product, and himself. He felt that this would take more than a 60-second phone call or form letter. No, he had to devise a way of obtaining a personal meeting with the prospect and he would need more than just a few moments with the prospect. But most affluent prospects have very little time to devote to solicitations and are protected by a picket line of employees who intercept sales callers before they ever get near the target.

These problems did not deter this ESP. He responded to the situation with one of the most extraordinary techniques ever developed. Stated very simply, he paid for their time. His main client base consisted of physicians. His technique enabled him to penetrate the various levels of sales interceptors that may be found in a physician's office. Yes, selling something to a physician is difficult. But this ESP never revealed that he was selling anything until he was speaking in person with the targeted prospect.

He would make an appointment to visit the physician. No one ever intercepted him. No one ever denied him a "for fee" visit/consultation with the physician.

When he visited the physician, he would say that he had a problem but not a medical problem. When the physician asked him to describe the problem, he would answer, "Doctor, you are my problem. I will pay you for a visit to help you with your investment needs."

This ESP told me that most physicians will listen to someone who pays them for their time. While other sales professionals would sit in one physician's office for hours waiting to make their pitch, this ESP was able to obtain the undivided attention and business of several physicians each day. While salespeople in fields ranging from pharmaceuticals to life insurance are trying to sell by stealing the physician's time, this ESP is paying for it.

Mr. Sensitizer

It is not easy to sell life insurance products. Often, prospective customers find it difficult to conceptualize the need for such products. This is especially true for affluent prospects who are under 40 years of age. Many of these prospects consider premature death so unlikely that it does not warrant the "high premium" associated with a large amount of life insurance. Those who have life insurance often purchase much less than they should.

How can marketers of life insurance encourage the affluent, especially the younger affluent, to become more sensitive to the need for their products? In a recent conversation with Ed Bean of *The Wall Street Journal,* I learned about a unique technique developed by an extraordinary sales professional whom Ed encountered several years ago.

This ESP concluded that verbal cues were not strong enough to convince insensitive prospects that they needed substantial amounts of life insurance, that visual cues had to be used to break down the resistance of such prospects.

He spent his spare time walking through cemeteries, where he sought fresh graves with flowers around and on top and with a gravestone or marker indicating that the deceased had died at under 40 years of age! He took pictures of such graves, focusing on the "critical dates." Then, when he encountered the usual objection ("But I don't need life insurance—I'm too young to think about such problems"), he would extract several of his "visual cues" from his briefcase and hand them to the affluent prospect. After a brief moment, he would suggest to the now sensitized prospect, "All of these people probably thought they were too young to need life insurance."

Mr. B. B.

One of the most innovative techniques in attracting affluent prospects was recently demonstrated by a business broker. Business brokers function as intermediaries. They facilitate the purchase and sale of businesses valued at less than $10 million.

One marketing objective of the business broker is to find prospects with dollars and an interest in purchasing businesses. Another marketing objective is to uncover business owners who are interested in selling their businesses. Often, the typical business broker has too many businesses for sale but not a large enough supply of potential buyers. Mr. B. B. developed a simple, yet productive, method for increasing his supply of potential business buyers.

Many Americans have a strong urge to start their own business. Some of these individuals are able to raise significant amounts of money for such undertakings. They are very sensitive to offers of information about how to successfully start their own business. Given his knowledge of these needs, Mr. B. B. offers *seminars for those interested in successfully launching a business*.

A small, inexpensive, but well-placed classified advertisement in the business section of newspapers in targeted cities is an important means of attracting affluent prospects who wish to become business owners. The seminars naturally include a discussion of how to start a business. In the course of the seminars, however, the topic of purchasing an existing business is also presented. In reality, some people have a much better chance of succeeding in business via the purchase route rather than the start-up method.

The seminar method provides Mr. B. B. with an effective means of attracting prospective buyers for businesses. It also provides him with a steady stream of potential prospects who may someday wish to sell their businesses.

Mr. B. B.'s seminar method is classified as a chumming technique. Why? Chumming suggests that the fish are attracted. Mr. B. B. actually charges the fish a fee to chase him! Early in their careers, many of the best ESPs learned that you often frighten prospects when you chase them. Attracting prospects is often much more productive than chasing them, because attracted prospects self-designate themselves as ready, willing, and able to be caught.

But even Mr. B. B. could benefit from some advice. He is beginning to recognize that attracting prospects is not the same as closing them. Many well-conceived seminars that attract a large number of prospects fail to generate business. One reason why this happens is that too many of the attendees have little or no money and no ability to borrow even moderate amounts. This proble ____ be avoided by (1) charging more than a token amount for admission, (2) indicating in promotional messages the dollar commitment that previous attendees have made in investing in businesses, and (3) providing credible symbols at the seminar that communicate the trustworthiness and the level of expertise of Mr. B. B. and his associates.

The third point is especially important in generating future business. Most people judge the expertise and trustworthiness of a marketer by the people with whom he associates. Mr. B. B. can greatly enhance his credibility by having several noncompeting professionals participate in or cosponsor seminars. Ideally, these professionals would be representative of several fields, including:

1. *Certified Public Accounting.* A CPA from a prestige firm would add credibility by association to Mr. B. B. The accountant should have considerable experience in valuing small and medium-sized businesses. Affluent business owners have a strong need to learn how much their business would sell for, given the current economy. For many business owners, this type of information alone is often worth the admission price.

2. *Tax and Contract Law.* Most affluent business owners are interested in determining the tax implications of selling their organizations. They also want advice about the significant components of a sales contract, such as payment schedules, contingency buying and buybacks, payment methods, and default.

3. *Banking.* Commercial loan officers from banks are often willing to make presentations to potential business buyers and sellers. Potential buyers typically need credit to start or purchase a business, while potential sellers often need to refer potential buyers to the proper credit source.

Mr. B. B.'s seminars for those interested in starting or buying a business will be much more productive when the program contains his message in concert with those of the other professionals mentioned. All of these professionals have a vested new business interest and will probably perform well at the podium. Asset managers, trust officers, financial planners, and security brokers would probably also be delighted to make a presentation at Mr. B. B.'s seminars.

Remember, affluent businessmen who sell their businesses often need advice about how to invest their money. Dollars in transition provide one of the greatest opportunities for any marketer of investments.

Yes, You Would Buy a Cadillac from Lester

Lester Pazol has been one of the top Cadillac salesmen in America for over 20 years. He is also an author and lecturer.

Lester says that his primary objective is not to sell but to be perceived by prospects and clients as trustworthy. He reasons that being perceived in this way greatly increases the probability of making sales. Lester told me that most sales professionals never reach ESP status because the objectives they choose place them under too much stress. According to Lester, most automobile salesmen feel that they must make a sale every time a prospect presents himself and thus regard each prospect as an adversary.

> They are taught by a formula that I call WUOOUC: "*w*arm the customer *u*p, *o*vercome his *o*bjections, and show an *u*rgency for the *c*lose," which is the American way of doing business. And if you don't buy, you're an idiot. That's not my philosophy. If I can get you to like, trust, respect, and admire me, it becomes an evolutionary process.
>
> If I say, "I'm not really interested in the sale but interested in you, and if the sale doesn't happen, I'll have given you the best advice that you can get," the customers now begin to want to be close to me because their goal is to get the best value. That's everybody's goal. So, I'm appealing to what they want. The best value. They now have the confidence in me to know that if I don't have what they want, I'll still guide them in the best direction. So, now I've created a psychological obligation on their part. If they don't buy from me, they are obligated to send me a customer.

Some may think that Lester is highly successful because he offers the lowest prices on Cadillacs. But more often than not, the prices of his offerings are higher than those of some other price/promotion-oriented dealers. Lester sells more than automobiles, more than price—he sells himself and his firm's commitment to high-quality service and response to customer needs.

Lester does not become defensive when he fails to close a sale.

Regardless, I'm the winner. I've accomplished a friendship—the aspect of the goal that I have equations for—I'll get what it is that I'm after. That may be a referral, a recommendation, good-will—it will come back to me. Out of a hundred [prospects], I'll likely sell 40–45. The national average is 15 percent. The point is that the 55 that don't buy from me become allies. This 55 snowballs, and all of my energy is being utilized; none of it is wasted. I'm just as nice to the guy that didn't buy as I am to the one that did buy.

We're in the numbers business, and you're only going to sell 35–40 percent of the vehicles if you're good and maybe 45 if you're super. So, the problem is handling the people you don't sell. Emotionally, you can get bent out of shape. You get down and call 10 people, and they say no. But your personality is so screwed up now that you might miss the next 10.

DR. STANLEY:

Surely, you meet some people with whom you have nothing in common? How do you go about working on a relationship with somebody like that?

MR. PAZOL:

You have to remember what I told you my goal is. I know certain things about people that I've studied. There are three things about people that I know for sure, and I'm positive that, without a doubt, everbody is like this. First, everybody is suspicious of anything you tell them that will benefit them. So, you know that right up front. The more things you say that would come back to benefit you, the more things you give them to be suspicious of. The second thing is that everybody is inhibited. Everybody is shy. So, when you present them with a nonshy person, they are almost always intrigued by it. They are curious and want to know more about you. And I am not a shy person by design. I know how shyness affects the other person and how my nonshyness affects them too. And, thirdly, once you've gained the respect of a person, he listens to you differently and becomes impelled to gain your respect. If you're in sales, there are only two ways he can gain your respect—buy from you or send you a customer. So, if you go after the relationship, you gain the respect and win the game. Maybe not in an immediate sale, but you are a winner. Now, you're dealing, not with the personality that's sitting there, but with three grooves in this brain. And everything you say or do is directed to those grooves and not to the sale of the product.

DR. STANLEY:

When you're talking to somebody, do you find they sort of gradually warm up to you, or is it like a light coming on when all of a sudden they realize . . .

MR. PAZOL:

They warm immediately because of the way I start the relationship. I don't give them a chance to not like me. I open the relationship PCRH = O = I. That's *personality* creates a *curiosity* that gives you time to establish *relationships* from which you can be *humorous,* conveying *objectivity,* and "I" is *interaction.* No matter how mad you get or how demeaning the customer is to you.

DR. STANLEY:

Is everybody that comes in there price sensitive? Or is there another issue involved.

MR. PAZOL:

No, they are all price sensitive, they are service sensitive, and they are value conscious. That's really the name of the game—regardless of their quirks. I had a lady in the shop, and she leased a car from a very big leasing client of mine. The horn went off in the middle of the night two nights ago. She brought it out. We supposedly fixed it and didn't. She called the head of the leasing company, and he called me. "Please take care of this lady—she's on my back," he said. So, I set up for her to come in the store and told her we'd loan her a car today. She's belligerent, antagonistic, and everything else. She walks through the door, and I said, "Clara, you know you're worrying yourself do death over nothing." She's not my client—the leasing company is; and for that reason I'm worried about Clara. She's just mean about the whole situation. I said, "Clara, you're worrying too much. You have on a blue dress; I'll get you a blue car to go with it. And you don't say a word to me. All you can do is holler about the damned horn. You're not enjoying your car because you're mad and upset. Relax." Her son is with her. I said to him, "Tell her to relax." She started laughing and walked off. I probably won't have another moment's problem with her . . . unless the horn goes off again.

DR. STANLEY

How do you deal with the tough pain-in-the-neck people?

MR. PAZOL:

Tough. People are unbelievably tough. But you don't change your personality. You continue with keeping it light and airy. When they get tough, you have a whole set of responses to clear questions. What if they ask, "Why is the other salesman $500 cheaper than you?" Ordinarily, your first response, especially after going through the American philosophy, says you're on the defensive. Why put yourself on the defensive? If you've established a relationship, you're at liberty to put some humor in. Say, "It's because this extra $500 goes into a special fund. I'm trying to buy my mother a new yacht. You know how hard it is to get good labor today."

If you say what they expect you to say, you're just a salesman. If you say something that makes them laugh, that will work. This is a defensive situation—something I call the "red flag questions." In [my] workbook, I have a whole list of these questions for every industry that will teach people how to sit down and do their own red flag questions. Here's for chemical sales: "Your prices are way out of line. Your service is not as good as it used to be. I've been using somebody else's product for years, and I'm happy with it." I ask each person in [my] class to sit down and write out the personal statements that come up and ask them to prepare what I call a "Listerine answer." That's a humorous statement. The reason I call it Listerine is because of that commercial that said, "I hate it, but I use it twice a day." In other words, they have such confidence in this product—they tell you it tastes like crap, and they still buy it. That's what you want to establish—that you have such a good value, you're so sharp, a knowledgeable expert in your field, that you don't have to act like an ordinary begging salesman. Not everybody is going to be relaxed enough to do this. But you have to get your confidence. One step at a time. It may take 10 years, but somewhere down the line you may get that confidence.

If someone asks you a red flag question and you give them your Listerine answer, basically what you're saying in a humorous way is that you're paying $500 more to me and I'm worth it. Without saying that, you're saying it. If you interpret every one of those questions and don't take it personally and realize that this person wants a good buy, that's all. He doesn't have any experience in this field, and he's begging for help.

DR. STANLEY:

Do you think that would work with any type of car or any product, or does it just work with an upscale product?

MR. PAZOL:

Any product. If you relate to somebody, you establish a relationship of interaction. That's when they really believe that you'll tell them the truth even if it means no sale. Once you establish what I call objectivity and you've established more than a customer-sales relationship, you can treat them as you would your brother. They will react in the same way. The second you get serious and start acting like this commission is more important than the relationship, you kill that liberty that you would otherwise have. Humor—it keeps the customer relaxed, and it keeps you relaxed. You can say a lot of things in the name of humor that you can't say seriously without putting a crimp in the relationship. You can say, "Look, Joe, you know you need this damned car, and you know I need the money; now, let's get on with the program." You've asked for the order, but you've left the tension out.

DR. STANLEY:

Do they come to you because they feel you can find them the specialty model that is in undersupply?

MR. PAZOL:

Well, they know that I'm the expert in my field, that I'm the dean of the Cadillac salesmen in America. That helps. I pursue that image. They might be able to go and get a cheaper price, but they won't be dealing with me. If they were to find a cheaper price, if they want to sell our relationship down the river for $200 . . .

DR. STANLEY:

Do you find that the top people want to deal with the top person. Do top salespeople want to deal with top salespeople?

MR. PAZOL:

Everybody wants to deal with the top person. They don't want to deal with some lemon. I use an old saying in my course, "My brain surgeon better drive up in a Rolls-Royce." They don't want to deal with somebody that needs them. They want to deal with somebody that doesn't need them. They feel that if the fellow doesn't need the money, he won't lie to them. So, the more you can convey that image, the better off you are and the more you've gained that respect I was talking about.

When you ask people like Lester a directive question, they will focus on the subject you raise. As a researcher, I have to go beyond a narrowly defined subject area in order to develop a more accurate picture of ESPs like Lester. In fact, the first question I asked him was wide open: "Tell me about yourself."

Open-ended, nondirective questioning of this type often provides a vehicle for measuring the respondent's needs, values, and self-image. What were the key words and phrases that Lester used to define himself? Among the more significant were the following: (1) "teaching at the university"; (2) "articles I have written"; (3) "my course on selling and stress reduction"; (4) "almost 30 years in the business, 22 years at the same Cadillac dealership"; (5) "college degree"; and (6) "credentials."

These key words and phrases tell Lester's story. He feels strongly that many people have a poor image of salespeople. Lester has a need to be viewed, not as a hawker, but as a true sales professional. Much of his self-image, and certainly of the image he communicates, reflects his accomplishments in the areas of writing and teaching as well as his accomplishments in sales.

Lester's personality exudes confidence and strength. Any prospect who talks to him can immediately sense that he is of a different breed than other automobile salespeople. He started his career selling Chevrolets, then moved up to Oldsmobiles, and finally to Cadillacs. As he moved up in make of automobiles, he also traded up to a more affluent clientele. Meanwhile, something else was taking place. He began to write about the psychology of selling and about how to deal with stress. Yes, he is different—and different by design. How many automobile salesmen teach at a prestige university? How many ever wrote two books (*The Nervous American: From Stress to Success* and *Winning the War Within*)? Talkers are often perceived as only hawkers, whereas writers are viewed as experts/professionals. The affluent prefer to deal with professionals like Lester.

DR. STANLEY:

Why is it that a lot of people don't make it in your industry?

MR. PAZOL:

Well, a lot of people use the car business as what I call a "bridge" job. They are waiting for their aunt to die or their boat to come in. They say they don't need a degree or diploma; they can just sell cars. They don't really go into it with the same intensity that a stockbroker or real estate agent would. There are a multitude of people who are able to get into the car business. The car business is never really treated with the dignity of one of the higher professions that require education and so on. So, you have a lot of people floating through with no credentials, just breathing bodies. They stay in if they hit it lucky, and if they don't, they get another bridge job. If the standards were raised, the car business would be a very lucrative pursuit. The problem is that the people don't have qualifications to get the job in the first place and aren't really looking at it as a career. The reason I got into it was that General Motors came to me in 1965 and asked me to go around the country and tell college graduates why they should become car salesmen—with myself being the epitome of the car salesman. At that time, I had been one of the top Oldsmobile salesmen in the country and had been with Chevrolet and was one of their top salesmen in the country. They told me to tell them not to go to IBM or the "piece of the rock" and to show them they could have it in the car business.

People ask me why I'm a good salesman. I don't know. I started reading a lot of books—psychology. I've read everybody—Freud and everybody else. So, I put together a seminar and started my own company in the sales seminar lecturing business in 1967. In about 73, I involved the stress program. It was an evolutionary process. It went from "Why I was able to do it" to "If you're uptight and nervous and if your goal is to sell, you automatically apply a pressure to yourself and inhibit your personality." Your personality is what does the most for you. If you're not functioning 100 percent, you're inefficient. Inefficiency in sales leads to inefficiency with your mate and your children, to heart attacks. People have heart attacks because their bodies are not efficient. The two courses I teach at the university every other quarter (one is called "Better Communications, Less Stress," and the other is called "The Easy Way to Selling") are both basically the same course—don't worry about the selling. To make it simple, I say, "Stop selling; make friends." If you believe your goal is to make friends, the sale becomes a by-product of a relationship. And if you go in and your goal is to make a sale, people become defensive—everybody's suspicious.

As I have often stated, there are two basic methods of marketing to the affluent—the traditional method, in which the marketer pursues the target, and the unconventional method, referred to as chumming by some ESPs, in which the target pursues the marketer. Only a minority of even ESPs have mastered the second method. Lester's image, enhanced by writing, teaching and word of mouth, is the base for his chumming system. After all, if you were a top sales professional who wanted to purchase a Cadillac, you would probably want to deal with the author of the book that helped you lower your stress and enhance your productivity.

DR. STANLEY:

Does all of your current business come from referrals?

MR. PAZOL:

I don't keep up with them; they keep up with me.

DR. STANLEY:

You don't have a Rolodex to keep up with them?

MR. PAZOL:

I don't do anything. I just sit by the telephone all day long. I say, "Hey, howya doing?" Like, trust, respect, and admire—they are looking for me. Salesmen have the second lowest credibility of any profession there is. Only politicians are lower.

There was a customer in the showroom just now—says he's a millionaire, in a double-breasted suit. Owns more property here than probably anybody else or at least as much as anybody else. I'm cutting up and clowning with him, and he says, "Can I go look at my car?" I said, "Yes, but don't touch it." I told him he had to bring me a bottle of Dom Perignon for letting him have this car, I'm doing him a favor. The reverse psychology intrigues them. They like the relaxed personality.

A relaxed personality is often found among top-ranked professionals in fields other than selling. Michael Spinks once told Tony Brown ("Tony Brown's Journal," WETV, Atlanta, Georgia August 9, 1987) how he coped with the pressure he encountered before and during a major fight. Spinks stated that he would have a difficult time ever winning if he became uptight at such times. He said that he trained himself to view each fight as just another sparring match. Like many top-ranked ESPs, Spinks did not take even big encounters too seriously. To do so would communicate a lack of self-confidence and strength.

MULTISTAGE MARKETING

Enlightened marketers more often than not attribute their success to their use of extraordinary marketing methods and to their proprietary methods of identifying prospects. How else can one explain why some sales professionals consistently outperform their peers by 200 percent, 300 percent, and even 500 percent or higher? Yes, they do market differently

Some enlightened marketers employ a method of multistage marketing that includes the following steps:

Step 1: Develop unique and timely methods of identifying high-potential prospects. Don't discount centers of influence and information conduits even if they are unlikely to make purchases. Don't purchase out-of-date prospect lists that are widely distributed. What good is a prospect's name if it is also known to several hundred of your competitors? How much value is there in a list of prospects who are not in the mood for your marketing and investment ideas?

Step 2: Contact and debrief these prospects, key informants, and influencers. Telephone debriefings can be efficient and productive in refining your list. Test the hypothesis that these prospects are ready, willing, and able to purchase, or at least to act as key informants or influencers. Often, it is better not to sell, but to listen, during this initial contact. When you review articles and news items about these prospects, always look for things that you have in common with them. It is much easier to gain a personal visit with a prospect if you can demonstrate that you share a common interest with him. If the prospect likes duck hunting and you do too, mention this sport when you talk to him. Most of the news items that you see will be ego enhancing for your target—e.g., "Judd Parsons, Top Mack Truck Sales Professional Award for This Year." Congratulate Judd in your initial and subsequent discussions. Ask him whether he would give you some advice about how to become an extraordinary marketer. Always focus on the prospect's needs, ego, achievements. Demonstrate that you carefully read the news item. The more knowledge you exhibit on Judd and his lifestyle in your initial discussion, the more impressed he will be with your intellect and the greater the probability that he will grant you a personal visit.

Step 3: Based on your debriefing, eliminate those prospects who are unlikely to be receptive to your marketing message. Encourage those prospects who qualify as potential clients to meet with you. Key informants are also worth visiting.

Step 4: Meet your prospect and continue to debrief him. If you determine during your initial visit that his current need can be fulfilled by your offerings, ask him to give you a significant portion of his business. If he declines to do this, find out what his objections are and then ask him for a small piece of his business. It is often easier to trade down from a large request than to trade up from a small one. Whether the prospect buys or not, ask him for his financial measurements—goals, asset composition, important dates (e.g., CD rollovers, retirement), and so on. Also ask him for referrals to persons who are likely to be interested in your offerings. Ask politely whether you may mention his name when speaking to those to whom he referred you.

Step 5: Recontact the prospect/client at the proper time, with a custom message based on your previous "sizing up" of the prospect/client. It is often more productive to use your first visit with a prospect as a debriefing interview and to ask for the business during subsequent visits.

Very often, when an affluent prospect turns your big request down, he feels a need to "do something positive" for you. If your prospect says no to your big request, view this as an opportunity to make a smaller request. If you are unable to close on a sale of any size, immediately ask for the names of other people who might need your offerings.

After a turndown, some enlightened sales professionals go one step beyond this. They ask the prospect to complete a brief questionnaire. The questionnaire details financial goals, family composition, dates of key financial events (rollovers, retirement, bonuses, etc.), asset composition, and income composition. Such data make it easier for these sales professionals to develop the right message and deliver it at the ideal future date.

ESP'S IN THE INVESTMENT INDUSTRY: TECHNIQUES EMPLOYED DURING INITIAL CONTACT WITH A PROSPECT

Very few of the ESPs whom I have interviewed use a canned sales pitch. Most ESPs tailor their selling approaches to the individual needs of prospects.

During their initial contact with a prospect, ESPs generally attempt to uncover needs for basic investments and related financial services. In this approach, the large majority of ESPs make no distinction with respect to the type of prospect. Business owners are just as likely to be debriefed about their needs as are other types of affluent prospects.

ESPs view the initial debriefing process as a very important ingredient in obtaining business from prospects. In fact, many ESPs feel that their chances of making a sale are enhanced if they do not ask for business during their initial contact with a prospect.

Most ESPs appear to have developed this approach by instinct, their own experience, and trial and error. Some gave credit to the sales training they received from organizations for which they had previously worked. Most felt that high pressure, canned, telemarketing methods were counterproductive. They found this especially true for larger prospects, such as those of business owners.

Almost all ESPs felt that the probability of consummating a sale in the future was influenced by the occupational title and job description that they communicated during their initial contact with prospects. ESPs typically defined their occupation as financial consultant, financial planner, vice president, and so on. Few, if any, defined their occupation as salesman. They described their function as one of enhancing the productivity of the prospect's financial assets.

In approaching affluent business owners, ESPs are likely to introduce themselves as experts in managing company financial assets. They de-emphasize trading and quick-return investments.

Interestingly, many ESPs have never been formally trained in selling relationships or in marketing to the business side of the affluent market. At the same time, other ESPs praise their sales experiences at such companies as IBM and Xerox, which specialize in marketing to businesses rather than individuals.

The traditional methods that ESPs oppose are (1) untargeted cold calling by telephone, (2) closing a sale during initial contact, (3) personal as opposed to business investing, and (4) short-term relationships, though these methods are endorsed by some ESPs who operate in major urban areas. Also, some ESPs believe that telephone cold calls are effective in selling certain types of high-credibility investments, such as municipal bonds.

ESPs from some areas in the country have an approach that appears to be very successful with small business owners. Many of these ESPs feel that the key to designing an investment offering for the small business prospect is to ask him questions about his business. This can be done during initial telephone conversations or face-to-face meetings.

Once the financial service needs of the prospect have been determined, the ESP can design an investment product concept and marketing theme to fit those needs. Discussion of this product offering may not take place until the second, third, or even fourth meeting. This method of consultative selling enhances the probability of making a sale, especially in situations where the prospect is making major investment decisions (e.g., decisions on pension and profit sharing plans.

The responses of ESPs regarding the initial theme have important implications that go beyond marketing tactics. The training of both new and established sales professionals should include greater emphasis on the how and why of marketing to the affluent business owner. That training should stress empathy for the goals and needs of the business owner. Prospecting should be taught on a continuing basis.

Marketing training for sales professionals should also include true-to-life small-business selling encounters. These encounters should include contacting and making appointments with small-business owners. The training should also include discussions of videotapes showing trainees debriefing pseudo-small-business prospects. Following each of these discussions, selected ESPs should be asked to critique the trainees and their methods. Investment firms should also conduct a survey of the top producers who deal with small-business owners. The survey would document the best methods of debriefing clients and of developing marketing themes based on the intelligence obtained from clients. This information should be included in each firm's sales training.

QUOTES FROM ESP'S CONCERNING INITIAL CONTACT TECHNIQUES

If I talk to individuals about their business and their retirement plan or if they are individuals interested in retirement benefits in general, they will always talk to me. They don't perceive I'm after their money.

I might call myself a consulting service coordinator. I believe that is vague enough that I can say that I am anything.

I just let them know that there are things in the corporate world that [our firm] is very good at—and I listen to them. You know, when I worked for IBM, that was the first drill we ever did when we walked in the door. How are you going to sell him something unless you know what he wants—emphasis on listening to the client. Finding out what his objectives are before you start.

I don't ask them on the first phone call. I just ask to meet them. I just ask for 20 minutes of their time. Again, my presentation is that I get in there and listen to them. I don't go with a preset notion of what their needs are. I let them tell me exactly what they are doing, what their needs and concerns are, and then attempt to fit financial planning with this. I use my title, which we all know is ridiculous, regional director of financial planning, which sounds very impressive. Probably about 80 percent of the time, they will say, "Yes, I'll give you 20 minutes of my time."

I think it is a matter of timing, because sometimes they are more receptive to discussing certain things than they are at other times.

I really don't know what I will say when I get them on the phone (initially). The hardest part used to be to get past the secretary. But now I know how to do it. When she asks if Mr. Big knows who I am, I respond that he should. I never lie to secretaries.

Timing is sometimes just luck when you're out there prospecting. It just so happened that I caught him in a receptive mood that Monday and was able to do more business with him.

The critical part of doing business with small business owners is to keep in touch with them (after your initial contact).

I am a consultant. I work with managed money, and I go into the thing about managed money. And probably 2 out of 10 times, the guy says, "Really, tell me more about that," or "How does that work?" or whatever. . . . The people, the press, whatever, look at us as stockbrokers, and my card doesn't say stockbroker. I am always with the consulting group [of the firm].

I'm not there to sell them a product. I'm there to sell them a service.

The smaller the client, the more you are going to hear about the family problems and the automobile and the college and the other stuff. The larger client, his focus [is on the business] because he is where he is and because he has accomplished what he has accomplished in his business.

I get prospects from the local companies and take a look at who the chief executive officers are. I call them up and tell them I want to talk to them about the company. A guy that owns a company in town that is publicly traded over the counter, he loves to tell his story, and all these guys love to tell their story. We are salesmen, but we have to be good listeners. I don't know anybody else that does that, that calls them up and says, "I would like to talk to you about your company."

I prospect with a letter that says you need [a minimum investment of] $100,000. And if you want a copy of the [audio tape that describes the offer and my philosophy], return this slip. I get a 2 percent return on that.

The guy is one of the largest privately held jeans manufacturers. I started a personal relationship with 25 bonds.

CHAPTER 5

SOURCES OF INFORMATION

Where does one go to gather intelligence about affluent prospects who are likely to be encountering a significant economic event or an upturn in their liquid wealth? There are many sources of such market intelligence. Some of these sources are so common and so close at hand that they are overlooked. Others are far more exotic and often not readily available.

I have stated that marketing to the affluent and fishing have much in common. In a very broad sense, there are two methods or categories of fishing. In the first method, the fisherman finds the fish, chases the fish, and hopefully catches the fish. Finding the fish is the foundation of this fishing method. The bulk of this chapter is devoted to the goal of finding and identifying suspected big fish who are ready, willing, and able to purchase.

The second method of fishing is based on the idea of attracting the target to the fisherman. This method, called chumming, is discussed in Chapter 7. It is important to note here, however, that the method is very useful. Not all affluent people can be identified. Not all affluent who are in an upside cash flow can even be suspected. Chumming is very useful in attracting the very latent affluent—those who rarely give anyone a hint that they are affluent.

The discussion in this chapter is not intended to cover every possible information source. It is intended, however, to stimulate marketers to utilize unconventional intelligence sources. It is also intended to serve as a base for developing new avenues of market insight.

The Houston Lament

During one of my presentations in Houston, Texas, several ESPs asked me to comment on the affluent market in the area. One of them pointed out that it was interesting to reflect upon the condition of the Houston affluent market before the oil crisis. Obviously, the affluent market had changed in Houston because of the "oil depression."

Much of my discussion in Houston centered on identifying wealth via news and other types of public information. "Dr. Stanley, your suggestions are fine under normal conditions, but we are not operating under anywhere near normal conditions—100,000 homes in foreclosure." I acknowledged the problem and then asked, "Did you notice the billboards down the road from our hotel? The same announcement is also in the classified section of this morning's newspaper—2,000 homes to be auctioned off this weekend. Don't you think the auctioneer will be in the right economic frame of mind after he gets his fee for selling those homes? Two thousand problems translate into one auctioneer's payday. What do you think he will do with the revenue he generates from the problems in oil country? Why not give him a call? His name and phone number are up on the billboard outside. But don't wait too long to call him; he may be euphoric for just a few days after the sale. Wouldn't you rather he open an investment asset account with you than purchase a yacht? Don't forget to ask for a list of those who purchased homes. What types of people can afford to buy homes when others can't make monthly payments? Often, they are affluent. Often, they have considerable dollars for buying homes in down markets for resale in peak periods."

AUCTIONS AND MARKET ACTION

Early one Monday morning, I found an auction notice in my mailbox at the university. Sent by one of my entrepreneur-oriented colleagues, the notice indicated that an estate of over 100 acres of land would be sold along with a nine-bedroom mansion, stables, a barn, and a horse track. My colleague's handwritten note stated that the property would sell for several million dollars.

I tacked up the notice in my office, where it remained for two days. A former student stopped by to discuss his career. Roland was a young, fairly successful insurance agent. He had always had a good aptitude for selling and was what one could call "pleasantly aggressive." It did not take too long to determine his purpose in stopping by. During the last two years, he had sold a great many $10,000 life insurance policies. However, he felt unsure about how to trade up to wealthier clients. A seminar on how to be a top producer in the insurance industry had made him keenly aware of the need to do this. At that seminar, he had been told that he should trade up and that the only difference between marketing $10,000 policies and $100,000 or $1 million policies was one or two zeros. Roland also wanted my advice on how to market financial planning services and fringe benefit offerings.

At the time of our meeting, Roland was like many marketers of financial services who had survived the first few years of the business. He had done so through hard work, aggressive prospecting, long hours, discipline, and an ability to deal with pain and rejection. In a nutshell, he had survived through blood and guts, not through finesse. He told me that his marketing strategy was quite simple: he considered any breathing person a viable prospect for his offerings. In essence, he was too busy surviving to do any real market planning or intelligence gathering.

Roland is thriving and will continue to thrive by using his shotgun or blast approach. But he will wear out a lot of shoes and orthopedic hose in the process. Without changing his marketing techniques, he will never become a top insurance marketer.

Roland finally spelled out why he was in my office. "Dr. Stanley, I want to know who the affluent are. Do you have a list that I could borrow?" I gave him the same response that I have given to dozens of my former students: "Roland, I can give you fish or teach you how to fish. If I give you a list of people who I know or suspect are affluent, what will you do after you have fully exploited the list? The top, self-made producers in insurance, securities, real estate, financial planning, autos, and yachts all have something in common. All of these winners know how to custom-develop their own lists. In other words, they know what cues and what information sources to use to identify who is likely to be affluent and who is not. And, equally important, they know when the prospect is in the mood to purchase."

I could tell that Roland was not very excited about the lecture. "But, Dr. Stanley, I can't spend months going to school to learn how to fish for the affluent." I explained to him that he did not have to stop working to learn how to fish. All he had to do was to start thinking about the clues that affluent people leave. "The affluent often leave a trail," I suggested. I then glanced at the auction notice.

I handed the notice to Roland. "OK, scholar," I stated, "here is your first lesson on becoming a top producer and affluent yourself." After carefully reading the auction announcement, he said, "I don't want to become a real estate investor; I want to market insurance to the affluent."

Roland had failed to read the signs of affluence correctly. I suggested that he take the notice home for further study.

Roland called me the following week to inform me of his progress. He said that much of the proceeds of the auction had gone to pay taxes, other liens, legal fees, and marketing costs and that the net proceeds had gone to 14 relatives of the deceased. He did not feel that a windfall of a few thousand dollars would place any of these prospects in the affluent category.

Obviously, Roland had not paid attention to the last class lecture he attended. In that lecture, I had told the class that in terms of concentration of six-figure incomes, auctioneers were among the top 10 occupations in America and that attorneys also ranked high. Both auctioneers and attorneys are most likely to say yes to Roland when they have received or contemplate receiving a large commission or judgment. But Roland's perceptions and behavior reflected the common view of the affluent. Roland assumed that the heirs to the estate were the most important target.

I explained to Roland that very often the people who put deals together or consummate agreements, such as marketers, sales professionals, agents, and auctioneers, are more affluent than the actual buyers or sellers of the property. I am sure, however, that he would love to sell life insurance, property insurance, and disability offerings to any family that has the financial ability to purchase a multimillion-dollar property.

Very often the public does not perceive marketers, sales agents, or even auctioneers to be affluent. Why? Because people often use a proxy variable to predict wealth. The proxy is occupational status. But the esteem that is associated with one's occupation is neither actual wealth nor a perfect predictor of wealth. The affluent sales/marketing occupational category is probably the most overlooked classification in marketing financial services.

Many auctioneers are prototypically affluent, but their cash flow often varies considerably. They are paid for performance, as are the majority of the affluent. When are the affluent who encounter wide fluctuations in compensation most likely to consider spending money for automobiles, major insurance coverage, securities, or big-league financial planning? The answer is usually when they are contemplating or have just concluded a major transaction.

The top producers in the financial services industries are concerned with six basic dimensions of intelligence gathering: (1) *When* will a significant amount of money change hands? (2) *Who* are the buyers, sellers, and intermediaries? (3) *Where* will the money change hands? (4) *How much* money will change hands? (5) *Why* is the sale taking place? and (6) *What* products or services will the actors need?

I told Roland that much of this information could be gathered by reading auction announcements. I advised him to get on the mailing lists of auction companies and to consult the classified sections of the newspapers for information on forthcoming auctions. I also advised him to call auction companies for additional information.

Most successful marketers are strategic readers who consume and digest information about the factors that influence their target markets. Most of the people in this country are not readers; they are television watchers who receive their current events information from television quiz shows and the seven o'clock news.

To be an effective marketer to the affluent, you must separate yourself from the pack. Read what others do not read. Read what will give you strategic advantage. The seven o'clock television news may be informative with respect to world events, and even entertaining, but it is too general, too shallow, too diffuse to provide a marketer with a relative advantage. The total number of words on a half-hour television newscast would fill only a bit more than half of a typical newspaper page (*New York Times Magazine*, July 27, 1986, p. 15).

I recommended to Roland that he reallocate the 30 minutes he devoted to network television news each weekday (7,800 minutes each year). "The really important information, Roland, is neither on network television nor in the front sections of the newspapers. The most important market information from news sources is often found in the back sections of the newspapers. Read the classified ads. Be especially sensitive to those sections where information is given about large sums of money that will be in transition. Auction notices are only one of dozens of important sections carried in the classifieds. But who reads the classified section? Most readers are buying. However, the best people in the world of marketing to the affluent are also reading. They read as sellers to those who are selling. Sell to sellers, not to buyers!"

After I finished my lecture to Roland, he commented that I was a genius for thinking of these ideas. I responded that I had acquired most of them by reading, interviewing ESPs, and listening to my dad's marketing wisdom. My final advice to Roland was to read more, especially in vehicles where the affluent left a track to follow. "And Roland, follow only fresh tracks. Market to those whose immediate financial position dictates an ability and willingness to spend."

Most affluent individuals are price sensitive most of the time. They can be prospected dozens of times and refuse to buy each time. Why? Because they are usually cash poor. Only rarely are they at the height of their cash flow. It is at these times that they are least sensitive to price, most sensitive to persuasive communications.

My first lesson in market timing was given to me by my dad. I can recall his telling me about how the wisest bar and grill operator marketed his offerings. For Tim Reilly, the timing of his marketing message and an unobtrusive way of communicating with his prospects were critical.

Via his own home style of marketing research, Tim determined that most of the workers in his trade area were paid each Friday. His bar and grill was located at a point between where these prospects lived and where they worked. Most of the prospects walked to and from the plants where they were employed.

Tim always had a large supply of unsalable stale beer. On Friday afternoons about one hour before the day shift ended, Tim would pour the stale beer all over the sidewalk outside his establishment. Many people in the area, including his competitors, thought that he was overly concerned with cleaning the sidewalk. But Tim had something else in mind.

The aroma of the tap beer emanating from the sidewalk acted as a highly productive *cue* that enhanced his prospects' perceived need for beer. Tim had released the right cue at the right time, at the right place, and at the right target—thirsty and hungry men with a weekly maximum of cash! On Friday afternoon, Tim's targeted prospects had the time to consume the product being offered and were the least sensitive to its price. Whether people are factory workers or factory owners, they spend when they have dollars to spend.

Often, market research that addresses the price sensitivity of affluent consumers badly misses a key factor. The maximum price that affluent prospects will pay for a product or service varies according to the prospects' (1) current or contemplated cash flow, (2) the length of time that they have to postpone the purchase, and (3) the characteristics of the product and its sponsor.

The first two factors are often not taken into consideration when new product or service offerings are being designed. If you ask a group of affluent respondents how much they would be willing to spend for financial planning, asset management, traditional trust services, universal life insurance, or even luxury durable goods, their responses will be unstable. The price that they say they will pay in the future and the amount they actually spend are often quite different. Someone who must have a financial plan designed within 30 days will be inclined to pay more for the plan than will someone who has 365 days to contemplate such a purchase. Also, someone who has just received a $200,000 year-end bonus will respond differently to the maximum price question than he would have before his windfall. Thus, both research questions and promotional messages should take optimal timing into consideration. Information about the time that economic events will take place is a critical issue in marketing to the affluent.

"SOMEONE WILL HAVE TO STAY HOME WITH THE GIFTS," OR TRACKING AFFLUENT GAME BY THEIR OWN INK PRINTS

Just a few days before I was married, my future mother-in-law had a suggestion for me. She indicated that someone should stay at home and guard the wedding gifts during the ceremony and reception. Apparently, the infamous "newspaper gang" was operating in the area.

What was the newspaper gang's modus operandi? These enterprising burglars were heavy readers of newspapers, especially the wedding announcements. They noted the names, address, and phone number of the bride's parents and the time and date of the wedding. They made their assault at the time of the wedding and reception. First, they would call the home of the bride's parents to see whether anyone was "guarding the gifts." If all cues indicated that the coast was clear, they would break into the home, removing the gifts and anything else that appealed to them. They were able to raid several homes in one day.

The exploits of the newspaper gang show that printed information can be used as market intelligence. Notice that the newspaper gang used the information contained in the wedding announcements for purposes other than those for which it was intended.

Often, people can read a newspaper day after day without perceiving the valuable marketing information that it contains. The newspaper provides critical information necessary to the timing and targeting of marketing programs. These key issues are most significant in marketing financial services and even expensive durable goods, such as automobiles.

The skills needed to draw out marketing intelligence from the newspapers cannot be acquired overnight. One must constantly improve those skills by trial and error. Always ask yourself: (1) How can this information be used as a marketing tool? (2) What are the implications of this knowledge? and (3) Does this knowledge give me important target and time dimensions?

Using information from newspapers for purposes other than those intended by the reporters provided the foundation for a best-selling book, John Naisbitt's *Megatrends* (New York: Warner Books, 1982). In his introduction, Naisbitt discusses a research method called content analysis. This method serves as a substitute for public opinion polls. By determining how much space newspapers devote to various topics, one can predict events as well as public opinion.

> During [World War II] intelligence experts sought to find a method for obtaining the kinds of information on enemy nations that public opinion polls would have normally provided. . . . it was decided

that we would do an analysis of the content of the German newspapers. (Ibid., p. 3)

We were able to find out

what was going on in Germany and to figure out whether conditions were improving or deteriorating by carefully tracking local stories (published articles in newspapers) about factory openings, closings, and production targets. (Ibid., p. 3)

Naisbitt points out that content analysis even made it possible to determine German military casualties.

You may ask what this has to do with marketing to the affluent. The answer is that affluent targets, like military targets, often answer key questions without fully realizing what they are divulging. The intelligent marketer understands that affluent prospects and their upside cash flows are often revealed in newspapers and other media. Most of these prospects never intended to communicate their identity or clues about their level of wealth or changes in cash flow.

Some marketers may regard analyzing newspaper stories as applicable only to very big business and very extensive business. But analyzing printed information for intelligence purposes can be productive on the smallest scale.

Obviously, our intelligence community in World War II required substantial resources to make predictions about the opinions and attitudes of an entire nation. However, individual events, whether they concern military matters or the affluent, can be predicted without making a major dollar commitment to intelligence.

Prior to the outbreak of World War II, predictions of forthcoming military actions were made by individuals as well as government organizations. A reporter wrote a series of published articles predicting German military activities. The predictions were so accurate that German intelligence, convinced that the reporter was receiving top-secret information, kidnapped him for purposes of interrogation. After several days of interrogation, the German intelligence command was shocked to learn that the reporter had been able to make his predictions by analyzing news stories. By examining news stories that announced changes in officer assignments and provided information on the expertise of these officers, he was able to predict impending military build-ups, the contemplated level of offensive thrusts, and the location of military resources—information that the enemy never intended to communicate.

Similarly, affluent people often divulge key information about their level of wealth, as well as the cash flow, without realizing that they are doing so. By examining any major newspaper in America, the market intelligence professional will find tracks leading to affluent prospects.

Very often, affluent targets unconsciously identify themselves and even their level of wealth by placing advertisements and news stories in the press. Every day, thousands of affluent prospects place classified advertisements in newspapers detailing the sale of their businesses, private aircraft, commercial real estate, yachts, and the like. Local, regional, and national newspapers carry hundreds of clues to the affluent each day. In addition, trade publications list businesses for sale within their industry.

Another method of marketing to the affluent relates to the classified section of newspapers and trade publications. Sellers of businesses are likely to be the most ardent readers of such sections. They often examine the offerings in these sections to assess the value of their own businesses. Many affluent prospects who contemplate the sale of various types of assets never publicize these offerings. Very frequently, however, they closely examine the character and price of related assets that are listed for sale in the classified sections. Those who do list in the classifieds will tell you that they have been contacted by other sellers who wish to reduce their uncertainty about the prices at which they are offering their businesses for sale. I once placed a classified advertisement for a 1957 Corvette. Several of the people who called me were sellers who were attempting to determine how much their own automobiles were worth.

Since the affluent often read the classifieds, not as buyers, but as sellers, the marketer should consider placing his promotional message in or near the classified section that the affluent sellers of assets will probably be reading. If the marketer's objective is to communicate with the affluent who are expecting significant increases in their liquid wealth from the sale of business or other assets, he may find it valuable to place strategically located classified advertisements that emphasize service or product offerings for those prospects. Marketers of such varied products or services as asset management and luxury retirement homes may find such tactics to be highly productive and very inexpensive. It is not unusual for business owners to spend 30 or 40 years effectively running their organizations. But more often than not, they are confused about what to do with the proceeds of liquidation.

Some sellers of significant assets, such as businesses, go into what some might consider a consumption frenzy. Such consumers may be very receptive to promotional messages for vacation homes, luxury travel programs, expensive automobiles, jewelry and collectable items, and decorating and architectural services. The transformation from a rather frugal and conservative lifestyle to one of frenzied consumption is often found among affluent entrepreneurs who contemplate selling or have recently sold their business, farm, commercial property, timberland, and so on.

A highly innovative classified advertisement was written by a young business school graduate who sought employment and an eventual equity interest in an entrepreneur's business. Advertisements of this type are most effective when placed in or near the Business for Sale section.

> Disappointed in your children? They have no interest in managing the business. You don't have to sell your business, adopt me. Your new son will run the business! Call Mark.

Thousands of young people hunt jobs with conventional and unimaginative weapons, but not Mark. He will probably succeed not only in finding the management job but also in becoming wealthy. Why? Because he is innovative and because he understands the needs of the affluent.

HOW FRED BUYS BOATS

I like to recall Fred, my best friend's father. Fred was a consummate reader of the classifieds and a very practical man. His line of work was the sale and rental of new and used construction machinery. He could accurately determine the value of used machinery, trucks, automobiles, and even boats and yachts.

Fred had a strong affinity for boats. He told me many times, however, that there was no need to purchase a new boat, that plenty of almost new boats all over the metropolitan area were just waiting for new owners. Many people—often affluent, middle-aged people—visit a boat show and buy what Fred called the image of a boat or yacht. Many of these people are onetime buyers. They never owned a boat before buying this one, and they will never buy another. For a middle-aged person who has never owned a boat and who has no mechanical aptitude, no sense of direction, no experience with navigation, the image of a boat or yacht is very different from the reality of a boat or yacht. Soon, the boat of such a person is likely to become a nightmare. Most of the people who really enjoy boating grow into it. They buy a small boat and then trade it in for a bigger boat; they constantly trade up.

One day, Fred's sons telephoned me. They asked me to join them in looking over a used cabin cruiser that Fred had expressed some interest in buying. Fred did purchase the two-year-old, 27-foot cabin cruiser, which happened to be in excellent condition, at a significant reduction from its original price. It had been in the water for only 2 months and in dry dock for 22 months. The doctor who sold the boat placed an advertisement in the classified section of a newspaper in which he indicated not only that the boat was for sale at a much-reduced price but that he would be *willing to finance its purchase*.

The advertisement showed that this doctor would soon have a substantial increase in his liquid assets, that he did not need the proceeds of the sale to pay off a debt on the boat, since the boat was not financed, and that he did not need the proceeds immediately, since he was willing to finance the boat for the purchaser.

Of all the classified sections in the newspaper, perhaps none is more important than the Businesses for Sale section. In addition, the classified sections of many trade journals often contain dozens of ads for businesses for sale. This area is important for several reasons. First, a great number of dollars will change hands. Second, entrepreneurs are often least sensitive to the prices of products and services when they are in the process of liquidating their business assets. Third, these entrepreneurs have a strong need for advice concerning how to invest the proceeds of the sale and what product and service purchases to make. Of course, the classified sections are not the only parts of newspapers and trade journals that provide clues about the affluent.

Randy of Atlanta

Extraordinary sales professionals (ESPs) are very perceptive about economic changes within their trade areas. While many sales professionals read newspapers for pleasure, ESPs are often strategic consumers of information who are quick to recognize and capitalize on newspaper accounts of affluent financial situations.

For more than a year, several Atlanta newspapers carried stories indicating that a real estate developer intended to buy out the Lake Hearn subdivision, which contained 114 single-family homes. Many of the homeowners in the subdivision had paid less than $100,000 for their homes. About $250,000 was paid for each home during the buy out. In a single day, over $25 million was distributed to the Lake Hearn homeowners. In discussion of future plans with several of them, I found that many had no intention of plowing back the bulk of these dollars into a home. Some stated that they preferred to invest their windfall. I know of only one security broker who aggressively pursued this affluent situation. Randy read the news stories about the Lake Hearn windfall and acted on the information they provided. He obtained the names, addresses, and phone numbers of the Lake Hearn residents from the city directory. Several of them are now his clients.

Affluent situations of this type will increase in the future. More and more developers will buy out subdivisions, farms, and businesses. Business owners in growing numbers are thinking strategically. They are more likely than ever before to give the liquidation option serious consideration even in their initial business plan. Affluent situations will also increase as a result of large legal settlements and judgments. These will be obtained largely by businesses rather than individuals. However, most of the businesses that gain such windfalls will be owned by a small number of principals. Other affluent situations that will increase in coming years will include early retirement of corporate managers with considerable stock in their fringe benefit packages, women becoming affluent widows, and sons and daughters becoming affluent heirs.

In fact, in a case more recent than that of the Lake Hearn subdivision, a developer has proposed to buy out another residential neighborhood in Atlanta. The modest homes in this neighborhood, which are on one-acre lots, will probably be sold to the developer for $1.3 million, more than eight times what their ordinary resale value would be. Some of the people who receive a windfall of this size want to invest most of it. Others feel impelled to purchase automobiles, boats, vacations, and so on. But rarely have marketers of such items taken the initiative and called on these soon-to-be-affluent. One respondent who recently obtained a home buyout windfall purchased an expensive station wagon for his wife, a luxury convertible for himself, and a cabin cruiser within three weeks after receiving the proceeds of the sale. Not one automobile or boat sales professional took a proactive role in seeking his business.

Sales professionals often overlook the fact that many consumers who receive economic windfalls are in a consumption frenzy just before and immediately after such events.

Richard D. Caller of the Family of D. Callers

Richard D. Caller is a heavy and strategic consumer of information. This young broker reads not only to enhance his product knowledge and forecast changes in the market but also to identify a different type of market opportunity—the major sales variety.

Richard consumes newspaper reports, magazine stories, and television announcements with the objective of identifying prospects for his investment products and services. He is especially sensitive to information about prospects and opportunities that have yet to develop fully.

He recently told me how he had identified a major market opportunity. While most of his colleagues were having lunch one day, Richard turned on the television in his office. One of the cable channels carried the story of a corporation that had just announced that it intended to buy back several million shares of its common stock. Richard immediately recognized that the impending transfer of ownership of millions of shares might create an opportunity for him.

Within 10 minutes after the news report was aired, Richard D.

Caller telephoned the office of the corporation's chief financial officer. The CFO's secretary told Richard that her boss was out of town and made it very clear that he never talked to stockbrokers. Richard considered hanging up on the secretary, but wisdom overruled his anger. He said to her, "Please tell your employer that Richard D. Caller called to inquire about the impending stock repurchase. Please remind him that your common stock has been on my recommended buy list, as well as my firm's, for over a year. I want to broker the buyback of the shares. Let me give you my office and home telephone numbers. Your employer may call me anytime, day or night. Please tell him that I expect to hear from him as soon as possible."

The following evening, the CFO phoned Richard. After a brief discussion, Richard was informed that he would be brokering several large trades, the first of which was for $4 million. The size of the other trades had not yet been determined at the time of this writing, but each of them is likely to be as large as or larger than the first. Richard had the impression that no other broker in America had taken the initiative of calling the CFO just at the right time.

INFORMATION AND IMAGE ENHANCEMENT

Developing and exploiting strategic information sources is useful beyond identifying prospects. Information on prospects plays a vital role in enhancing the image of sales professionals. Affluent prospects always attempt to judge the quality of the sales professionals who call on them. They view sales professionals who develop dossiers on prospects as being intelligent, perceptive, and empathetic. "If that salesman is smart enough to know a lot about me before we ever meet, he probably knows a lot about his product and my needs."

Tom R. and His Dossier Method

Tom R. did not major in marketing research. In fact, he never took a marketing course. Nonetheless, he developed a highly productive method of identifying affluent prospects. He has his own style of obtaining new business.

After Tom captured a significant amount of the securities market in the city where he lives, he sought new market opportunities. For this purpose, he developed a dossier method that he has employed successfully in towns and cities outside his normal trade area.

Tom targets several areas and then researches the economic events that take place in each of them. He does this by subscribing to the local newspapers and cataloging every article they publish on significant economic events in the lives of local residents. He may catalog these items for many months before visiting an area. When he arrives in a targeted town, he carries with him his dossiers on those residents whom he suspects to be affluent.

Tom believes that there are three reasons for the success of his method. First, people are favorably impressed with sales professionals who spend their time studying the backgrounds and especially the achievements of prospective clients. Second, the affluent often feel that experts "are from out of town." Third, many affluent people do not want anyone in their own town to know about their financial affairs. They believe that confidentiality will be more effectively maintained if they patronize an out-of-town broker rather than one from their own town.

Drake of St. Norbert's

Dear Mr. Morris:

For several years, I have been an investment adviser for many prominent families in your community. Often, these clients have asked me to help them develop an investment strategy in terms of major-sized cash proceeds from the sale of their business, inheritance, etc. Several of my clients, like you, have been awarded significant sums of money from legal settlements.

As I followed your case in the newspaper, I was particularly impressed with your courage and fortitude in ''taking on a large company.'' I applaud your victory. I would be delighted if you would allow me to personally visit with you and your family next week. Let's plan on talking by phone and firming up a meeting. I have established an excellent reputation in

```
helping solve the investment problems associated
with sudden cash windfalls.
     I am looking forward to sharing my ideas with you.

Sincerely,


Drake
Financial Consultant
```

Ten days after writing a letter of this type, Drake visited Mr. Morris. Following a 30-minute presentation of his investment philosophy, he asked Drake to invest $300,000 of his million-dollar award.

In discussing Drake's success in prospecting Mr. Morris, three issues became clear. First, up until the time Drake closed the sale, none of his competitors had approached Mr. Morris. Second, the ideal affluent prospect is one who has or will have a great deal more liquid wealth than he has ever had before. Third, prospects are favorably impressed by sales professionals who flatter them by praising their achievements or by categorizing them with "other prominent" prospects.

Somewhere in the Middle of Four Figures

Vanity is a trait of many affluent prospects. Some very clever marketers have developed methods of identifying, stimulating, and selling affluent prospects who are very vain. Often, affluent prospects whose picture appears repeatedly in newspapers and magazines are likely to have a stong need to be complimented on their personal appearance as well as their social or economic achievement.

I have encountered several enterprising marketers who prospect by what might be called the picture method. One afternoon, I received a telephone call from a young man who introduced himself as someone very interested in my research on the affluent in America. He then said that he was in the business of marketing to the affluent and would like to stop by my office and discuss some of the problems he encountered with them. When I asked him how he had found out about my interest in the affluent market, he replied that he had read the interviews I had given to *The Wall Street Journal* and *Forbes* magazine. He also said, "Dr. Stanley, I can tell you're a quality scholar from the way you dress. You dress very well. May I ask where you purchased your suits?" I told him, thinking to myself that this young man was very perceptive. We chatted for a few more minutes. At the conclusion of our conversation, this perceptive character invited himself to my office so that he could get a personal view of the high-quality researcher and high-caliber dresser. I assumed that he was in the market for my consulting services. How proud I was of myself!

The young man arrived precisely on time. I was impressed with how well he was dressed—he was a perfect "10" in terms of business apparel. However, I was surprised that he was carrying a suitcase. "Perhaps he is on a tight schedule," I thought. Was he on his way to the airport or just returning from an important trip?

After introducing himself, he asked me to describe some of the more productive methods of marketing to the affluent. My response centered on identifying targets, understanding need events, and matching cash flow patterns with marketing messages.

His response to my comments took the form of a clever debriefing. "Dr. Stanley, are you often called on to deliver important speeches to large audiences?" Yes," I replied. At this point, I assumed that he wanted me to give the keynote address at the next managers' meeting of his firm. "Dr. Stanley, are you scheduled to deliver one or more speeches in the next few months?" "Yes." "How many people will be in your audiences?" "Thousands." "Wow," I thought, this fellow wants a really super speaker. I'm the one he needs. He has come to the right person, the source of superior marketing intellect." "Are you satisfied that your wardrobe will make the right impression on your audience?" "Ah, ah, I'm not sure."

"Dr. Stanley, would you stand up for a moment—I just want to get your measurements. You see, my company provides customized personal wardrobe selection for successful people like yourself. You have better things to do than shop around all day looking for the suits and accessories that are right for you. Our clients include many well-known senior corporate executives, surgeons, entrepreneurs, and high-performance sales professionals. They all have similar needs. They realize that success is directly related to one's personal appearance. Also, they hate to take time from the productive pursuit of their careers to fight the crowds at shopping centers. I measure and fit my customers in their office, often while they are doing business on the phone. We custom-fit each client and manufacture all our suits. We also offer top-of-the-line shirts and ties.''

Up to this point, I had assumed that I was selling this fellow. Why else would I have my offensive team on the field? But I began to realize that he was hitting me with some ESP lightning bolts. However, I regained my composure sufficiently to inquire about the price of these symbols of success. I was told that all of them were actually very modestly priced considering the time savings and customizing. The young man went on to say, "Our suits range in price from $600 to somewhere in the middle of four figures." I asked what he considered the middle of four figures. "Why, around $5,000 or $6,000," he replied. "Our shirts start at $30, and most people buy six at a time. In fact, I will show you the fabric selection from the case I just happen to have with me. Have you ever seen such fine fabrics?" I agreed that the fabrics were excellent. I also pointed out that I had just taken a very heavy hit from a former student who sold suits at Brooks Brothers. "He just finished golden-fleecing me." The young man then asked when I might be in the market for his service and whether I knew anyone who might be interested in his offerings. I told him when he should call on me again and gave him the name of a top producer in the security business. I also suggested that he make a presentation on how to dress to the 60 members in my executive MBA class. "Most of them will be interested in dressing up for their graduation," I told him.

What can marketers learn from this extraordinary sales professional? It is not enough to know that certain persons are affluent. Information about affluent prospects has value only if it is timely, since only timely information makes it possible to schedule solicitations when they are most likely to be well received. Correspondingly, the identities of the affluent and timely information on them are most valuable if they are known only by the sales professional. The ESP in this case does not buy lists of the affluent. He develops his own lists by thoroughly digesting current media reports about the affluent. He constantly scrutinizes newspaper and magazine reports about executives who will be promoted, entrepreneurs who are taking their companies public, politicians who have won or will probably win important elections, and lawyers who have been featured in business periodicals. Such information provides him with the identities of people who are ready, willing, and able to spend money and who are likely to be insensitive to price and very sensitive to saving time and energy. Such prospects are inclined to place a priority on the informational or advisory content of market transactions. While most sales professionals are reactive, this young man is proactive. While his peers spend most of their time waiting for prospects to appear at a retail store, he is constantly researching the affluent, prospecting the affluent, and initiating sales contacts with the affluent.

Few of the people who are constantly mentioned in the press are ever contacted by sales professionals soliciting their business. This is one of the major reasons why this young man is a top producer in his field.

Affluent prospects who are often mentioned in the press are, by definition, exceptional marketers in their own right. People clever enough to master the art of marketing themselves via public relations pieces in the press are very likely to have high incomes. This means that many of these exceptional marketers have significant amounts to invest. Also, I have found that press reports about the affluent influence their moods and temperaments.

For example, take the young achiever who has just been promoted to partner and whose annual income has increased from $65,000 to over $200,000. He is likely to be euphoric for at least a few weeks after his promotion is reported in the press. He is also very likely to be receptive to messages delivered by marketers of expensive custom clothing, automobiles, vacation homes, and insurance and by enlightened marketers of investment services. But remember that euphoria does not last forever. And also remember that those marketers who are first to identify prospects in the "right mood" have the best chance to *close the sale*. Several major categories of capital gain are listed in Table 5–1. Enlightened sales professionals will be sensitive to information about impending transactions within these classifications.

TABLE 5–1
Capital Gain Categories

Capital Asset Category	Average Gross Capital Gain	Number Receiving Capital Gain	Description of Capital Gain Category
1. Corporate stock	$12,498	3,426,181	Stock in any corporation, and warrants. Excluded from this classification were stock options or privileges, calls, puts, spreads, and straddles.
2. Securities other than corporate stock	2,133	504,074	
U.S. government obligations			Bonds, notes, and other evidences of indebtedness issued by the U.S. government and its instrumentalities or possessions.
State and local government obligations			Investments in obligations of states or U.S. possessions, including obligations of political subdivisions and the District of Columbia
Other bonds, notes, and debentures			Includes securities issued by corporations, banks, and insurance companies.
3. Commodities, including futures contracts	18,931	197,285	Most sales or exchanges of crops or staples resulting from an obligation to buy or sell a fixed quantity of a commodity on a specific date at a fixed price; except for a hedging transaction, a capital gain or loss resulted if the commodity future was a capital asset.
4. Capital gain distributions	2,071	944,965	Long-term capital gains distributed or credited to stockholders in the form of cash or other property by regulated investment companies and real estate investment trusts.
5. Share of capital gain or loss from partnerships and fiduciaries	9,701	1,070,164	Capital gains and losses allocated by partnerships and fiduciaries to partners and beneficiaries, respectively, who, in turn, reported distributive shares on their individual income tax returns.
6. Capital gain distributions from small business corporations	7,948	62,382	Long-term capital gain distributions from earnings and profits of electing small business corporations (reduced by the special tax imposed at the corporate level) taxed through each stockholder.
7. Liquidation distributions	29,476	44,106	Cash or other property received by a stockholder when a corporation was liquidated.
8. Lump-sum and other retirement plan distributions	7,061	50,237	Lump-sum payments to employees from a qualified annuity plan or from an exempt trust that formed part of a pension, profit sharing, or stock bonus plan.

TABLE 5–1 (*continued*)

Capital Asset Category	Average Gross Capital Gain	Number Receiving Capital Gain	Description of Capital Gain Category
9. Sales or involuntary conversions of certain depreciable and other property	14,270	323,830	
Involuntary conversions by casualty or theft			Depreciable business property, or nonbusiness property, held for more than nine months, that was compulsorily converted into money or other property not similar or related in service or use to the converted property. Loss (or gain) was after adjustment for any insurance proceeds and was otherwise eligible for long-term capital loss (or gain) treatment.
Involuntary conversions by other than casualty or theft			Trade or business property held for more than nine months and compulsorily converted, e.g., by seizure or condemnation. Loss (or gain) was after adjustment for any insurance proceeds and was otherwise eligible for long-term capital loss (or gain) treatment.
All other livestock, except poultry, including certain livestock used in trade or business			Unless covered under 12 (depreciable livestock), cattle, hogs, horses, mules, donkeys, sheep, goats, fur-bearing animals (such as mink), and other mammals, if held for draft, breeding, dairy, or sporting purposes. Cattle and horses were included if held for 24 months or more; the holding period for other animals was 12 months or more.
Cut timber			Timber that was cut, if owned, or held under contract to cut, for more than 12 months, if an election was made to treat the cutting as a sale of property used in the taxpayer's trade or business.
Other farmland with unharvested crop			Farmland with unharvested crop that was sold (with no retention rights or options) or exchanged at the same time and to the same person, if the land was held for more than 12 months. Crops included fruit and nut trees.
Qualified trade or business assets and transactions not elsewhere classifed			Business assets (either real property or depreciable personal property) eligible for long-term capital gain treatment that could not be classified by type of asset or transaction.

TABLE 5–1 (continued)

Capital Asset Category	Average Gross Capital Gain	Number Receiving Capital Gain	Description of Capital Gain Category
10. Qualified gains on nonfarm depreciable business and personal property, except certain buildings	7,668	494,917	Property held for more than one year, if the gains exceeded pre-1969 accumulated depreciation and if the property (except livestock) was tangible (e.g., machinery or equipment) or intangible (e.g., patents or copyrights). Tangible property included certain real property (except buildings) if used in specified industrial activities or if used for specific purposes described in the Code.
11. Qualified gains on other depreciable real property, including certain buildings	39,320	144,893	Real property (not included in 10, above) held for more than one year, on which gains were realized. However, property on which gains were due to the excess of accelerated over straight-line depreciations for 1964–69 was only partially included depending on how long the property was held; property on which gains were due to excess depreciation after 1969 was not included at all.
12. Qualified gains on farmland with unharvested crop and livestock, except poultry, used in trade or business	8,387	399,363	Farming property held for more than one year on which gains exceeded the post-1969 (a) difference between accelerated and straight-line depreciation and (b) accumulated farm losses. Capital gain on farmland was further limited to amounts in excess of accumulated deductions for soil and water conservation expenses for the most recent years. Restrictions did not apply if nonfarm AGI or net farm loss was less than the amounts stated in the Code.
13. Standing timber	9,382	63,050	Investment property held by the taxpayer that was sold and treated the same as the sale or exchange of any capital asset.
14. All other farmland	49,932	6,184	Includes farmland held for more than one year, with expenditures for soil and water conservation or land clearing, on which gain was realized.
15. Oil and gas property	212,017	1,284	Operating mineral interests in oil and gas wells or geothermal deposits, the gain on which exceeded intangible drilling and development costs expensed over the lesser amount that could have been deducted currently if the costs were capitalized.

TABLE 5–1 (continued)

Capital Asset Category	Average Gross Capital Gain	Number Receiving Capital Gain	Description of Capital Gain Category
16. Personal residence	30,811	1,009,772	Principal residence or the home in which the taxpayer lived unless a "new" residence or home of at least equal cost was purchased within two years.
17. Nonbusiness real estate	25,483	725,029	Unimproved real estate, rights-of-way on property, rental property, and all other real estate other than that reported as farmland with unharvested crop, other farmland, real estate subdivided, residences, and business assets.
18. Prior-year-installment sales	6,974	1,421,364	The classification was used for deferred payments received from sales or exchanges of capital assets.
19. Other types of assets	7,871	1,449,447	Other assets (e.g., mortgages, nonbusiness bad debts, life interests in estates, termination payments to employees, patents, and foreign currency conversions). Also includes property or transactions that the taxpayer did not specifically identify and stock options, privileges, calls, puts, spreads, and straddles.
All capital asset categories	$18,044	8,405,189	

Source: *Internal Revenue Statistics for Individual Returns, 1981.* Internal Revenue Service, Washington, D.C., 1986. Compiled by Bobby Clark and David Paris.

THE CRUISE METHOD

I once asked Tom C., of Washington, D.C., one of the biggest producers in the securities industry, how he found his affluent prospects. I anticipated a lengthy and complex response. Were his methods elaborate? Computer based? Did they involve an analysis of proprietary financial statements, state-of-the-art geocoding, or a sophisticated network of professional observers? None of these things. His most important method for identifying affluent prospects can be summed up in one word: *cruising*.

Most ESPs realize that owners of small and medium-sized businesses often have many dollars to invest and many have told me they identify such owners by driving through industrial areas and business districts and looking for the names of the businesses. Anytime they see a business with a name like Robert's Tool and Die or Peterson's Construction Machinery Company, they assume that the business is probably owned and operated by a Mr. Roberts or a Mr. Peterson.

Tom C. gave the following account of his brand of cruising.

> My wife bursts into tears whenever I do this, and I do this at least three times a week. When I drive up by this little place that says DeCardell Printing, I'll stop my car and go in and ask if there is a DeCardell. . . . or I take some articles that I have written or something, I go in and introduce myself, and I say, "I do business in your chain of grocery stores, and I would like to introduce myself." Kind of a low-pressure thing. . . . I put leisure clothes on, and I stop by and say, "Well, this is my day off. I have been doing business with you for five years, and I just wanted to stop in and introduce myself."

I interviewed another cruising ESP. In his early 30s, this ESP had made over $300,000 in one year from commissions on security sales. He told me that he lived and prospected in the Detroit metropolitan area. When he told me this, I bet him that I could guess what type of business his top client was in. He accepted the bet. "Your best client, in terms of size of portfolio, is a tool and die manufacturer." After seeming to go into shock for a moment, the ESP asked, "Can you predict the changes in the market with the same accuracy?"

My guess had a fair chance of being correct because the anatomy of wealth in Detroit indicates that suppliers to the automobile industry are very often quite affluent business owners. Those suppliers include a high concentration of often affluent tool and die manufacturers.

After we discussed my guess and the anatomy of wealth in Detroit, I began to realize that this young ESP was very perceptive about recognizing wealth. What methods did he employ in identifying and prospecting the affluent?

> My main target is the business owner. I look (while cruising) for buildings that are ideally in the low-rent commercial areas, you know, the ones that somehow avoided being shut down by OSHA. . . . This tells me that the owner does not throw his money around,

that he has money in his pocket, not in the rugs, office rent, wallpaper, and office equipment. If he has been in business for five years or longer, and is in the "right" type of business, like tool and die, chances are very high that I have located someone with lots of dollars to invest. He is probably wealthy, not only because of his business revenue, but also because he is frugal as hell. Very often, when I talk to these types of prospects, I find that they have never been discovered by my competition. I especially like to find these types who are in their 50s and early 60s and have been in business for 20 years or longer. They have a pile of money.

The cruise method has enabled many ESPs to succeed, not only because of its inherent efficacy but for other important reasons. One reason is that not all businesses and not all business owners can be found on so-called affluent prospect lists. It is quite common for American business owners to own several businesses. Often, their individual businesses will not appear in anyone's millionaire directory. But added together, the revenue and wealth of all their businesses is quite substantial.

Another reason why the cruise method has been productive for many ESPs is that it permits them to rely on their own abilities. As one superproducer stated recently, "I'm the best in person. . . . I do almost all of my prospecting in person. . . . My own eyes are my sources. I'm not dependent on others."

Obviously, the cruise method does not fully account for the success of the ESPs who employ it. Most of the ESPs who cruise also have an uncanny ability to gain (1) entrance to the prospect's place of business; (2) the confidence and endorsement of interceptors, such as secretaries; (3) an interview with the targeted business owner; and (4) a positive response from the affluent business owner. Not all sales professionals are suited for cruising and subsequent cold calling on business owners. Those who are have a natural aptitude and personality for manipulating both the interceptors and the business owners.

SOURCES OF INFORMATION ABOUT
AFFLUENT BUSINESS OWNERS

Identifying prospects who are business owners is critical for ESPs. Most of the top producers believe that they have superior selling skills. They also believe that a substantial portion of the small-business prospects has yet to be captured. From their perspective, the key is to find the method of locating these prospects. Usually, top producers who have direct sales responsibility develop their own source lists. These lists, which are often lists of small-business owners, are the product of the top producers' insight, intellect, and curiosity. Great variations exist among the lists. Each ESP seems to have his own formula for identifying business owners.

The sources developed by top producers in the securities business are as much a competitive weapon as superior proprietary products and creative communications. Quality source material provides a barrier against competing registered representatives. This perceived relative advantage is coveted by the top producers.

Some of the sources of small-business prospects include:

- *The Macmillan Directory of Leading Private Companies*
- Dun's Business Identification Service
- *Directory of Women-Owned Businesses*—National Association of Women Business Owners
- *Business Owner's Reverse Directory*
- Standard & Poor's Stock Reports—Over the Counter
- *Standard & Poor's Register of Corporations, Directors, and Executives*
- Secretary of state—list of pension plans
- Newspaper reports on small businesses
- Telephone book lists of retailers
- *Who's Who in Trade Associations*
- Secretary of state—list of recent incorporations
- *Contacts Influential*
- *Pension and Profit Sharing Plans Directory*
- *Blue Book of Pension Funds*—Dun's Marketing Service

INTERPERSONAL SOURCES OF INFORMATION

Two especially important sources of information about the identities of affluent prospects and changes in their cash flow are accountants and attorneys. Very often, accountants and attorneys are among the first to be informed about changes in their clients' financial lifestyles. Also, many affluent prospects never give any outward signs of their wealth. A statement from a millionaire entrepreneur puts it simply: "How much am I worth? Only my accountant and my attorney know for sure."

Along these lines, an accountant wrote to me, suggesting that there may be more millionaires in America than has been estimated.

Dear Dr. Stanley:

Recently, I read in the *Times* an article concerning your study of millionaires. It piqued my curiosity when you were quoted as stating that the number of millionaires in 1984 was 832,602. The exactness of this figure is what intrigued me. It has occurred to me that your figure may be understated. I believe there are a lot of low-profile individuals in the country who have carefully amassed small fortunes in real estate and who, on the surface, would never be recognized as or believed to be millionaires. I personally know and work with four such persons in my capacity as a CPA. Perhaps your analysis somehow provides for including such individuals. In any event, I felt intrigued enough to at least make an inquiry of you.

Very truly yours,

H. L.
Certified Public Accountant

Charles of Louisiana

One of the reasons that Charles became a top producer in the securities industry was his ability to impress many CPAs in his trade area with his knowledge of how the tax law affects alternative investment opportunities. Much of Charles's business with the affluent has been a direct result of information he obtained from a number of CPAs. Charles was kind enough to share with me some of his thoughts about the role of CPAs in his marketing strategy.

DR. STANLEY:

> What is your source of information to identify a prospect? Think about your last good prospect—where did the name come from?

CHARLES:

> Almost invariably, it is going to be a CPA. Lots and lots of referrals. I do lots of business with CPAs. I probably have 20 different CPAs that I'm doing business with, and they send clients, which I think is somewhat unusual.

DR. STANLEY:

> What kind of business do you do with them?

CHARLES:

> Stock business, municipal bonds, some business with their corporations—that kind of stuff. Some insurance. I get insurance referrals from CPAs.

DR. STANLEY:

> How did you cultivate that, Charles?

CHARLES:

> Just figured they knew where the money was.

DR. STANLEY:

> Say I'm an accountant. How are you going to approach me?

CHARLES:

> Of course, I really don't do any prospecting anymore, but early on, I knocked on doors, sat down with people, and I know a lot of tax law, so I could talk with them and develop rapport. I go to the right person in local firms. I don't get many referrals from the national firms.

DR. STANLEY:

> What do you think got them on your side?

CHARLES:

Knowledge of tax law. Not only that, but they become not only referrals but also clients. I need to know all of the tax laws. I subscribe to a lot of stuff—taxation for accountants and all that stuff, and I read it. We host some dinners in the year, qualifying for their ongoing education—for CPAs.

Steve H.

Many industry experts consider Steve H. to be the premier marketer of municipal bonds. He has also trained many others who have become ESPs in the municipal bonds area. During an interview, I asked him about his market orientation.

I tell the young guys, OPM-DPM, which is Other People's Money, Dead People's Money. And people who control OPM-DPM are just more professional to speak with.

One of Steve's favorite targets in terms of OPM-DPM is attorneys. It is certainly true that many attorneys play an important role in influencing the investment decisions of their clients. They are often an important influence on the investment of large sums of money that are in transition for only a short period of time. This money may come from estates, trusts, foundations, business liquidations, court awards, and real estate sales. The precise times when such situations will exist are not usually predictable.

Steve is in constant contact with attorneys who influence where and how OPM-DPM will be invested. Attorneys are among the first to know when large sums of money will be in transition. They are a critical source of market intelligence. In such situations, market intelligence refers to *when* the money will be in transition, *who* will receive the money, and *how* much money will be in transition.

Attorneys are often asked three important questions by clients who receive transition dollars. They ask attorneys where they should go for quality investment advice, what investment vehicles are most suitable given their need for low risk and their aversion to paying taxes, and why specific referrals are made.

Steve positions himself in the minds of important attorneys as an expert in providing advice and investments relating to transition dollars. In short, he provides the right message to the right people at the right time. The people in this case are attorneys who have a big-league influence on big-league transition dollars.

Attorneys are important for another reason besides their influence on transition dollars. Attorneys are among the most affluent occupational segments. Legal service firms generate about $50 billion a year in receipts, of which legal service partnerships account for about $25 billion. Of the $25 billion in revenue, about $10 billion is net income and about $6 billion is paid out in salaries and wages.

SELECTED COMMENTS FROM ESP'S

You can drive around town, and you can see a business, a small business, that looks like it is getting bigger or better.

The luncheon—just get the reverse directory of a business community, and just send out invitations to it.

Dun and Bradstreet. Probably a list that is used a lot, but I still try to get an appointment.

I read five to six newspapers a day, and I always find something that I don't know, in the marketing sense, that I can use in my business.

I have a list of the biggest privately held companies in town. You can get them anywhere. Libraries have them. I send my sales assistant down to the library. There are a lot in your business section.

I've used *Contacts Influential*. In our area, it is just a book that you lease that lists all businesses in the greater metropolitan area.

I've used a Local Venture Capital Forum. They bring in a group that is looking to go public or looking to raise dollars. This is an open forum, inviting top business people in the area who have invested in venture capital in the past.

I work on the board and do fund raising with them [his alma mater].

Set up a booth as an exhibitor [at the state medical society meeting]. . . . Get a lot of names and locations so that we will be able to see them later.

I have the Northeast territory. If you own a manufacturing plant or small business, your name appears on the list. God forbid if your business begins with an *A,* because probably 30 times a day all of the brokers who are probably going to last about six months in our industry will pick up the phone and call.

If I see a guy in the paper, I'll go to some of my associates, I have a couple of CPAs, somebody on the board at the savings and loan. Funny, I've a 74-year-old guy that runs my concrete company; he knows everybody. . . . I'll say, "Can you get an introduction for me?"

I think everybody would be amazed at how many guys there are who haven't been found in the entrepreneurial sector.

It was a response to a newspaper. He might have been to an annuity seminar, but the guy stumbled in the door. . . . I'm talking to him and suddenly discover, gee, he has $4 million, and obviously he became a very good client.

The insider trading list of the SEC published every month is my best source.

I want to get this out to the young guys. When you read the paper, you shouldn't be reading the articles, you should read the ads—a list of 100 affluent charter financial analysts with phone numbers and addresses.

We have an industrial development commission and a chamber. You can imagine how many names of small businesses you can get out of start-up stuff—250 last month we got, I think, for the fourth quarter.

CHAPTER 6

A BIG-LEAGUE ORIENTATION: FOCUSING ON THE AFFLUENT

WHO ARE THE AFFLUENT?

Recently, I told a group of top producers in the insurance industry that too often marketers of insurance products chase the pseudoaffluent and not the real affluent. My research shows that most of the affluent are not enamored of wearing diamonds or driving imported luxury automobiles. Keep in mind that the average American millionaire realizes significantly less than 10 percent of his net worth in annual income. As C. Eugene Steuerle, assistant director, Office of Tax Analysis, Department of the Treasury, stated:

> This data is especially rich in information on reported rates of return on closely held assets, as the sample consists of farmers and businessmen with substantial amounts of such assets at the time of death. For the purposes of this article, the ratio of realized income to value of wealth shall be referred to as the realized rate of return or simply the rate of return. The realized rate of return differs from the actual economic rate of return by the amount of unrealized income or other income on capital not reported on the tax return.
>
> For this sample the size of the *realized rate of return on all wealth is found to be around 2 percent*, much less than would be recognized if that wealth were invested in the lowest-paying savings account. Even when wage income is added to capital income (because of the difficulty of separating the two components), the amount of realized income is still less than 4 percent of the total value of assets (C. Eugene Steuerle, *The Relationship between Income and Wealth,* OTA Paper no. 50, Washington, December 1982).

Thus, in spite of having considerable wealth and substantial annual increases in wealth (in unrealized form), the typical American millionaire may personally be cash poor. This possibility is certainly supported by the large number of top producers in the insurance industry who have focused on the concept of having "the business pay the premiums." Often, the realized income of American millionaires is not enough to support an ostentatious consumption lifestyle. I cannot count the instances where millionaires have arrived at my interviews driving nondescript, full-size, American-made automobiles. These automobiles often appear to be well used and fairly old. It may be difficult for even the American millionaire to purchase many luxury goods if his realized income is less than 4 percent of the total value of his assets.

Deceptive Vehicles

Even the affluent with the highest levels of realized income are not all purchasing expensive automobiles. Table 6–1 lists the makes and models of the motor vehicles most recently purchased by 34 households with annual incomes of $1 million or more. It also lists the second and third automobiles most recently purchased by these households. It is important to note that fewer than 20,000 American households out of nearly 90 million, or about one household in approximately 4,600, have incomes in the seven-figure or higher category.

The data in Table 6–1 show that while such luxury imports as Mercedes-Benz and Porsche are certainly represented, they do not dominate the auto-buying behavior of the American households that produce seven-figure annual incomes. Moreover, domestic compacts and subcompacts are well represented in the data.

In a national study of 2,862 buyers of new imported motor vehicles, *Newsweek* magazine included the following automobiles in its definition of luxury sedans: Audi 5000, Jaguar, Mercedes-Benz, Peugeot 604, Saab 900 Turbo, and Volvo GTL and 760 GLE (see Table 6–2). The results of this study indicate that many buyers of luxury imported automobiles are not affluent in terms of income. Prospect 100 buyers of new luxury imported cars, and what will you find? Fewer than 30 of these buyers have annual household incomes of $100,000 or more; more than one third have incomes of

TABLE 6–1
Automobiles Recently Purchased by Households with Annual Incomes of $1 Million or More*

Make of Car	Model of Car	Number of Households
Most Recent Purchase		
Buick	Apollo/Skylark	2
	Riviera	1
Cadillac	Coupe de Ville, Sedan de Ville	5
	Seville	2
Chevrolet	Chevelle	1
	Impala, Caprice	1
Ford	Galaxie, LTD, Squire Ranch Wagon, XL	1
	Bronco	1
Mercedes-Benz	No model specified	4
Mercury	Capri	1
Nissan	Sentra	1
Oldsmobile	Vista Cruiser, Supreme, Cutlass	3
Pontiac	Ventura	1
	Firebird, Trans Am	1
Porsche	No model specified	2
Saab	No model specified	1
Volkswagen	Dasher/Quantum, Rabbit, Scirocco, Jetta	3
None owned		3
Second Most Recent Purchase		
BMW	No model specified	1
Buick	Skylark/Apollo	1
	Estate Wagon, LeSabre	1
	225 Limited, Electra, Park Avenue	1
Cadillac	Coupe de Ville, Sedan de Ville	1
	Biarritz	1
	Seville	1
Chevrolet	Celebrity, Chevelle	1
Dodge	Dodge Van, Sportsman, Voyager	1
Jaguar	No model specified	1
Jeep	Suburban Wagoneer	1
Lincoln	Continental Mark II/IV/V	1
Mercedes-Benz	No model specified	4

TABLE 6–1 (concluded)

Make of Car	Model of Car	Number of Households
Mercury	Bobcat, Lynx	1
Motorhome	No model specified	1
Oldsmobile	Eighty-eight	1
	Ninety-eight	1
Plymouth	Horizon	1
Pontiac	Bonneville, Grand Am, Grandville	1
Volkswagen	Dasher/Quantum, Rabbit, Scirocco, Jetta	1
No second car		11
	Third Most Recent Purchase	
Austin-Healey	No model specified	1
BMW	No model specified	1
Cadillac	Biarritz	1
Ford	Bronco	1
	Truck	1
Mercury	Park Lane, Colony Park, Montclair, Marquis, Commuter, Marauder, Monterey	1
Nissan	Sentra	1
Oldsmobile	Eighty-eight	1
Pontiac	Bonneville, Grand Am, Grandville	1
Porsche	No model specified	1
No third car		24

* Source: Affluent Market Institute Data Base, projections from computer analysis of Federal Reserve Board, *Study of High Income Households*, 1983.

under $50,000; and fully one half have incomes of below $63,500. The artifacts often associated with the affluent in advertisements are reflective of the myths rather than the realities regarding the affluent population in America.

The Cream of a Very Large Crop

In researching very affluent farmers in America, I identified a number who were estimated to have seven-figure incomes. I thought it would be interesting to see how a group of security brokers would

respond to this information. I mailed the names of several dozen of
these affluent farmers to the national sales manager of an aggressive Wall Street–based firm, who I thought would appreciate this
information. This manager had been a very productive sales professional whose career success was based largely on prospecting
among what some refer to as the latent affluent. These are persons
with affluent incomes or net worth but relatively low occupational
status. I reasoned that someone who had cut his teeth on prospecting among this segment would be excited to learn about farmers
with seven-figure incomes and sent him the following "Urgent–
Top Secret" message:

```
TO:   MARKETING COMMANDER

URGENT—TOP SECRET

SIGHTED LARGE AFFLUENT CONVOY ON WESTERN HORIZON.
HEAVILY LADEN WITH LIQUID ASSETS. TARGETS IDENTIFIED
BELOW. SUGGEST IMMEDIATE ACTION FROM THE BEST OF YOUR
WOLF PACK. GOOD HUNTING!

T.S.
U. AFFLUENT
```

As soon as the sales manager received this information, he air-
expressed it to several of his branch offices. I spoke with him two
weeks after this. He seemed somewhat depressed when I asked
him how his sales force had responded to the "affluent convoy of
farmers."

"Your information was quite accurate as far as I can tell from
those who contacted these prospects, but most of our guys never
attempted to make contact. They don't seem to believe that
farmers have any money."

There are over 2 million farmers in America. I estimate that
most of them are nowhere near affluent. But I also estimate that
nearly 2.0 percent of these farmers are affluent in terms of either
net worth or income. However, even seasoned sales professionals
are often misled by the popular press. Newspapers all over America have been printing stories of bankrupt farmers who overex-
tended themselves and could not repay their bank loans. But there
are also many farmers who own highly productive farms, have no

TABLE 6–2
Household Income Characteristics of Buyers of New Imported Cars

Annual Household Income	All Buyers (percent)	Buyers of Luxury Sedans (percent)
	100.0	100.0
Under $15,000	6.4	0.3
$15,000–$19,999	7.2	0.8
$20,000–$24,999	10.6	3.2
$25,000–$34,999	18.1	6.3
$35,000–$49,999	24.8	26.2
$50,000–$74,999	19.4	24.2
$75,000–$99,999	5.7	10.5
$100,000–$149,999	4.3	13.0
$150,000 and over	3.5	15.5
Unweighted base (number)	2,624	367
Median ($000s)	39.6	63.5
Mean ($000s)	49.8	85.4

Source: Newsweek, Inc., *1983 Buyers of New Important Cars* (New York: Newsweek, 1983) p. 33.

outstanding debt, and receive a disproportionate share of the $26 billion annual government farm subsidy. According to IRS statistics, the affluent income category that has the largest percentage of households with farm income is the top income category—$1 million or more annual income.

Market information must be accurate and timely. But the accuracy and timeliness of market information are irrelevant if a barrier of ignorance concerning the realities of the affluent market exists among its potential users.

Nearly everywhere I visit in this country, people tell me, "You know, Dr. Stanley, there is an awful lot of wealth in this city." Actually, millionaires can be found in every city and every state. However, wealth in this country is highly concentrated. It is highly concentrated not only by states and by cities but also by neighborhoods, especially the so-called upper-class and upper-middle-class neighborhoods. However, according to Jonathan Robbin, founder of the Claritas Corporation and developer of a neighborhood consumer taxonomic system (PRIZM), "about one half of the millionaires in America do not reside in top clusters [upper-class and upper-middle-class neighborhoods]." Robbin also suggested during a recent interview that the consumption lifestyles and income characteristics of households are more closely related to neighborhood "quality" than is actual wealth. This was not surprising to me since in a recent study on which we collaborated, we found that more than 700 neighborhoods in one metropolitan area had at least one household with income-producing assets of $1 million or more. Is there anything prestigious about living in a neighborhood 200th, 300th, or 400th best in one metropolitan area?

While neighborhood taxonomic systems will certainly identify high concentrations of wealth, most of the households that reside in the so-called prestigious neighborhoods are not in the millionaire league. In fact, many people who live in neighborhoods whose average house value is in the top 5.0 percent in America do not generate six-figure incomes. I estimate that in 1984 fewer than one half of the households that lived in homes valued at $300,000 or more had annual incomes of more than $100,000. A major objective of many people who live in upscale neighborhoods is to demonstrate upper-middle-class membership. Perhaps these people all completed a course in social class theory in which their instructor told them that society would rank them as upper middle class if they (1) had high status occupational positions (corporate executives, professionals, or owners of major businesses), (2) owned a large home, (3) lived in a prestigious dwelling area, and (4) had income from inherited sources or earned sources (W. Lloyd Warner et al., *Social Class in America* [New York: Harper Torch Books, 1960, p. 123).

Proprietors of small businesses (the segment I estimate to contain the largest number of American millionaires) are ranked fifth or third from the bottom on a seven-point scale of status characteristics. On the other hand, one can be very upper middle class and have a level of net worth nowhere near seven figures and an income of less than six figures. It is my belief that the number of households in America that are interested in looking wealthy is far greater than the number that are interested in being wealthy.

The Really Big Market

Looking at the affluent market in terms of consumers, individual investors, families, and or households is important but one-sided. One should not attempt to market to the affluent without first determining how they become affluent. Most of the affluent households in America, whether defined by income ($100,000 or more per year) or by net worth ($1 million or more), are headed by business owners. This fact has been revealed many times by the research that I have conducted. Most people think of the affluent as consumers of homes, automobiles, clothing, and, of course, personal types of insurance products. However, this is only one side of the affluent market. *My research discloses that the relationship between wealth and the ownership of privately held/closely held businesses is highly significant.* With the exception of inherited wealth, fortunes are most often in the possession of the founders of successful business organizations.

The relationship between wealth and business ownership was also revealed in a recent study of the affluent by the Federal Reserve. This study and some of my research findings provided NBC News with an interesting report.

Late on the night of March 4, 1986, when I returned home from teaching the university graveyard shift, my answering machine was lit up like a Christmas tree. A number of my former students had left messages informing me that I had been mentioned by John Chancellor in his "NBC Nightly News" commentary. Chancellor stated:

> One million American millionaires by the end of this year. One millionaire for every 100 households by next December. That's the prediction of market researchers, and it is supported by new figures from the Federal Reserve Board. The Fed says it has found a dramatic increase in the number of people at the very top of the income scale.
>
> Who's making it? People in commercial and investment banking, insurance, and real estate, along with entrepreneurs. Doctors and lawyers do well, but they're not at the top of the scale.
>
> Other studies show that old money, inherited money, is not the path to riches. Professor Thomas Stanley, an expert on wealth at

Georgia State University, says that most millionaires are self-made and hardworking. He says ethnic backgrounds are changing, that only 40 percent of today's millionaires are white Anglo-Saxon Protestants; the rest are of East European, Italian or Irish stock. The Federal Reserve study shows that nonwhites and Hispanics are beginning to show up in the high-income categories, although very few of them are big rich. But 20 years ago, there were hardly any.

The other thing we are learning is that a million isn't what it used to be. The average income for a millionaire is about $120,000 a year. That's four or five times what the average family brings in, but it's not megabucks.

In fact, having a million millionaires may require new terminology to describe the really rich. Really rich, these days, begins with 10 million. The rest are just ordinary millionaires.

I was delighted that the popular press was beginning to understand the realities of the affluent market in America. Of the millionaires in this country, 80 percent are first-generation millionaires. Most of the millionaires in this country have both a financial and a managerial interest in a small or medium-sized corporation, partnership, or sole proprietorship. Yet some still believe that America is the land of big business. This is not the case.

- The Federal Reserve estimated that in 1986 equity in noncorporate businesses totaled $2,409 billion. This figure exceeded the estimated value of all the shares traded on the New York Stock Exchange as of February 1986 ($2,200 billion).
- Obviously, this figure would be appreciably higher if household ownership in privately held/privately managed business corporations were included.

Despite these facts, many marketers have failed to address the needs of the affluent as seen through the eyes of the business owner. This lack of sensitivity to the business side of the affluent market provides an opportunity for innovative marketers. The current size and recent growth of small and medium-sized businesses in this nation have made that side of the affluent market especially significant. More and more, America is becoming the land of the seller, the home of the business owner.

- There will be more than 90 million households in America in 1990. At that time, nearly 20 million businesses will be operating in this country, or 1 business for every 4.5 households.
- The ratio of the number of households to the number of businesses is declining. The growth in the number of businesses is approximately three times as great as the growth of the household population. While the number of businesses has been increasing at a rate exceeding 6 percent per year, the number of households has been increasing at a rate of less than 2 percent per year.
- The number of businesses has been increasing by nearly 1 million per year; sole proprietorships have accounted for over 70 percent of this growth.
- About 12 million sole proprietorships, 1.7 million partnerships, and 3.2 million corporations were conducting business in this nation in 1985.

But when one addresses the business side of the affluent equation, it is important to be selective. Why? Most businesses in this country are quite small. Many fail within a year after opening; others never become more than marginally profitable.

- Most businesses are small in terms of revenue generated. The average annual income from sales and operations for a sole proprietorship in 1985 was only $42,940, and the average annual income for a partnership was less than $200,000. In the same year, the average annual business receipts for a corporation were approximately $2.2 million.
- Only 40,700 of the 11,928,573 nonfarm sole proprietorships in business in 1985 had annual sales of $1 million or more.
- Of the 1,713,603 partnerships in this country in 1985, only 56,000 (3.3 percent) had annual business receipts of $1 million or more.
- Although the average revenue of corporations is much higher than that of the typical revenue generated by sole proprietorships or partnerships, most corporations have annual sales of under $1 million. Only about one out of five corporations has annual sales of $1 million or more. Even

more striking is the fact that less than 1 out of 10 corporations has annual sales of over $5 million.

• About 72 percent of all sole proprietorships that reported receiving revenue had positive net incomes.

• Only about one half (51.4 percent) of the partnerships that operated in this country in 1985 had any net income.

• Of the 3,170,701 active corporations in existence in 1984, only 1,777,779 (56.1 percent) reported having any net income.

Most affluent individuals own one or more businesses. However, most business owners are not affluent. Affluent in this context refers to those with at least six-figure incomes and/or with $1 million or more in net worth.

Certain types of businesses are more likely than others to produce wealth for their owners. But the type of business is not the best predictor of the profitability of a particular business. I have found hundreds and hundreds of business types to be associated with the creation of wealth. However, a consistent finding does emerge from my research. The quality of the business owner/manager is the single most important factor in explaining the organization's performance and, correspondingly, the owner's net worth.

Recently, I estimated the average cash balances held by various types of corporations (see Table 6–3). Obviously, these cash balances will vary even within the same type. But the variation among types is considerable.

Examine the factors that account for the wealth accumulation of a typical American millionaire. He owns or owned a business that generated annual receipts of between $500,000 and $5 million. (This revenue range accounts for more than four out of five self-made business owner millionaires.) His business is or was likely to be in the top 10 percent of all firms in its industry in terms of profitability.

Yes, wealth accumulation depends on much more than the business owner's choice of industry. How he operates his business, his consumption lifestyle, his propensity to invest, how long he has been in the business, luck, and many other factors are significant. Among the ranks of affluent business owners, one will find the cream of the industry crop in everything from livestock

TABLE 6–3
Cash Holdings of Active U.S. Corporations Categorized by Industry

Industry	Number of Corporations	Mean Cash Holdings (Rank)	Mean Business Receipts	Mean Assets	Percent of Mean Receipts (Rank)	Percent of Mean Assets (Rank)
All	2,925,933	$ 184,865	$ 2,104,284	$ 3,198,222	8.8	5.8
Banking	14,021	21,951,154 (1)	2,062,322	180,909,112	1,064.4 (1)	12.1 (4)
Petroleum (including integrated) and coal products	2,106	1,583,508 (2)	266,277,538	210,623,644	0.6 (57)	0.8 (56)
Insurance	7,900	1,550,645 (3)	26,359,309	108,361,448	5.8 (15)	1.4 (54)
Tobacco manufacturers	96	1,234,666 (4)	326,512,635	459,920,885	0.4 (58)	0.3 (58)
Credit agencies other than banks	35,434	905,668 (5)	324,555	24,358,870	279.0 (2)	3.7 (38.5)
Motor vehicles and equipment	2,991	872,677 (6)	47,852,254	55,618,759	1.8 (50.5)	1.6 (53)
Primary metal industries	4,237	662,764 (7)	28,552,268	34,134,573	2.3 (45)	1.9 (50.5)
Transportation equipment, except motor vehicles	4,179	550,726 (8)	16,890,783	15,337,546	3.3 (36)	3.6 (40.5)
Electrical and electronic equipment	17,105	451,776 (9)	10,200,108	11,051,140	4.4 (23)	4.1 (36)
Chemicals and allied products	10,145	409,606 (10)	21,285,792	21,373,705	1.9 (48.5)	1.9 (50.5)
Food and kindred products	15,411	333,413 (11)	18,369,054	10,484,407	1.8 (50.5)	3.2 (43.5)
Holding and other investment companies, except bank holding companies	46,939	324,406 (12)	558,009	8,597,421	58.1 (3)	3.7 (38.5)
Security, commodity brokers and services	10,579	312,483 (13)	1,412,375	14,036,041	22.1 (5)	2.2 (48.5)
Paper and allied products	3,942	299,931 (14)	15,884,861	13,598,596	1.9 (48.5)	2.2 (48.5)

TABLE 6–3 (continued)

Industry	Number of Corporations	Mean Cash Holdings (Rank)	Mean Business Receipts	Mean Assets	Percent of Mean Receipts (Rank)	Percent of Mean Assets (Rank)
General merchandise stores	9,958	292,430 (15)	14,401,838	11,136,049	2.0 (47)	2.6 (47)
Electric, gas, and sanitary services	10,980	270,391 (16)	24,412,483	43,808,621	1.1 (56)	0.6 (57)
Coal mining	3,543	243,349 (17)	4,984,680	4,845,385	4.9 (19)	5.0 (33)
Machinery, except electrical	26,708	235,535 (18)	5,898,663	6,841,259	4.0 (28)	3.4 (42)
Instruments and related products	6,174	226,952 (19)	7,556,288	6,274,736	3.0 (39.5)	3.6 (40.5)
Leather and leather products	2,273	222,501 (20)	5,553,718	3,260,142	4.0 (28)	6.8 (19.5)
Textile mill products	5,075	214,457 (21)	7,771,371	4,609,119	2.8 (42)	4.7 (34.5)
Communication	12,634	170,313 (22)	10,033,406	19,432,528	1.7 (52)	0.9 (55)
Heavy construction contractors	18,341	162,927 (23)	2,928,117	1,661,172	5.6 (16)	9.8 (8)
Oil and gas extraction	27,876	151,809 (24)	5,839,737	5,606,788	2.6 (43)	2.7 (46)
Nonmetallic minerals, except fuels	3,509	148,986 (25)	1,814,683	2,190,543	8.2 (7)	6.8 (19.5)
Stone, clay, and glass products	9,975	137,101 (26)	4,434,457	4,266,471	3.1 (38)	3.2 (43.5)
Fabricated metal products	42,325	113,374 (27)	2,673,635	2,071,475	4.2 (25)	5.5 (27.5)
Apparel and other textile products	15,957	111,512 (28)	3,142,332	1,491,090	3.5 (33.5)	7.5 (17)
Metal mining	1,748	111,264 (29)	2,480,272	6,425,527	4.5 (21.5)	1.7 (52)
Transportation	91,856	98,575 (30)	2,299,561	2,104,727	4.3 (24)	4.7 (34.5)
Rubber and miscellaneous plastics products	10,713	96,938 (31)	3,836,740	2,524,096	2.5 (44)	3.8 (37)
Lumber and wood products	14,203	93,380 (32)	3,275,742	3,082,247	2.9 (41)	3.0 (45)
Printing and publishing	37,904	88,229 (33)	2,208,207	1,596,550	4.0 (28)	5.5 (27.5)

Industry					
Miscellaneous manufacturing; manufacturing not allocable	19,063	83,117 (34)	2,087,663	1,481,953	4.0 (28)	5.6 (25)
Groceries and related products	24,065	83,052 (35)	6,476,311	1,185,664	1.3 (55)	7.0 (18)
Furniture and fixtures	8,523	81,891 (36)	2,360,385	1,289,432	3.5 (33.5)	6.4 (22.5)
Miscellaneous wholesale trade	208,897	79,325 (37)	3,755,851	1,439,739	2.1 (46)	5.5 (27.5)
Food Stores	44,583	71,604 (38)	4,618,746	922,211	1.6 (53)	7.8 (15)
Hotels and other lodging places	18,936	70,696 (39)	1,132,113	1,366,053	6.2 (11)	5.1 (31.5)
Insurance agents, brokers; service	51,637	68,064 (40)	335,067	404,051	20.3 (6)	16.8 (1)
Machinery, equipment, and supplies	52,653	66,270 (41)	2,034,929	1,243,998	3.3 (36)	5.3 (30)
General building contractors and operative builders	113,656	60,234 (42)	1,003,491	708,102	6.0 (13.5)	8.5 (10)
Building materials, garden supply, and mobile home dealers	40,527	43,067 (43)	1,197,658	542,458	3.6 (32)	7.9 (13.5)
Automotive dealers and service stations	82,634	43,051 (44)	2,797,144	663,908	1.5 (54)	6.4 (22.5)
Amusement and recreation services	58,945	37,407 (45)	603,357	676,711	6.1 (12)	5.5 (27.5)
Apparel and accessory stores	45,326	36,048 (46)	956,591	445,517	3.7 (31)	8.0 (12)
Special trade contractors	150,348	35,357 (47)	690,909	280,265	5.1 (18)	12.6 (3)

TABLE 6–3 (concluded)

Industry	Number of Corporations	Mean Cash Holdings (Rank)	Mean Business Receipts	Mean Assets	Percent of Mean Receipts (Rank)	Percent of Mean Assets (Rank)
Furniture and home furnishings stores	36,118	33,662 (48)	821,590	414,091	4.0 (28)	8.1 (11)
Business services	210,496	32,070 (49)	506,692	364,153	6.3 (9.5)	8.8 (9)
Agriculture, forestry, and fishing	91,320	31,202 (50)	664,077	552,009	4.7 (20)	5.7 (24)
Real estate	295,119	27,928 (51)	103,018	538,245	27.1 (4)	5.1 (31.5)
Miscellaneous retail stores	175,135	26,218 (52)	846,197	327,952	3.0 (39.5)	7.9 (13.5)
Wholesale: retail trade not allocable	4,805	24,466 (53)	538,159	233,459	4.5 (21.5)	10.4 (7)
Auto repair, miscellaneous repair services	75,448	23,081 (54)	417,550	302,371	5.5 (17)	7.6 (16)
Other services	403,952	22,852 (55)	354,185	156,820	6.4 (8)	14.5 (2)
Eating and drinking places	114,846	21,166 (56)	626,026	313,427	3.3 (36)	6.7 (21)
Personal services	51,929	19,651 (57)	324,562	179,210	6.0 (13.5)	10.9 (6)
Nature of business not allocable	20,134	14,741 (58)	231,559	131,296	6.3 (9.5)	11.2 (5)

Source: Affluent Market Institute data base estimates, Internal Revenue Service tax returns, 1981.

breeding to paint contracting to data processing. There are winners in the game of wealth generation in almost every conceivable industry. But in almost every industry, most business owners are not affluent and will never become affluent. Industry statistics are not substitutes for identifying the individual winners who own and manage particular businesses. The identification of affluent individuals is discussed in Chapter 5, "Sources of Information."

Despite the drawbacks of the industry statistics, they are useful in helping the marketer develop some sense of direction. The profitability data for American corporations provide important clues about affluent targets. When a list of the most profitable corporate industries is reviewed, several factors become evident. Many of these industries are dominated by a relatively small number of large publicly held corporations. Among these industries are petroleum refining, computers, tobacco manufacturing, utility services, and petroleum and coal product production.

Selected Profitable Corporate Categories

There are several criteria that can be used to identify categories of industries that often produce considerable profits for owners. One of those criteria is the proportion of corporations within an industrial category that have positive net income. This criterion gives some indication of the inherent profitability of a category. This criterion coupled with one other—the number of corporations in the category—was used in defining the industrial categories listed below. Each of these categories comprises at least 1,800 corporations. At least 70 percent of the corporations in each category report positive income. This is considerably higher than the norm for all corporations, which is only 56.2 percent. Such corporate categories include:

Manufacturers of specialty apparel/accessories. This industry is composed of nearly 2,000 corporations. Four of five have positive net income. Members of this industry manufacture everything from belts to bows. Often, they occupy market niches that shelter them from the stormy competition prevalent in commodity apparel.

Manufacturers of optical, medical, and ophthalmic goods. There are many highly profitable, privately owned firms in this industry of approximately 3,000 corporations. The average net corporate income in this industry is in excess of $500,000.

Manufacturers of meat products. This industry comprises nearly 2,500 corporations, of which 74 percent have positive net incomes. The average net income of a corporation in this industry is $350,000. Manufacturers of specialized meat products may be found in all sections of the country. The products of many of these manufacturers fit the needs of ethnic and/or regional preferences. Often, their businesses are significantly more profitable than producers of livestock.

Manufacturers of industrial machinery. Many small backwater firms make up this industry of nearly 4,000 corporations. Of these corporations, 7 out of 10 are profitable, with an average net income of nearly $300,000.

Wholesalers of farm products and raw materials. Often, intermediaries in America are more affluent than the majority of producers. More than 6,000 of these wholesalers have net positive incomes.

Manufacturers of dairy products. Over 2,000 corporations in this country manufacture dairy products. More than 1,400 of these corporations have a positive net income. Ben and Jerry are not only humorous; they are astute observers of where one can make money.

Accounting, auditing, and bookkeeping services. This industry comprises over 17,000 corporations. There is a considerable amount of money to be made even outside the Big Eight.

Wholesalers of motor vehicles and automotive equipment. More than 15,000 of the firms in this industry report positive net income.

It is beyond the parameters of a single chapter to analyze all of the industry categories that reflect corporate America. However, four industries have been selected for scrutiny in Table 6–4. These four serve as a base for enabling marketers to develop an appreciation for wealth generation and clues on proper targeting of corporations, executives, suppliers, and ESPs.

TABLE 6–4
The Affluent Business Network

Industry of Corporation	Dimensions and Key Characteristics*	Affluent Opportunities within the Corporations of This Industry	Affluent Opportunities within the Ranks of Suppliers to the Industry	Affluent Opportunities among the ESPs Serving the Industry
Tobacco manufacturing	Industry composed of fewer than 100 manufacturers. Ranks 3rd overall in average receipts per corporation. Ranks in the top quarter in percentage of corporations with net income, average net income for corporations with net income, and average return on receipts.	Industry dominated by several large publicly held corporations. Limited opportunity for marketers who seek affluent business owners. Some marginal opportunity to address the needs of top corporate executives. However, many of these individuals are heavily prospected. Also, the total number of affluent executives is relatively small. Some opportunity in terms of addressing the needs of executives, even middle managers, who are leaving the firm and have mid-six-figure to low seven-figure accumulations in pension/profit sharing plans. Some opportunites for marketing to key suppliers for those who gain the endorsements and referrals of key executives.	Tobacco manufacturers are often served by highly profitable suppliers, including advertising agencies, public relations firms, lobbyists, law firms, medical science consultants, and production consultants. Most of these key suppliers are privately/closely held corporations or partnerships. Many tobacco manufacturers pay a premium to quality suppliers. Major affluent opportunities reside among the ranks of suppliers.	Affluent opportunities exist for marketers who target the ESPs representing the suppliers to the tobacco industry. Such ESP categories include media sales, tobacco brokering, marketers of advertising agency services, paper sales, production equipment sales, and sales of printing services.

147

TABLE 6—4 (concluded)

Industry of Corporation	Dimensions and Key Characteristics*	Affluent Opportunities within the Corporations of This Industry	Affluent Opportunities within the Ranks of Suppliers to the Industry	Affluent Opportunities among the ESPs Serving the Industry
Alcoholic beverage wholesaling	Nearly 5,000 corporations. More than 70% have positive net income. The average net income for corporations with net income is over $300,000 from approximately $7 million in average receipts.	Industry composed of large number of private corporations. Most of the corporations in this industry owned and managed by individual/family. Significant opportunities to address the needs of the owners/managers of the more profitable firms. Affluent owners of these types of businesses often overlooked by many marketers. Affluent owners have need for both personal and corporate investment services. Organizations of this type are often able to make rapid patronage and investment decisions.	Opportunities to market to suppliers limited. Largest suppliers are large alcoholic beverage manufacturers. Other suppliers include truck dealers, office supply companies, accounting firms, insurance agencies.	Such opportunities may exist. ESPs are often found in the insurance sales area. Also, some ESPs emerge from office supply and truck sales.
Regulated investment companies	Nearly 2,000 corporations. Over 70% have a positive net income. Ranks 1st overall in receipts per corporation.	Conventional wisdom suggests that it is difficult to sell investment products to people who are in the business of selling these products themselves. However, a growing trend among ESPs is to target sales professionals in their own industry.	Significant opportunities exist in targeting suppliers of this industry. Many of these suppliers are extremely wealthy owners of businesses. These suppliers include law firms, printers, small/medium-sized computer and systems companies, office supply companies, economic research consulting companies, direct mail specialists, and marketing consultants. Reciprocity is a grossly underutilized marketing tactic.	Such opportunities probably exist, especially among suppliers providing printing, computer specialities, and direct mail services.

| Nursing and personal care facilities | Over 7,000 corporations. Nearly 80% have positive net income. | Industry still composed of large number of privately held corporations. The most profitable corporations often have multiple units. Multiple units are generally indicative of profit motives as opposed to other motives. Despite the growth of the market for nursing and personal care facilities, affluent owners are still underprospected. Owners of these types of organizations are often accessible and are often quick to make changes in their personal and business lifestyles. | Some opportunities exist for targeting affluent suppliers in this industry. Among the more important suppliers are personnel recruiting firms, hospital supply companies, laundry and cleaning supply services, and wholesale food suppliers. | Some ESPs have been found in personnel recruiting companies and wholesale food suppliers. |

* Source: Affluent Market Institute data base estimates, Internal Revenue Service tax returns.

The Anatomy of the Privately Held Business Environment within the Metropolitan Area

No single estimate or identification method is perfect in locating millionaire households. An alternative or supplement is to approach the problem from a wealth generation perspective.

Most of the millionaires in America are first-generation millionaires. Typically, their wealth has been generated from entrepreneurial pursuits. Thus, it is important to recognize what categories of business are associated with the presence of millionaire entrepreneurs. The business taxonomic method proposed herein is a radical departure from the practice of targeting millionaires by their neighborhood, yet it may have equal or greater efficacy in identifying these very wealthy prospects. This method has values that go beyond identification and targeting. It also provides a basis for the development of a market segmentation strategy.

Even the most elementary industrial marketing textbooks indicate that various types of industries are often highly concentrated. For example, the New York City metropolitan area has a high concentration of apparel manufacturers and the Detroit metropolitan area has a high concentration of tool and die manufacturers who service the automotive industry. Marketers will find it valuable to understand the anatomy of wealth generation within targeted metropolitan areas. A growing trend in marketing to the affluent is the exploitation of clusters of wealth within specific industries. Some enlightened marketers focus on industries with a high concentration of affluent business owners. These marketers often find that knowledge of industries of this type helps them understand the financial service needs of business owners. Some of these marketers have gained a reputation as authorities with respect to servicing the needs of business owners in particular industries.

The business taxonomic method provides marketers with a productive targeting vehicle. It also suggests a hierarchy in terms of the relative market value of business and the corresponding wealth of entrepreneurs within a targeted area.

Table 6–5 illustrates performance and pro forma market value estimates for privately held businesses with sales of $1 million or more within a metropolitan area. The number of privately held

TABLE 6–5
Pro Forma Market Value Estimates for Privately Held Metropolitan Area Businesses with Sales of $1 Million or More

Standard Industrial Classification		Number of Firms in Category	Ranked by Market Value	Estimates	
				Return on Sales (Percent)	Total Market Value ($000s)
3079	Plastic products	180	5	4.9	585,354
5511	Automotive dealers	374	10	1.7	455,940
5812	Eating places	401	14	4.2	455,490
2752	Commercial litho printing	163	17	5.4	414,558
8911	Engineering and architectural services	162	22	5.7	382,014
5084	Industrial machinery and equipment	450	26	2.5	318,150
1711	Plumbing, heating, air-conditioning	200	30	4.1	293,112
5081	Commercial machines and equipment	260	35	4.5	279,048
5161	Chemicals and allied products	110	60	3.3	179,388
5085	Industrial supplies	160	61	2.5	170,700
5039	Construction materials	140	81	3.1	131,058
3544	Special dies, tools	101	90	5.5	106,758
3841	Surgical, medical instruments	19	111	5.6	95,592
2011	Meat-packing plants	21	126	1.0	79,800
2051	Bread, bakery products	22	143	3.7	64,260

companies with annual sales of $1 million or more by standard industrial classification (SIC) code can be estimated from data supplied by Dun and Bradstreet. Using pro forma net profit figures, an estimate of total market value is illustrated. The total market value of the million-dollar firms within selected SIC categories can also be estimated. This is a crude approximation. However, it provides a reasonable estimation of the value of privately held businesses within each SIC in a metropolitan area.

Not All Affluent Business Owners Incorporate

It may seem surprising to some observers, but some millionaire business owners never incorporate. Such business owners often indicate a strong reluctance to operate anything but a sole proprietorship. There are a number of reasons for making this decision.

Some feel that they have better control of their business if it is not a corporate entity. Some feel that the added paperwork and regulations associated with changing from a sole proprietorship to a corporation detract from the real purpose of a business.

Only a small percentage of sole proprietorships ever generate the wealth associated with entering the millionaire ranks. However, if only 2 in 100 owners of sole proprietorships become affluent (a conservative estimate), a discussion of sole proprietorships would be important. Why? First, this percentage is approximately twice the average for American households. Second, if millionaires constitute 2 percent of the owners of the over 13 million nonfarm and farm sole proprietorships in America, this means that there are 260,000 such millionaire business owners. It is difficult to ignore this sizable market.

What types of sole proprietorships account for a disproportionate number of the affluent? This is a difficult and complex question. Often, a successful sole proprietor is also the sole producer/marketer of a specialty product or service that fits no real industry type. In fact, if one examines profitability figures by industry, one ambiguous category is consistently at or near the top. Whether one addresses corporations, partnerships, or sole proprietorships, the category "not allocable" is at or near the top of the profitability dimension. Not allocable contractors, wholesalers, and manufacturers are often highly specialized firms that have proprietary knowledge of their specialty and market and little or no competition. Given the performance characteristics of such firms, one would expect their owners to be affluent.

Nevertheless, there are drawbacks to prospecting the owners of "not allocable" businesses. One drawback is that individual "not allocable" firms are not easy to identify. Many of these firms have no trade association to exploit. Another drawback is that prospecting among such owners precludes a major thrust of the concept of marketing to the affluent, namley focusing on clusters of affluent prospects. Leveraging one's marketing knowledge among the affluent portion of the 6,812 highway and street construction contractors will probably yield greater benefits than focusing on the 31 "not allocable" contractors, despite the fact that as a group these 31 contractors are among the most profitable category of business in America.

The course opposite to exploiting "not allocable" businesses is to look at industries that contain a high portion of profitable organizations. Table 6–6 ranks selected categories of sole proprietorships according to the percentage that report positive net income.

If an industry contains a very high proportion of firms that produce net income, this indicates that the industry possesses ad-

TABLE 6–6

Rankings of Selected Categories of Sole Proprietorships according to the Percentage with Net Income

Category	Total Number of Businesses	Percent with Net Income	Comments and Suggestions
1. Men's and boys' clothing and furnishings stores	1,645	100.0	Target those with multiple outlets.
2. Billiard and pool establishments	1,114	100.0	Often a cash business.
3. Offices of osteopathic physicians	1,001	100.0	Return on receipts over 50%.
4. Wholesalers of alcoholic beverages	1,624	99.8	Focus on those that sell the most important brands.
5. Furriers and fur shops	2,223	99.7	One of the least prospected affluent groups in America.
6. Freight transportation arrangement	6,414	99.5	Average return on receipts over 20%.
7. Mobile home dealers	4,718	95.4	Target those that have been in business for more than five years. Do not overlook owners of mobile home parks.
8. Highway and street construction contractors	6,812	92.5	Follow news reports and news releases about the firms that have been awarded city, county, or state contracts.
9. Carpentry and flooring contractors	312,842	92.0	Ask the general contractors whom they recommend as subcontractors for carpentry and flooring.
10. Offices of chiropractors	18,928	91.5	The typical office has a return on receipts of over 36%. Whom do law firms recommend?
11. Roofing and sheet metal contracting	53,539	91.4	Target those that are winning school, municipal, state, and corporate business.
12. Drug stores and proprietary stores	14,128	90.9	The most profitable proprietary stores have multiple outlets. See your yellow pages.

TABLE 6–6 (concluded)

Category	Total Number of Businesses	Percent with Net Income	Comments and Suggestions
13. Wholesalers not allocable	18,651	90.8	Everything from flowers to tobacco.
14. Coal mining	717	90.7	Average receipts nearly $500,000; average return on receipts 16.2%.
15. Drapery, curtain, and upholstery stores	17,508	90.3	Ask the decorators of model homes who does their drapery, curtain, and upholstery work.
16. Agriculture/veterinary	16,367	89.7	The variation in income among these professionals is very high. See their accountants.
17. Taxicabs/passenger transportation	42,975	89.5	Multiple-vehicle transportation operations a primary target.
18. Other local and interurban passenger transportation	16,945	89.4	Bus and van passenger transportation companies are often over-looked by marketers.
19. Dental laboratories	15,246	89.4	Ask the endodontists for the names of the better-quality, high-volume dental labs.
20. Primary metal manufacturing	4,972	89.2	Average return on receipts over 20%.
21. Painting, paperhanging, and decorating contractors	180,209	88.8	Which are the consistent winners of contracts offered by area businesses and government agencies?
22. Offices of dentists	77,439	88.2	Focus on orthodontists, endodontists, periodontists, and dentists with multiple units.
23. Bowling alleys	1,456	88.1	Bowling still lives, but not necessarily in the fashionable suburbs. And who markets to affluent professional bowlers?
24. Fruit stores and vegetable markets	10,463	87.4	Why are so many Asian-Americans going into this business (especially Korean-Americans)?
25. Offices of optometrists	16,919	86.9	Even the small operations are often profitable. Specialists and multiple-unit types are important targets. See membership directories of the state association and the American Optometric Association.

Source: Affluent Market Institute data base estimates, Internal Revenue Service tax returns, 1984.

vantages that go beyond the qualities of its business owners. Approximately 70 percent of all the nonfarm sole proprietorships in America have positive net incomes. In some industries, however, all of the sole proprietorships have positive net incomes. Coupled with the net income criterion is another important dimension—the number of member firms. Except for coal mining, all of the industries listed in Table 6–6 comprise at least 1,000 firms.

Obviously, only a minority of the firms in each of the industrial categories listed will produce substantial wealth for their owners. Within the categories listed, marketers must prospect selectively. Table 6–6 gives several suggestions regarding the more productive sole proprietorships

Affluent Suppliers

Why not look for affluent targets among the major corporate giants? There are several reasons why these corporations are not viable targets for marketers to the affluent. *First,* by definition, there are only 500 firms in the Fortune 500. This is in reality a small segment when one considers that there are over 3 million corporations and that the American millionaire population numbers over 1.2 million. *Second,* few employees of major corporations become millionaires. Obviously, the top three or four executives in major firms are often very well paid and often have a considerable number of dollars invested in the corporations that employ them. *Third,* the names of these top executives are public information. Even their salaries and stockholdings to the penny are made available by the SEC and the financial press, including *Forbes* magazine (see "The Boss," *Forbes,* June 15, 1987). Since the names and wealth of the leaders of industry are so widely available, these people are heavily prospected. They are constantly being approached and, in many cases, hounded relentlessly by hundreds of brokers, financial planners, fund raisers, and so on. In short, they may prove to be a very unproductive target for most marketers. They are a long shot at best. Some ESPs (a very small percentage) have been successful in marketing to this group, but an individual sales professional would find it extremely difficult to capture the pension, profit sharing, cash investment business of any Fortune 500 company.

Beyond the top executive segment, is there any other value in relating to major corporations? Many corporations, as well as many other well-run organizations, are very selective in the suppliers they choose to patronize. Very often, the owners/managers of firms that supply the quality corporations are among the most likely to be affluent. Also, the sales of supplies to these corporations are often consummated by some of the most affluent ESPs. These sales professionals act as commissioned employees or as independent sales agents. It is important to remember that often the best suppliers and the best sales professionals serve the quality corporations.

Another point should be made about profitable industries. Some profitable industries are not dominated by a small group of giants. Many of the privately held and closely held corporations in those industries generate considerable wealth for their owners/managers as previously discussed in Table 6–4.

Affluent ESPs

Dear Marketer:

One of the largest affluent occupational segments in America is the ESP category. In spite of their high incomes, these top sales professionals are often overlooked by those who target the affluent. Why do so many sales professionals ignore the ESP segment? First, there is tremendous ignorance in the marketplace about the relationship between wealth and occupation. Sales and marketing positions, according to my estimates, account for 5 of the top 10 occupations in America in the generation of six–figure incomes.

Another reason why the ESP segment is often underprospected is that this market is highly fragmented. ESPs are found in a very wide variety of industries (see Table 6–7). They are typically the cream of their industries' crop of thousands of sales professionals. Thus, they are not easily clustered by any target market strategy. You are not likely to find large numbers of ESPs working for the same firm.

The third reason why ESPs are often ignored relates to their job activities. ESPs are often a moving target, in the field making calls and traveling. Most ESPs are employed by small and medium–sized firms that may be overlooked by sales professionals. And even sales professionals who do prospect the owners/managers of smaller firms may never consider prospecting the sales professionals of those firms.

It is often difficult to convince even top producers that many ESP prospects are employed by small and medium-sized family businesses whose sales are under $10 million. But more often than not, ESPs are found in

TABLE 6-7

Offerings and Targets of Selected ESPs (sales professionals generating incomes from commissions of at least six figures)

Product/Service Sold	Targets
Contracting General Paint	Developers, businesses, municipalities
Food manufacturing Private label products Soy bean products	Grocery store chains, food stores, groceries, restaurants
Textiles Carpet yarn Material Sheets	Carpet manufacturers, clothing manufacturers (blue jeans), retailers
Carpet products	Wholesale distributors
Women's apparel	Chains of women's specialty stores
Building products—lumber	Wholesalers, retailers, manufacturers
Automobile engine parts	Original equipment manufacturers, retailers, wholesalers
Office supplies	Banks, hospitals, real estate, communications companies, direct mail
Office equipment	Education, banks, law firms, Fortune 500 companies, general business
Paper products	Wholesalers/distributors of soft drinks
Printing (commercial)	Office supply companies, ad agencies, fast-food chains, airlines, consumer packaged goods manufacturers
Cleaning products	Automotive, grocery, paint stores
Industrial manufacturers Patented hoses Water valves Power transmission products	U.S. government, corporations, hardware stores, chain retailers, manufacturers
Computer software, hardware, systems	Telecommunications companies, utilities, field services, banks, government, schools, law firms, manufacturers, wholesalers, retailers

TABLE 6–7 (concluded)

Product/Service Sold	Targets
Air-conditioning and refrigeration products	Building contractors, industrial developers, consulting engineers
Motors and production innovations	Food processors, forest product companies, foundries, textile manufacturers
Weapons—aircraft	Third World countries
Medical equipment	Hospitals, medical centers, research facilities, doctors, laboratories
Communications equipment	Broadcasters, government, oil companies, airlines, hotels
Transportation—wholesale	Beverage companies
Building materials—wholesale	Retailers, contractors, building materials dealers, utilities, manufacturers of building materials
Heavy equipment	Paper and pulp plants; chemical and utility plants; carpet manufacturers; lumber manufacturers; contractors; builders; rock, coal, and marble producers; land developers; government
Paper products—wholesale	Hospitals, printers, restaurants
Food products—wholesale	Food and grocery stores, meat markets, restaurants, caterers
Automobiles—retail	Affluent consumers
Appliances—retail/wholesale	Appliance stores and builders
Investment services	Banks, savings and loans, manufacturers and wholesalers of distilled beverages, affluent consumers, small and large businesses, corporations
Insurance services	Financial industries, individuals, small firms, major businesses
Real estate—commercial and residential	Affluent individuals, businesses (retail and commercial), industrial and commercial developers
Advertising services	Businesses, cable systems, networks, ad agencies
Personnel services	Industrial businesses, corporations, distribution centers, big retailers
Consulting services	Real estate, chemical companies, other industries
Accounting services	Privately held corporations

just such businesses. They are well compensated, and they certainly earn their living. Typically, they are responsible for generating sales of goods and services that are not supported by advertising, sales promotion, or even public relations dollars.

In spite of some inherent obstacles in finding ESPs, this segment can prove lucrative for those who target the affluent. In fact, I recommend that ESPs be given special attention by novice sales professionals. ESPs are an ideal target for this group. Novice sales professionals can often gain insights about how to improve their own sales methods by interacting with prospects and clients in the ESP category. Also, ESPs often have a Rolodex filled with the names of other affluent prospects.

ESPs are especially sensitive to the character and needs of other sales professionals. This is especially true with respect to novice sales professionals. ESPs have, by definition, considerable courage, and they admire other sales professionals with the same quality. Aspiring ESPs can easily demonstrate this quality to those who have already achieved ESP status by asking for their business.

But how can one find prospects within the ESP population? The method I employ for research purposes can also be used in prospecting. I tell my survey team to telephone organizations listed in business directories that have sales between $5 million and $250 million. The members of the survey team are instructed to simply ask for the name and telephone number of each organization's top sales professional. In more than 90 percent of the calls, this information is given without hesitation. The same approach can be used in identifying affluent sales managers.

If one wants to become an ESP, there is no better target than ESPs.

Sincerely,

Thomas J. Stanley, Ph.D.
Chairman, Affluent Market Institute

TJS:sw

MUCH OF WHAT GLITTERS IS NOT GOLD: THE PSEUDOAFFLUENT

People who spend considerable amounts of money for clothing are not necessarily affluent. In fact, during sessions with focus groups of millionaires that I have conducted, sponsors have made this sort of comment: "These people [the respondents] can't be millionaires; they don't look like millionaires, they don't dress like millionaires, they don't eat like millionaires, and they don't have millionaire names." My response to such comments was, "Do you want to study American millionaires or television actors who look like millionaires?"

I find that the managers representing the firms that typically sponsor focus group interviews with millionaires wear more expensive clothing and jewelry than do most of the millionaire respondents. I have observed that among focus group participants the most popular watch is Seiko, a fine timepiece, moderately priced. This is also the most popular brand among CEOs of the Fortune 500 companies (see "Life among the Business Elite," *The Wall Street Journal,* March 20, 1987, pp. 20–21). But among the managers of sponsoring organizations the proportion of expensive watches is at least twice as great as the proportion among the millionaire respondents. Rarely do these managers have six-figure incomes or $1 million in net worth.

When Grey Advertising recently released a study dealing with the income boundaries of the so-called ultraconsumer, I was not surprised by the results. The ultraconsumer category consisted of persons who aggressively seek luxury consumer goods. According to the study, people who are well dressed may not be well heeled financially. At what level of income did the Grey researchers find consumers of $700 suits? Was it in the $100,000, $200,000, or $1 million annual income category? Actually, the threshold annual income of such consumers was $25,000.

Grey Matter, a Grey Advertising publication, stated, "Frequently, the driving force behind luxury consumption isn't age, income, or career status—it's attitude" (Chris Burritt, "Men's Apparel Manufacturers Try Hard to Tailor Sales to Suit 'Ultra-Consumer' " *Atlanta Constitution* August 14, 1986, p. 1C). The attitude of many self-made millionaires in America is that they should not flaunt their wealth. I can recall a conversation I had with a decamillionaire immediately after completing a series of focus group interviews. He just wanted to set the record straight. He had underestimated his net worth on the screening questionnaire. "I put down $1 million. I'm worth at least $10 million, but please don't tell anyone. I don't want my children kidnapped."

How Can a Professor Live in This Neighborhood?

When my wife and I attended a neighbor's recent cocktail party, it did not take the attendees long to start quizzing me about who has the money in America and how affluent our neighborhood is.

During the course of the inquisition, a woman asked an interesting question: "How can you, Dr. Stanley, a professor, live in this neighborhood?" I asked her for clarification, "What do you mean by *how can?*" Her response was that this was an affluent neighborhood. In fact, she stated, "Our children are the richest kids who go to our local high school!" "How do you know that this is an affluent neighborhood?" I asked her. "Look at the size of the homes, professor." I then said, "The size of a home is a better predictor of the size of one's mortgage than the size of one's net worth."

I explained that I had purchased a lot in the neighborhood, not for prestige, but in order to be 10 miles closer to downtown and that I had made the purchase when the real estate market was at its lowest level. During an interview, millionaires in the real estate business had told me, "Now is the time to buy". In addition, we had built our home and thus saved about 40 percent of what it would have cost if it had been standing there. I also explained that I had had my students survey the neighborhood before we moved into it. "At the time of the study, most of the households in the neighborhood had incomes under $75,000, including the family that lives in the classic colonial—your household." Often, I pointed out, middle managers employed by major corporations feel compelled to live in upper-middle-class neighborhoods even if they can barely afford the payments. Her response to these revelations was, "Well, you obviously inherited your money." I told her that the only thing I had inherited was a series of educational loans! Our conversation then ended.

Clearly, my neighbor, like most Americans, did not understand the point I was making. Conspicuous symbols of wealth are better indicators of one's credit use than of the size of one's investment portfolio. Remember that the principal objectives of the American millionaire are to minimize realized income and to maximize long-term unrealized income. The average millionaire in this country realizes significantly less than 10 percent of his net worth in income each year, whereas many middle managers making $75,000 per year realize over 40 percent. As a result of taxes and socially defined consumption patterns, such managers have few or no discretionary dollars to invest. More people in America look wealthy than are wealthy.

Re: M.D.'s versus McD's

Dear Dan:

I was delighted to hear that you are continuing your successful penetration of the affluent market. You must be very proud of capturing the pension plan of the surgeon you referred to during our last conversation. However, don't let your pride in this instance overwhelm your objective assessment of the affluent market. A physician who nets over $500,000 in income per year is not at all typical, nor is the fact that his net worth exceeds $2 million.

The impression that you gave me was that you are considering allocating much more of your marketing resources in the direction of physicians. This change in orientation may adversely influence the marketing track record you have established in prospecting entrepreneurs.

I must caution you against changing your current market focus. Your success in marketing to business owners has rarely been duplicated by anyone in your age category. Your first taste of success with marketing to medical professionals may be a mixed blessing. It is too easy to think that every physician that you will call upon will be so accessible, so responsive, and so affluent.

There are several reasons why the physician market

is not productive for many marketers of investment products and services. *First,* most physicians are overprospected by your colleagues, as well as scores of other types of sales professionals, including those from the insurance industry, the real estate industry, consulting services, financial planning, and the luxury vehicles industry. They are often overprospected because most people, including sales professions, assume that all physicians are affluent. Also, the names, addresses, and telephone numbers of these targets are readily accessible via the telephone directory.

Perhaps overprospecting would not be as serious a drawback if all physicians were affluent. Herein lies the *second* problem with targeting physicians. Many physicians, in fact more than one half, have annual net incomes of less than $100,000 before taxes. According to the American Medical Association's *Socioeconomic Characteristics of Medical Practice, 1986,* the pretax median annual net income of a physician in this country was $95,000 in 1986. This means that one half of the physicians made less than $95,000 in that year.

You may suggest that $95,000 is a substantial annual income. Only about 2 in 100 American households have higher incomes than this category. It is easy to believe that the typical physician, because of his high income, accumulates a great number of investable dollars. The issue of net worth is the *third* factor to consider when examining the physician market. It has been my experience in interviewing many physicians that they are in relative terms underaccumulators of wealth.

There are several reasons why so many physicians, even many of those who generate significant incomes, never achieve true financial independence. Often, their time and intellect are totally committed to their profession. Other matters, including the development of investment plans, are often low on their priority list.

Some physicians are very gun-shy about dealing with marketers of investments. That gun-shyness comes from previous experience with investment ideas that returned little or any value. This is especially true in cases where some so-called tax-advantaged investments proved to have no tax advantages or even any type of investment performance.

Many physicians do not start making affluent salaries until their mid-to-late 30s or their early 40s. In addition, medical school graduates typically face the burden of repaying educational loans, a market that is growing more and more competitive, and rapidly rising start-up costs, as well as high operating fees, such as liability insurance.

Often, people today, including physicians who barely reach the six-figure income level, mistakenly perceive themselves to be affluent. They believe that they can afford many "affluent artifacts," such as luxury homes, automobiles, and furnishings. The perception that a low six-figure income translates into true affluence is often formed many years before the individual finally attains this plateau. All too often, physicians look at income in nominal terms—for example, they may think that a $100,000 income has always meant and will continue to mean that one is affluent. Such an attitude typically leads people to judge their income as having much more purchasing ability than it really does. Many physicians purchase according to nominal definition of income and not in terms of dollars adjusted for inflation.

The fact is that (according to the American Medical Association's *Socioeconomic Characteristics of Medical Practice, 1986*) the average annual net income after expenses and before taxes for physicians changed very little in terms of purchasing power from 1975 to 1985. The average in 1975 was $56,400, while the real income average in 1985 was only $56,600. Too many higher-income people today, including many physicians, think that they are living on a 1975 six-figure income.

In addition to the unrealistic perception of the buying power of their current incomes, physicians have a compounding problem that needs to be addressed.

Our social system ascribes extremely high occupational status to physicians in America. It is the prestige associated with one's occupation that dictates consumption habits. Those with high status feel compelled by society's mandates to purchase expensive artifacts denoting that status. Too many physicians and their families consume according to status characteristics although their incomes are often far below the social esteem associated with the title of medical doctor.

The inability of physicians to hold on to money and invest wisely is reflected in a letter that I recently received from the department head of a major medical college. Excerpts from this letter follow.

Dear Dr. Stanley:

I enjoyed very much the news account of the millionaire segment of our population. Your statement, as reported by the magazine's reporters, that physicians were among the least likely to be in a position of accumulating any significant wealth was not entirely surprising to me. As I look around me, I find numerous examples of physicians without any preparation for or demonstrated skill in handling the relatively high cash flow that passes through their hands.

At the present time, I am charged with the responsibility of identifying goals for and a method of bringing the principles of resource management into the curriculum of undergraduate medical students. I can find no precedent for this. Neither am I certain that it can be done, but I'm willing to give it a try.

I would appreciate learning a little bit more about your studies, and in particular about your observations regarding physicians and members of the other professions.

After I get into this a little further, I may well give you a call. When and if this course on resource management ever gets under way, I plan to draw from a lot of sources, among them your own studies.

   Finally, I just wanted to say that I was particularly amused by your little anecdote about millionaires who were reluctant to share their life secrets
until you came up with a $100 honorarium. That cer-
tainly was important evidence supporting your observations about what makes the average millionaire tick.

Sincerely,

Professor
Department Head, M.D.

   Given the realities of the physician market in this
country, why change your focus from affluent business
owners? I hope that you are not confusing the occupational prestige of physicians with their level of
wealth.
   In spite of their high incomes when compared with
those in other occupational groups, only a minority of
physicians are wealthy. I estimate that less than 1 in
10 physicians in this country is a millionaire.
   This ratio must be placed in the proper perspective.
Dan, perhaps you are mislabeling your target. Don't
target M.D.'s, target McD's. In *McDonalds: Behind the
Arches* (Toronto: Bantam Books, 1986), John F. Love estimates that one in four of the McDonald's franchisees
are millionaires. Society does not ascribe the same
social status to hamburger vendors as it does to physicians. But wealth in America is not the same as occupational status. How many times have you and your competitors visited a McDonald's to buy but not to sell?
It is sometimes difficult to believe that the typical
McDonald's hamburger vendor is more than 2 1/2 times
as likely as a physician to have a net worth of $1 mil-
lion or more.
   Obviously, there are many more physicians than Mc-
Donald's franchisees in this country. But there are
also many more millionaires among the ranks of business owners in this country than among the ranks of

physicians. Remember, people who feel compelled to demonstrate their high status, such as physicians, are more often than not spender types, not investor types. As I have stated many times before to you and you colleagues, the conspicuous artifacts of wealth are substitutes, not complements, of net worth. *Why do you seek investors among the spenders?*

Dan, if you are still interested in the physician market after reviewing my comments, allow me to make some suggestions. You may find it productive to contact the author of the above letter. Ask him whether he would be interested in having you teach/guest—lecture at the medical college. I am sure that medical school students would benefit from your presentations of investment alternatives for physicians. In addition, you would be able to associate yourself with many of the medical school faculty. Most medical school faculty are paid over $100,000 a year independent of outside income, such as consultation, book royalties, and retainers from corporations.

A tremendous amount of prestige goes along with lecturing at a medical school. You could use this element of your résumé to enhance your credibility with the medical community in your trade area. You have already made a good first step in developing a reputation among physicians. I understand that the affluent surgeon who is currently your client has an international reputation. He is a frequent contributor to leading medical journals, an officer in the American Medical Association, and a speaker at the national American Medical Association conferences. Less experienced surgeons often ask your client for his opinion regarding complex cases.

Clearly, your client is greatly respected by the medical community. You should place a priority on gaining his endorsement and Rolodex. As the security broker of record for this opinion leader, you would probably capture the business of many of his colleagues. Seek his support in becoming a main platform speaker at the national AMA conference. Ask him for a referral to the medical trade journal on which he serves as a reviewer. This would probably enable you to publish an article about investment opportunities for medical practices.

It is very important to be selective when you prospect medical professionals. The income generated by physicians in various specialties varies considerably. Table 6—8 illustrates the average net incomes of physicians, by specialty and according to percentile.

You will note that the average income for a physician at the 75th percentile is $140,000, substantially above the average for all physicians. Surgeons and radiologists at the 75th percentile level have incomes of approximately $200,000. These two groups are especially important in your trade area, New England, since in New England both are likely to have higher incomes than the national average. The 75th percentile surgeons in New England have an estimated income of $230,000, and the 75th percentile radiologists have an estimated income of $243,800. Focus on clusters of the affluent, such as radiologists who work in group practices. Some of these groups pool their pension dollars and other fringe benefit dollars.

Examine your current client list, and determine

TABLE 6—8
Distribution of Physicians Net Income after Expenses, before Taxes, 1985 ($000s)

	Mean	25th Percentile	50th Percentile	75th Percentile
All physicians	$113.2	$65.0	$95.0	$140.0
General/family practice	77.9	50.0	70.0	95.0
Internal medicine	101.0	60.0	89.0	121.0
Surgery	155.4	90.0	130.0	197.0
Pediatrics	77.1	50.0	70.5	95.0
Obstetrics/gynecology	122.7	78.0	117.5	158.3
Radiology	75.2	90.0	150.8	200.0
Psychiatry	88.6	55.0	80.0	105.0
Anesthesiology	140.2	98.0	128.0	169.3

Source: *Socioeconomic Characteristics of Medical Practice, 1986* (Chicago: American Medical Association, 1986).

whether you have any clients who are sales professionals in the pharmaceutical or medical equipment areas.
If you do, ask these clients about their perceptions
of the productivity of the various medical practices
upon which they call. Also, prospect physicians who
have multiple offices. Multiple outlets are often indicative of a practice that is managed by a physician
who has a stronger profit motive than many of his colleagues. Maybe you will be one of the few that can capitalize on an affluent market segment that has a total
annual pretax income of more than $50 billion.

Please keep me posted on your progress. I'm sorry
you could not share our last fishing experience in the
Adirondacks, but it is not every day that one's wife
gives birth. Congratulations.

Sincerely,

Thomas J. Stanley, Ph.D.
Chairman, Affluent Market Institute

WHERE TO FIND THE AFFLUENT

Why a Big-League Orientation?

A growing number of marketers, especially those who market financial services, are focusing on the affluent market in America
because the affluent market accounts for a disproportionate share
of this country's wealth and income. Here are several examples of
the quality of this market:

- Although only about 1.4 percent of the households in America have an annual income of $100,000 or more, this segment
  accounts for approximately 11 percent of the total income of
  all households.
- Two tenths of 1 percent of the individuals in America own
  more than 10 percent of the net worth in America,
- Less than 1 percent of the households in America account

for over 50 percent of the capital gains from the sale of equity securities.
- Households with annual incomes of $100,000 or more receive nearly 40 percent of the dividends from investments.

These statistics are often reflected in the disproportionate amount of income that a small part of their clients generates for security brokers, financial planners, insurance sales professionals, and private bank professionals. It is not unusual to find that less than 10 percent of a security broker's clients generate 65 percent of his commissions. During a recent interview, in fact, a top producer in the investment area reported that the top 5 of his more than 1,000 clients accounted for more than 20 percent of his income.

Like the use of investment services, the use of credit services is directly related to affluence.

- The average American household spends less than $2,000 per year on interest on loans. However, households with annual incomes of $100,000 or more spend over $16,000 on interest on loans per year.
- Although some people believe that the very affluent do not borrow heavily, the opposite is true. Less than 20,000 of the estimated 88,797,000 households in America have annual incomes of $1 million or more. However, these households spend about $88,000 for interest annually on personal loans.

Many ESPs have developed their own methods of determining who the affluent are and how to market productively among the affluent. They have also discovered how to discourage "nonprofit" customers and prospects from making inroads on their time, a skill that is very important for sales professionals. I recently stated to one of my clients that a major portion of his investment clients were

"marginal" because they contribute only $416 in total annual contributions on average. Also, they have little potential in terms of sales of conventional brokerage products that are marketed by personal methods. On the average, they are almost 60 years of age. Some monopolize more of the registered representative's time than the most profitable clients. . . . Consider selling traditional and untraditional services to this group by alternative methods, such as telemarketing and direct mail.

During an interview, I asked Roger Thomas, an ESP employed by Edward D. Jones, how he dealt with the problem of "marginal" prospects and clients.

DR. STANLEY:

Roger, tell us about the people that were the hardest to deal with and how you dealt with them. People who took up a lot of your time and didn't give you a whole lot of business.

MR. THOMAS:

My biggest time wasters were widowers. Widowers would just be hungry for a place to hang out. And they would come down to the office, and they would want quotes all day long, and they were stocks they didn't own. Or if they owned them, they owned 5 to 10 shares. They wanted service all the time. They wanted to just visit. They were lonely. There was nothing for them to do. I tried to turn that into a positive, however, by starting a men's club. I would invite them to my office three mornings a week. I'd open up real early, and I'd have coffee and all the morning papers from all over Moline, Peoria, Chicago. And I would invite them in and say, "No women; no phone calls, guys; just the men's club; come in and have coffee." It was over at 8:30, and at 8:30 I would clearly say, "Guys, I have to get to work." And they stopped coming around. But I gave them a reason to get together early. They would come in my office, and then they would get the hell out of my hair the rest of the day. They were great old guys, but they were just lonely.

DR. STANLEY:

But did they invest any money, Roger?

MR. THOMAS:

Very little.

DR. STANLEY:

They didn't have it or they just didn't invest it?

MR. THOMAS:

Very little. They kept it in the banks. They wanted. . . . I mean, they did a little business. They'd do $2,000 from time to time.

Roger's approach to dealing with "time wasters" in a small town setting is very different from the approaches employed by urban-based brokers. These brokers often find it important to qualify candidates for their services. This is often done during their first contact. One Philadelphia-based ESP recently put it this way: "I tell them immediately that if they don't have, at the very minimum, $100,000 to invest with me, I can't help them." Other ESPs whom

I have interviewed will serve only prospects whose net worth is $5 million or more.

It is not unusual for extraordinary sales professionals to communicate demarketing messages via the mass media. James C. Hansberger is an ESP and senior vice president for Shearson Lehman Hutton, Inc. A recent article about investment counselors defined his target market as follows: "His client's net worth ranges from around $2 million to $20 million, with a very few in excess of $100 million" (Carol P. Neill, "The Nouveau Triangle," *Business Atlanta,* June 1987, p. 126). Demarketing messages of this type are very important for many ESPs. Communicating to the general population one's ability to provide services will generate many inquiries from persons who will never qualify as profitable clients. Thus, untargeted communication may be less productive than no communication at all. It is important to remember that fewer than 1 American households in 10 has accumulated enough wealth to potentially be a profitable client for a financial counselor.

Demarketing has its drawbacks. There are inherent problems associated with setting an absolute minimum with regard to initial size of purchase and investment, income, or net worth. Such demarketing can repel the future affluent, prospects who are not affluent today but are likely to become affluent in the future. Some ESPs are guilty of ignoring the future affluent. However, one must remember that most ESPs "trade up" to more and more affluent clients over the years.

Most of the ESPs who now have high minimum wealth requirements will agree that this was not always the case. Such ESPs will report that very affluent prospects are unwilling to patronize sales professionals who lack considerable experience. Thus, many of these ESPs "cut their eyeteeth" marketing to prospects whose levels of wealth were much lower than those of their current clients. As these ESPs became more successful, they gradually traded up to more affluent clients and prospects.

Many top ESPs, however, will not ignore prospects with a potential for becoming affluent, including some prospects who currently do not come close to meeting the minimum wealth requirements of some ESPs. Marketers who target the affluent are well advised to examine the emerging affluent market in America.

In interviewing hundreds of American millionaires, I have

found that most of them had been ignored or poorly treated by one or more marketers to the "affluent." Memories of such experiences can rankle for a lifetime. Most of today's millionaires inherited only their drive, determination, and educational loans. They still patronize many of the people and organizations that recognized them as future winners.

How Should You Allocate Your Marketing Torpedoes?

Some words of caution about marketing to the affluent are needed. Often, prospects and current customers who appear to be big game affluent are, in reality, decoys. In the course of my studies, I have found a rather interesting segment of the American market, namely, the pseudoaffluent. The pseudoaffluent have one major goal in life. What is this goal? It is to look as if they are affluent. Remember, actual wealth and the visual symbols of wealth are not complementary. I can tell you from my research that there are decoys even in the wealthiest neighborhoods in America. So even with neighborhood targeting methods, you will find households that have very little, if any, discretionary money with which to buy your products. Have you ever noticed that some of the most wealthy-appearing members of your clubs are always behind in their dues?

You must try to avoid spending your valuable marketing resources chasing images of dollars instead of real wealth. As a sidenote, a big producer from the insurance industry recently told me what he does when he encounters a pseudoaffluent prospect who does not have the dollars needed to pay the premiums on an important policy. He develops a budget for the family to follow. With these strict budget controls, there will always be money to pay premiums. This method often works, but it can be very time consuming.

How should you allocate your marketing resources? Distribute your efforts according to the expectation of return. Often, even ESPs are too democratic in allocating their precious time to various segments. In fact, I find that some of the most marginal customers and prospects take up a disproportionate amount of your time. Obviously, there is a need for a systematic way of investing effort and service where they will generate the largest return.

In response to this need, I have developed the client/prospect value matrix (see Table 6–9). Plot all of your current and prospective customers along three dimensions: (1) estimated value of current business, (2) estimated future level of business, and (3) referral or patronage opinion leadership potential. There are at least eight types of customers/prospects—(two levels of current business) × (two levels of future business) × (two levels of referral business).

The matrix assumes that current business is your most important category, that money in hand or imminent is worth two promises. However, future business, in turn, is given greater weight than promises of referral business. Some have been well rewarded for such allocations. It is important to remember that the matrix does not cover all cases and situations. Often, successful market-

TABLE 6–9
Resource Allocation Matrix for Marketers of Investment Services

Value of Relationship			
Current	Future	Referral	Prototypical Clients/Prospects
High	High	High	Vince: Affluent entrepreneur and future decamillionaire
High	High	Low	Thor: Moonlighting professor and millionaire with a passion for investing
High	Low	High	Colin: President of retired affluent business owners association and treasurer of retirement village
High	Low	Low	Maryanne: Waitress who wins million-dollar accident award
Low	High	High	Wesley: Aspiring attorney and shoe-in to make partner in top law firm
Low	High	Low	Eileen: Young author of first novel that receives praise from top literary critics
Low	Low	High	Alvin: Pastor at Church of the Affluent Entrepreneurs
Low	Low	Low	Todd: Conspicuous consuming middle manager of major international corporation who lives by the creed that it is better to look affluent than to be affluent

ers set long-range plans to capture very affluent targets. However, the matrix is useful as a planning tool for those marketers who feel a need to improve the way in which they relate to various types of opportunities.

After you plot your customers/prospects, ask yourself how well you have allocated your time in terms of potential business. If you are like most people, you will find that your efforts and your potential benefits are not in complete harmony.

To enhance your understanding of this concept, I would like to relate a real-life case history. Vince, a 43-year-old self-made millionaire, is a partner and senior vice president of sales for a highly profitable growth company that produces specialized computer systems. His annual income is in the $300,000 range. On average, his firm has $420,000 in its corporate checking account and over $2,200,000 in its pension and profit sharing program. Several sales professionals work for him who make as much as or more than he does, and he knows a great many of the top sales professionals throughout the industry. For this reason, headhunters are constantly calling him for leads. He is also known and respected by many affluent suppliers and buyers of high-tech products and services.

Vince is a prospect in the number one category. Why? He has significant investment needs today; his personal and business needs are very likely to grow in the future; and he can make referrals to at least 50 other affluent prospects. Give the Vinces of the world a disproportionate share of your marketing resources.

How does Vince compare with Todd, a middle-level executive for a major corporation? Todd looks like a top prospect. He is 39 years old, and his annual income combined with his wife's puts him in the $100,000 category. He lives in a top neighborhood, drives a high-performance European luxury import, and is a member of a quality country club. He has nearly $9,000 in investable assets. He is having a very difficult time paying his current bills, and he had to borrow money to buy an IRA. Typically, he moves every 18 months. Obviously, Todd is not in Vince's league. He is in the number eight category. He has no business investment needs, and he would not be a good reference channel. The Todds of the world should be given your least amount of time in spite of their affluent appearance.

The value of the Vince and Todd types is not as difficult to comprehend as that of some of the other clients and prospects encountered. Alvin is the pastor of a church with a very high concentration of affluent business owners. He has very little of his own money to invest, and he is unlikely to ever become financially well off. However, he has a considerable amount of credibility with many of the affluent members of his congregation.

Only one ESP in the investment area ever offered to assist Alvin with his personal investment needs. This led to the eventual brokering of the church's funds with the same ESP. Recently, Alvin asked the broker to give a series of seminars about investment and retirement planning. Several of the broker's most important client relationships resulted from his initial sensitivity to Alvin's needs.

Eileen differs from Alvin because of her ability to generate future wealth. She is a 31-year-old first-time author. Although she has yet to receive any royalties, her book has received high praise from several major critics. Eileen differs from Alvin in another way, too. Like many authors, she does not associate with or have a significant influence on wealthy people.

Wesley is a young, aspiring attorney. His ability to perform in the courtroom is exceeded only by his ability to generate new relationships. During his short career, he has never been paid more than $65,000 a year, but he is the member of his firm who is most likely to become a partner during the next 12 months. The average annual income of partners exceeds $250,000. Currently, he has very little to invest, but his account has great value because of his wealth-producing potential. Beyond this factor, he will influence the investment and related behavior of many clients in the future.

Maryanne was a full-time waitress for most of her adult life. Several years ago, she was permanently injured due to the negligence of her employer. Recently, a jury awarded her $1,750,000. Although she has a considerable amount of money to invest today, she will have little influence on or contact with other wealthy individuals. Given her stated objectives for use of the money, including a new vacation home, accessories, and autos for family members, her wealth is likely to decline quickly.

Colin is the 88-year-old president of a retired entrepreneurs association and the treasurer of his retirement village. He has personal liquid assets in the seven-figure range. Because of his age, he cannot be considered an important target for future personal business. However, he is respected for his investment ideas by members of both his business association and his retirement community. He also counsels business owners who are contemplating retirement. Colin is always looking for individuals who will speak to his association's monthly meetings.

Thor is a professor of engineering at a major state university whose moonlighting exploits have made him a millionaire. Thor gave over 50 speeches last year and he is the author of two widely adopted textbooks. In addition, he has two major consulting contracts, one with the U.S. government and the other with an important defense contractor.

Thor has much wealth to invest today, and he will probably have even more wealth to invest in the future. However, like many moonlighters, he does not associate with other very affluent individuals. His closest friends include far less affluent faculty members, graduate students, and neighbors.

The Geographic Distribution of the Millionaire Population

Many, perhaps most, millionaires grossly underestimate their wealth. Many never realize the amount of their real wealth until they have an estate plan prepared. This issue is especially important today. The growth figures for the affluent population in this country indicate that a major market opportunity exists for those who are willing to pursue it.

- During the years 1982–85, the number of U.S. households increased at an average annual rate of 1.8 percent. The number of households with annual incomes in excess of $100,000 increased at an average annual rate of over 20 percent— 740,206 in 1982 versus 1,221,813 in 1985.
- The number of U.S. households in the $50,000–$75,000 annual income category increased by approximately 21 percent from 1984 to 1985—4,657,702 to 5,650,810.
- In 1982, there were 8,406 households with incomes of $1 million or more. Just three years later, there were 19,106. This seven-figure income group grew at an average annual rate of 42 percent.

Table 6–10 provides estimates of the American millionaire population and decamillionaire population (those with net worths of $10 million or more) by states as of January 1987. Accompanying these estimates are estimates of the respective levels of concentration per 100,000 households.

The millionaire population has increased at a nominal rate of more than 20 percent over the last two years. In January 1985, it was estimated that there were 832,602 American millionaire households. In January 1987, the level had reached 1,239,713. In both percentage and number, this change is the largest in the past 15

TABLE 6–10
Estimates of Millionaire Population within States

Northeastern States		Midwestern States	
Connecticut	28,925	Illinois	71,153
Maine	2,914	Indiana	22,355
Massachusetts	32,724	Iowa	11,735
New Hampshire	4,209	Kansas	13,043
New Jersey	55,853	Michigan	47,802
New York	116,826	Minnesota	20,488
Pennsylvania	52,445	Missouri	21,305
Rhode Island	3,889	Nebraska	6,288
Vermont	1,535	North Dakota	2,794
		Ohio	48,225
Southern States		South Dakota	1,845
Alabama	12,512	Wisconsin	19,578
Arkansas	6,232		
Delaware	3,673	Western States	
District of Columbia	5,585	Alaska	5,477
Flordia	57,634	Arizona	12,906
Georgia	21,480	California	170,382
Kentucky	11,969	Colorado	19,983
Louisiana	22,897	Hawaii	5,263
Maryland	29,296	Idaho	3,160
Mississippi	6,869	Montana	2,791
North Carolina	19,939	Nevada	5,366
Oklahoma	18,276	New Mexico	5,032
South Carolina	9,443	Oregon	11,256
Tennessee	16,013	Utah	5,464
Texas	102,085	Washington	23,820
Virginia	29,859	Wyoming	3,361
West Virginia	5,759		
U.S. total	1,239,713		

TABLE 6–10 (continued)

*Estimates of the Number of Millionaires
per 100,000 Households for States*

Northeastern States		*Midwestern States*	
Connecticut	2,462	Illinois	1,679
Maine	664	Indiana	1,103
Massachusetts	1,506	Iowa	1,096
New Hampshire	1,111	Kansas	1,395
New Jersey	2,012	Michigan	1,442
New York	1,751	Minnesota	1,309
Pennsylvania	1,189	Missouri	1,112
Rhode Island	1,068	Nebraska	1,039
Vermont	768	North Dakota	1,131
		Ohio	1,206
Southern States		South Dakota	707
Alabama	855	Wisconsin	1,108
Arkansas	703		
Delaware	1,583	*Western States*	
District of Columbia	2,225	Alaska	3,060
Florida	1,243	Arizona	1,068
Georgia	977	California	1,731
Kentucky	883	Colorado	1,612
Louisiana	1,461	Hawaii	1,566
Maryland	1,804	Idaho	888
Mississippi	762	Montana	918
North Carolina	852	Nevada	1,408
Oklahoma	1,456	New Mexico	962
South Carolina	803	Oregon	1,064
Tennessee	898	Utah	1,063
Texas	1,726	Washington	1,383
Virginia	1,407	Wyoming	1,847
West Virginia	811		

U.S. total 1,396

*Estimates of Decamillionaire Population for States
and Americans Living Overseas*

Northeastern States		*Midwestern States*	
Connecticut	2,323	Illinois	4,472
Maine	117	Indiana	1,051
Massachusetts	2,007	Iowa	519
New Hampshire	207	Kansas	789
New Jersey	3,254	Michigan	2,223
New York	10,569	Minnesota	1,060
Pennsylvania	3,062	Missouri	1,231
Rhode Island	230	Nebraska	313

TABLE 6–10 (continued)

Vermont	52	North Dakota	97
		Ohio	2,893
Southern States		South Dakota	70
Alabama	699	Wisconsin	918
Arkansas	374		
Delaware	255	*Western States*	
District of Columbia	525	Alaska	129
Florida	5,171	Arizona	735
Georgia	1,076	California	11,410
Kentucky	719	Colorado	1,173
Louisiana	1,811	Hawaii	214
Maryland	1,339	Idaho	142
Mississippi	401	Montana	111
North Carolina	1,019	Nevada	496
Oklahoma	1,482	New Mexico	230
South Carolina	381	Oregon	525
Tennessee	1,026	Utah	282
Texas	9,241	Washington	965
Virginia	1,285	Wyoming	241
West Virginia	298		

American households in foreign countries   604

Total number of American households   81,816

*Estimates of the Number of Decamillionaires
per 100,000 Households for States
and Americans Living Overseas*

Northeastern States		*Midwestern States*	
Connecticut	198	Illinois	106
Maine	27	Indiana	52
Massachusetts	92	Iowa	49
New Hampshire	55	Kansas	84
New Jersey	117	Michigan	67
New York	158	Minnesota	68
Pennsylvania	69	Missouri	62
Rhode Island	63	Nebraska	52
Vermont	26	North Dakota	39
		Ohio	72
Southern States		South Dakota	27
		Wisconsin	52
Alabama	48		
Arkansas	42	*Western States*	
Delaware	110		
District of Columbia	209	Alaska	72
Florida	112	Arizona	61
Georgia	49	California	116
Kentucky	53	Colorado	42

TABLE 6–10 (concluded)

Louisiana	116	Hawaii	64
Maryland	83	Idaho	40
Mississippi	45	Montana	37
North Carolina	44	Nevada	130
Oklahoma	118	New Mexico	44
South Carolina	32	Oregon	50
Tennessee	58	Utah	55
Texas	156	Washington	56
Virginia	61	Wyoming	118
West Virginia	42		

American Households in Foreign Countries	427
U.S. total	91

Estimates based on the Stanley Wealth Equation, copyright, Dr. Thomas J. Stanley, 1987. All figures are estimates as of January 1987.

years. The number of households in America increased during the same time at an annual rate of only 1.5 percent. The millionaire population has increased at a rate almost 15 times faster than the household population in America.

Two major components underlie the growth of the millionaire population. About one third of the recent growth can be attributed to the so-called stable factors. These factors include predictable changes in the value of small and medium-sized businesses owned by millionaires, real estate values, and conservative investments in the financial arena. The long-term annual rate of growth of the millionaire population is less than 9 percent in nominal terms.

During 1985 and 1986, much of the growth in the millionaire population, perhaps as much as two thirds, was a direct function of (1) the unusually positive stock market, (2) sales of private businesses that were grossly undervalued prior to being reappraised and sold, and (3) major increases in sizable windfall bonuses, realized business profits, sales commissions, and profit sharing.

The short-term change in the millionaire population is, by definition, short term. A downturn in the equity market can have a major influence on the size of the millionaire population. On average, about one third of a millionaire's wealth is held in equities. Even a modest decline in the equity market will probably reduce its size. Also, it is estimated that during 1986 the greatest number of businesses valued at between $1 million and $10 million were sold by private owners. Many of these businesses were sold because of the tax law changes concerning capital gains. Many of these businesses were sold at prices that were considerably higher than their owners had anticipated. Some of the growth of the millionaire population in the last year was a function of the real versus underestimated value of privately held businesses. However, it is likely that the number of businesses that will be sold on an annual basis will not reach the 1986 level again during this decade.

The number of American millionaire households residing abroad is especially noteworthy. This segment was not part of the original wealth equation until this year. I estimate that 9,152 American millionaire households reside overseas. This is not a large number when it is considered that the average number per state is approximately 24,800. However, this segment is important in terms of concentration of millionaires. The concentration of millionaires on average per state is 1,396 per 100,000 households. The concentration for "overseas" millionaires is 5,691 per 100,000 or four times as great as the domestic average. The overseas decamillionaire population is also important for the same reason. On average, 91 in 100,000 American households have a net worth of $10 million or more, while 427 in 100,000 American households living in foreign countries are decamillionaires. This level of concentration is approximately 470 percent of the average for all U.S. households.

As of January 1987, it is estimated that there are 81,816 American decamillionaires. In January 1982, there were only an estimated 38,855 decamillionaires. The decamillionaire population has more than doubled in five years, *increasing for this period* over 110 percent. California has the largest number of decamillionaire households, with 11,410, while New York is second, with 10,569. Almost one half, or 40,863, reside in only five states. These are California, New York, Texas (9,241), Florida (5,171) and Illinois (4,472). In terms of concentration of decamillionaires living within the United States, the District of Columbia is in first place, with 209 per 100,000 households. Connecticut is second, with 198, and New York is third, with 158.

It is important to note that these estimates of the millionaire population are based on statistical analysis and not on a head count of each millionaire. Under the best conditions, these analyses account for less than 50 percent of the variation in wealth. The estimates provided should be viewed as approximations and not as perfect predictions of these populations.

Technical Appendix 4 at the end of this book discusses targeting by geodemography.

MEETINGS

Ode to Big Daddy

We left Cos Cob harbor at 0600 hours on a bright Sunday morning in September. As soon as we cleared the channel, my colleague and captain turned on his two-way radio. Immediately, we received the message that we had anticipated: A large school of hungry bluefish was attacking baitfish in the harbor of Greenwich, Connecticut. We arrived and strategically positioned ourselves in the middle of the frenzied bluefish. The captain suggested that I fish with the Big Daddy lure. This so-called lure looks more like the fat end of a baseball bat than a baitfish! I said that this lure was so big that it would probably scare the fish. The captain, a seasoned veteran, replied, "To catch big fish, one must throw big bait." He also suggested that Big Daddys should not be cast on the water but launched in the direction of their intended target. Not long after my Big Daddy hit the water, an 18-pound bluefish grabbed it and headed for open sea. Twelve minutes later, I landed this magnificent game fish. For several hours that morning, the bluefish continued to attack everything that the five occupants of our boat threw at them. Afterward, we determined that whoever threw the largest lure in the water seemed to catch the largest fish.

This experience is directly related to marketing to the affluent. If a marketer of investments, for example, approaches an affluent prospect with an offer of a small dollar amount of securities, the prospect may indicate a preference for another marketer, one who launches Big Daddys rather than minnows. The more affluent the prospect is, the more receptive he will probably be to significant offers. The affluent often judge the quality of the marketer and his offering according to the dollar size of the proposal. The big-league affluent rarely have time to deal with a multitude of small fish. Typically, they find it appreciably easier to deal with a small number of large offerings than with a large number of small offerings. In addition, they perceive marketers of small offerings as oriented to "minor league" clients. Their reason for this perception is quite simple: Experts in their respective fields market and service the big league. Yes, the affluent use proxies to determine the character of the marketer. However, only a minority of sales professionals target very big fish or even have a Big Daddy in their tackle box; an even smaller minority target large schools of very big fish.

Peak Concentrations of the Affluent

Abruptly, at 1043 hours on the morning of our fishing tour, the bluefish stopped feeding. Upon turning to our sonar scope, we found that they had disappeared. Even the $500-a-day fishing guides who were operating near our boat told us that they had lost contact with the bluefish. How does the feast and famine of fishing relate to the affluent market? If someone were to ask me where and when I had found the highest concentration of large bluefish, I would give the latitude and longitude of Greenwich Harbor and the hours 0600 to 1043 on a Sunday in September. If I were asked where and when the highest concentration of the affluent could be found, I would estimate that between 1800 and 0600 hours on weekdays it could be found, coincidentally, in Greenwich, Connecticut. There are many other high concentrations of the affluent in neighborhoods throughout America. However, like schools of game fish, the affluent have a tendency to change their location. Most of the really affluent of Greenwich do not work in Greenwich.

Where is the highest concentration of the affluent between 0800 and 1800 on weekdays? I would estimate that on a typical weekday the highest concentration can still be found in the Wall Street district of Manhattan. There are, however, irregular patterns in the concentration of the affluent.

One of the most affluent daytime clusters in America is an office filled with security brokers. It is not unusual for hundreds of productive sales professionals to be housed in a single office building. ESPs often think strategically in terms of big league prospects and big league concentrations of the affluent. Concentrated targets enable one to concentrate his marketing efforts. Many mediocre sales professionals spend more time traveling from prospect to prospect than they do actually selling. ESPs in growing numbers, however, focus on clusters of prospects who are in close proximity.

Trade Conferences

Once I was asked to deliver a speech on millionaires to the members of Sales and Marketing Executives, Inc. SME is a professional organization for senior sales and marketing managers and executives. After I spoke, a member of the audience asked for my definition of a millionaire. I said that a millionaire was defined as someone with a net worth of $1 million or more. He then stated that many of the people in the audience were in that league and that he would be more interested in learning about people whose annual income was $1 million or more.

What are the marketing implications of that exchange? Where was the highest concentration of the affluent in Atlanta on that evening in May? And every first Monday of every month? Clearly, it was at the SME meeting. Interestingly however, few, if any, marketers of investments, insurance, or expensive durable goods attend SME meetings. This is an oversight since seasoned sales professionals have always been and will continue to be a major portion of the affluent market in America. Most of the ESPs whom I have interviewed have told me that they are very susceptible to sales pitches. Incidentally, SME meetings are highly conducive to selling since many of the formal impediments to selling are absent from these meetings and since most successful sales and marketing executives are well informed on the income and wealth characteristics of their peers.

Three Days in Orlando, Florida

When 10,000 people are waiting for you to speak, you can become fearful. You can become especially fearful if those people are the membership of the Million Dollar Round Table, an organization numbering some of the best sales professionals in the insurance industry. But fear is often a catalyst for ideas.

Just before. walking up to the podium, I was asked by the fellow sitting next to me, "Where is the most affluent neighborhood in America?" I was unable to answer him personally. Of course, there are many very affluent neighborhoods in America. Directing promotion to the affluent according to neighborhood income and wealth characteristics is a technique that many product and service marketers have used successfully.

However, rarely do marketers direct their resources to the "other affluent neighborhoods." Why not target the affluent according to industrial neighborhoods or according to the means that the affluent use to commute to and from work? Some clever marketers have been known deliberately to seek out affluent prospects for car pool membership and seat selection on commuter trains and buses. Just think how many very affluent prospects spend a dozen or more hours a week commuting to and from an affluent industrial area. Often, they commute by train or bus. What a fine opportunity for the enlightened marketer. No telephones, no secretaries to interrupt your conversations with the prospect. And perhaps more important, little or no competition.

What about the importance of affluent industrial neighborhoods to marketers of financial services? A heavy concentration of affluent business owners may be found in almost any established industrial area, industrial park, or industrial neighborhood in this country. More than a few top producers in the insurance and securities industries achieved their status by cold-calling on entrepreneurs at their place of work. Consider the fact that in some industrial areas dozens of affluent entrepreneurs are within a few acres of one another. Often, the number of affluent prospects per acre, block, or zip code is higher in industrial areas than in Greenwich, Connecticut!

Where else can one find the affluent in America? The best way to answer this question is to go back to the question I was asked at the Million Dollar Round Table conference. Before I gave my prepared speech, I said this to the audience:

> Someone just asked me where the most affluent place in America is. Let me tell you all. For three days in July, it is located at the Million Dollar Round Table conference in Orlando, Florida.

Yes, the affluent are often in motion, often not at home. Very often, they are active business owners, professionals, executives, and so on. They are likely to be at the top of their chosen fields. Very often, they are on top because of the priority they place on gathering information in regard to the direction their fields are taking, the changes in the market for their goods and services. They are also keenly interested in obtaining information on competitive threats, new strategies, new product and service offerings, retraining, and new ideas. Where do they gain such information? At the conferences of their industries' international, national, regional, state, and local trade associations.

Marketers who target the affluent should attempt to prospect at the trade conferences where very high concentrations of the affluent can be found. Increasing numbers of ESPs have been prospecting at the place and time that will give them the highest probability of marketing success. Many sales and marketing professionals think I am joking when I state that very often the best way to reach the affluent is to spend two, three, or four days at a trade show or conference of business owners or professionals. "How can I sell my competition, Dr. Stanley?" Some very innovative security brokers in the country are now targeting fellow brokers for direct investment offerings. Not only are they succeeding, but many of them attribute their ESP status to "selling the competition." These ESPs aim at concentrated schools of fish with Big Daddy–type offerings.

A Minnesota-based ESP in the securities industry told me that a team of New York brokers had recently sold direct investments to him and several of his colleagues. "I guess I'm like all the other salesmen in the world. I just can't say no to an interesting offer. I bought a direct investment in a firm that has a system for transforming normal cattle herds into prized beef. It just sounded so logical. I'm still very excited about it."

Where besides the Million Dollar Round Table conference can high concentrations of affluent prospects be found three or four days a year? They can be found at meetings of the American Bar Association, the Association of Certified Public Accountants, and the American Medical Association. They can also be found at meetings of entrepreneurially-oriented industries—building contracting, heating and air-conditioning contracting, and the like. Affluent professionals and business owners attend these meetings with their receptors open. They seek advice and wisdom about how to improve their businesses and their personal lives. Rarely do marketers of products and services directed to the affluent appear at such meetings. Enlightened marketers, however, will recognize that the greatest return on their resources can be generated at meetings of this kind. They will determine when and where future meetings of the affluent will take place.

Most sales professionals fail to recognize that the affluent market is composed largely of business owners and that the most successful business owners are typically those who actively seek information about their careers and businesses. Obviously, part of what they want to know is how to invest their profit sharing and pension dollars and whom to patronize in making such investments.

Marketers to affluent business owners should become knowledgeable about the key trade associations and their publications and conferences. During a recent keynote address to several hundred marketers of asset management services, I was struck by the fact that although dozens of marketing booths had been set up at the hotel where the conference was being held, in an effort to sell the attendees everything from investment services to software programming to promotional printing, none of these attendees had ever set up a booth or given a speech at a conference of affluent business owners! It would take these attendees several hundred days of traditional prospecting to encounter the number of affluent business owners that they could meet at a major conference. And even if they did not meet a great many prospects at such a conference, the list of attendees could be a very valuable piece of marketing intelligence.

Marketing at meetings of the affluent is important for reasons other than the concentration of prospects. First, people attend such meetings, not to avoid information, but to consume it. Second, the people who speak at such meetings—and to a lesser extent the people who have booths at such meetings—have been traditionally regarded as providers of valuable information. In other words, the credibility of the organization and its membership rubs off on those who market at such meetings. Speaking at conferences should be a goal of every marketer to the affluent. Speakers at conferences are, by definition, experts. Their message is considered credible because of the third-party endorsement that the organization has given them. There is no better way to persuade than to be regarded as a purveyor of credible information. Credible information is that which is endorsed by highly respected third parties. Third, marketers are likely to find few, if any, competitors at such meetings, and these meetings produce leads on many business owners in the latent affluent category—the category comprising individuals with significant wealth who have not been discovered by competitors. Many wealthy business owners provide few, if any, clues about their true wealth. Their offices are often located in rundown industrial neighborhoods that discourage marketers from visiting. Their business may be highly profitable though relatively small in dollar sales. It may not appear on any list of businesses, and its owner is not recognized as a corporate leader. Small businesses produce more millionaires in America than any other segment of the economy.

Marketing oneself to a trade association is not difficult. However, it does take planning and a commitment of time and energy. One of the problems associated with such marketing is the choice of target. There are thousands of trade associations in this country, many of which contain low concentrations of affluent members.

The level of affluence of a trade association's members is directly related to the profitability of the firms that those members own. Table 6–11 lists some of the more profitable types of business organizations and related trade associations and publications. As a first step, the sales professional should examine the profitability figures for selected industries. Ideally, those industries will consist of small and medium-sized independent businesses. Table 6–11 indicates many wealthy prospects may be found among the owners of such organizations as laundries, dry cleaning and garment services, vegetable and melon farms, general construction contractors, firms providing legal services, and certified public accounting firms.

After identifying important trade association targets, the sales professional should determine specific targets upon which to focus. Profitability is only one criterion. A number of ESPs have targeted trade associations of which they had previous knowledge or with which they were affiliated. Some of them were fortunate enough to have had current clients who were important figures in their respective trade associations. Others, because of previous experience, had superior knowledge about the important players within the targeted trade associations and marketed to them.

TABLE 6–11
Selected Partnerships: Profitability and Trade Association Information

Type of Partnership	Number of Partnerships	Indications of Affluence*	Trade Associations, Conferences, and Publications†
Laundries, dry cleaning, and garment services	6,940	91.9% have net income Return on receipts, 23.4%	International Fabricare Institute Membership, 10,000 Annual convention usually held in the spring Publications include *Bulletins; Fabricare News;* and *Focus*
Vegetable and melon farms	1,968	81.1% have net income Rank 13th of all partnerships by average net income (for those with income), $114,200 Rank 2nd by return on receipts (75.8%) for all partnership with net income	United Fresh Fruit and Vegetable Association Membership, 2,500 Annual convention held every February Publications include *Produce Merchandiser; Outlook;* and *Annual Directory*
General contractors/ construction	25,574	Rank 14th of all partnerships by net average income (for those with net income), $110,700	Associated General Contractors of America Membership, 33,000 Annual convention usually held in March Publications include *Construction Monthly; Contractor's Annual Roster;* and *National Associate Member*
Plumbing, heating, and air-conditioning contractors	4,252	84.4% have net income Rank 24th of all partnerships by average net income (for those with net income), $73,400 Rank 29th by return on receipts (23.5%) for all partnerships with net income	National Association of Plumbing—Heating—Cooling Contractors Membership, 6,300 Annual convention held every October Publications include *News; Leadership Directory;* and *Who's Who in the Plumbing—Heating—Cooling Construction Industry*
Legal services	25,152	95.7% have net income Rank 4th by average net income (for those with net income), $417,800 Rank 14th by return on receipts (42.3%) for all partnerships with net income	American Bar Association Membership, 313,564 Annual convention held every August Publications include *American Bar Association Journal; Directory;* and several other periodicals and journals

TABLE 6–11 (concluded)

Type of Partnership	Number of Partnerships	Indications of Affluence*	Trade Associations, Conferences, and Publications†
Certified public accountants	3,708	85.7% have net income Rank 6th by average net income (for those with net income), $315,100	American Institute of Certified Public Accountants Membership, 231,000 Annual convention usually held in the fall Publications include *Journal of Accountancy; Practicing CPA;* and *Membership USA*

* Source: Affluent Market Institute data base estimates, Internal Revenue Service tax returns, 1984.
† Source: Trade association information, including information on membership, conferences, and publications, is from *Encyclopedia of Associations,* 21st ed. Detroit: Gale Research, 1987.

Daniel and Maryann

One of the best ways to illustrate how one can successfully market to a trade association is to provide a prototypical case example. Maryann sells expensive retirement homes located in exclusive resort areas. She rarely gets repeat business, though referral business is imporant for her. Her problem is that once a prospect has been closed, he is no longer a client.

Daniel is a security broker who believes that the best protection against patronage atrophy is a steady source of new prospects. "You always lose clients, especially active traders. . . . New clients are what my world is all about. . . . My most productive time is spent prospecting for new blood."

Both Daniel and Maryann contend that their business is a numbers game. They believe that as long as they come into contact with large numbers of affluent prospects, they will succeed in closing a substantial number.

Since Daniel and Maryann obviously need a constant supply of new prospects for their offerings, spending a great deal of time penetrating a single trade association may be counterproductive for them. However, marketing via trade associations can be done in other ways. It might be advisable for them to rent and operate exhibits and booths at selected trade association conventions and conferences.

Daniel may wish to focus on a somewhat different set of trade

han Maryann. He may be most successful in targeting
the conventions sponsored by the trade associations
s. Accountants, especially those who own their own
practices, are among the most affluent occupational groups in
America. They have a need for both personal and business investments. But even more important, they are a major source of patronage endorsements. It is not unusual for one CPA to serve over
100 affluent clients. Such CPAs have a great deal of critical information about people who have money to invest and when those
people are most likely to need investment advice.

Attorneys are, in general, even more affluent than accountants. For this reason alone, they are a viable target for both Daniel
and Maryann. However, Daniel will find that attorneys are also
important influencers and actual financial service patronage deci-
sion-makers for many affluent individuals. They are often among
the first to know who will be selling a business, going public with a
business, receiving a cash settlement, inheriting wealth, and receiving royalties.

Daniel would be wise to consider manning a booth at national
and state bar association conventions. These will provide him with
access to heavy concentrations of very influential affluent prospects.

Maryann would be wise to scan trade association publications
that list businesses for sale. Such sales are often an indication of
two key factors in her prospecting equation—money in transition
and retirement.

The Daniels and Maryanns of the world of marketing should
have a copy of the *Encyclopedia of Associations,* published by
Gale Research Company of Detroit, on their "books to buy" list.
This publication provides important details on the key trade associations of various industries—for example, size of membership,
location and dates of annual convention, important publications,
and who's who.

"Teach Them to Fish"

Even top producers need sales stimulation from time to time. Sales
managers, wholesalers, and even producers of products and services often attempt to manipulate their sales force to increase their

production. Such manipulation is sometimes related to a single line of products or services. Take, for example, the problem that mutual funds have in encouraging brokers, insurance agents, and financial planners to sell their offerings.

Brokers alone have hundreds, even thousands, of investment products they can sell to clients. A large mutual fund recently asked me to suggest a strategy that it could use to enhance its share of the mutual fund market. My response to this request was made in the form of a presentation and written statement entitled "Market Share Expansion: Targeting Investors or Marketers?" My suggestions centered on the concept of blending trade association marketing strategies and sales contests.

Dear Marketer:

Much too much of today's marketing literature is oriented toward packaged goods. A lot of this information is inappropriate for the marketing of investments, especially those targeted to the affluent market. Your firm's main target should be brokers and not the so-called individual investor. Too often, its competitors spend inordinate amounts of money on advertising to the ultimate investor. They are often guilty of trying to impress friends, colleagues, and competitors with such promotional campaigns. In reality, the affluent are influenced by brokers, financial planners, and insurance agents. However, highly credible news stories and articles about your firm will have a major effect in favorably influencing both its brokers and its clients. You will find that public relations dollars are much more productive than advertising dollars when aimed at the investor as well as the broker.

With the track record that your funds have established, it is not unreasonable to request that your public relations firm place 10 or 12 stories and articles in credible media sources, such as *The Wall Street Journal, Barron's,* and *Forbes.* Reprints of these articles and news stories should be aggressively distributed to your brokers and prospective brokers. Transcripts and videotapes of interviews with your key employees should also be distributed to

wholesalers and selected brokers. This type of information creates the impression among brokers that your
firm and its offerings are of superior quality. Brokers will also feel that your firm is committed to
helping them sell their mutual funds to affluent investors.

You will recall from my presentation that new business is the broker's lifeblood. Even the biggest producers in the investment industry will tell you that
their number one need as brokers is information about
and access to affluent prospects. Your competitors
have not responded to this basic, yet very important
need. I am proposing that your organization develop a
proactive marketing program that will capitalize on
this void in its market.

The majority of wealthy investors in America are
business owners. These, of course, include owners of
professional services. The typical affluent prospect
has three fundamental investment decisions to make—
decisions about investing (1) personal dollars, (2)
corporate cash, and (3) pension and profit sharing
dollars. The highest concentrations of affluent
business owners in America can often be found at trade
association conferences. I would estimate that the
largest of these concentrations can be found at the
annual conference of the American Bar Association.
This conference is held each August. Currently, there
are 313,564 ABA members. The legal industry produces a
disproportionate share of the nation's affluent. Law
partnerships alone account for over $25 billion in
revenue and $10 billion in net income. The entire in-
dustry generates over $50 billion in revenue. In addi-
tion to their own wealth, attorneys often control or
influence the disposition of DPM/OPM (dead people's
money/other people's money). In other words, they are
important patronage opinion leaders for investment
service professionals.

How should your firm relate to this affluent segment
and at the same time cater to security brokers? I would
recommend that strong consideration be given to sponsoring a unique type of sales contest for brokers. The
contest winners would have their greatest profes-

sional need fulfilled—access to a new source of affluent prospects. There is no stronger incentive for a broker than the possibility of gaining new affluent clients and thus enhancing his ability to catch fish. Top sellers of investment vehicles during the contest period would receive the following prizes:

A sales booth at the ABA annual conference. All expenses paid for the winner and spouse, including transportation, booth rental, hospitality suite, brochures, and lodging.

Wholesalers from the contest winner's market area to act as missionary sales professionals at the conference. In other words, they will assist in drumming up business for the contest winner during the conference. All sales of mutual fund offerings made during the conference, regardless of who consummated the sales, would be credited to the contest winner.

A preconference direct mail campaign. This campaign will be direct at important decision makers who are partners of "affluent" law firms. The objective of the campaign would be to sensitize prospects to the need to visit the contest winner's booth at the conference. The campaign would also inform the prospect of the availability of a free analysis of personal and partnership investing programs. This type of offering will not only attract new business, it will serve as a vehicle with which to debrief targeted prospects and their firms.

Public relations support and offerings. The contest winner will be given free consultation by the firm's public relations firm. The public relations firm will analyze the current communications objectives of the contest winner. Following this analysis, it will make recommendations about how to fulfill those objectives. The public relations firm will also generate at least one "ghost written" article for the contest winner. This article should be written with the intent of being published in a credible vehicle. One possible outlet would be the trade publications read by attorneys. The public relations component of the contest will enable the contest winner to enhance his reputation and image among prospects and current clients.

Image consultation. The contest winner will be offered a free consultation with an image consultant. Analysis of this type would include suggestions about everything from hairstyle and clothing to stationery and office decor.

A contest of the type described above would be much more useful in fulfilling your company's needs than would awarding sports cars or other consumer artifacts to the winner. The publicity generated by the "marketing enhancement contest for brokers" is likely to exceed anything that comparable efforts have achieved in the industry. This type of promotion will encourage brokers to take the initiative of calling your firm's wholesalers for details about the contest and your mutual funds.

Obviously, not every broker will be interested in marketing on a national basis via major trade association conferences. However, the most aggressive brokers are always interested in *trading* up to prospects and clients with more dollars to invest and *trading* out beyond their current, self-imposed market boundaries.

What can your firm offer brokers who have a more regional or even a local orientation? The prize in such contests would be similar to the grand prize described above. However, instead of providing a booth and accessories at the national ABA conference, the firm can award "runner-up" winners with space at statewide conferences. For example, the broker who sells more of your funds in Colorado than anyone else but does not qualify as the national contest winner would be given a state prize. This prize would include a booth at the annual conference of the Colorado Bar Association, Colorado Association of CPAs, or the Colorado Association of Cattle Ranchers. Those aggressive state winners who do not qualify for the national prize could be stimulated in the future by competing nationally for the grand prize. The grand prize could change each year. Attorneys may be the best target for this year's contest. In subsequent years, however, conferences and trade associations for accountants, contractors, dry cleaners, and other "affluent" groups should be given consideration. At the state level, wholesalers should play a key role in selecting the ideal trade association in the context of a sales prize. Every state generates wealth differently. It may be counterproductive to have all of the statewide prize winners receive booth space within the same industry grouping.

A contest that emphasizes the enhancement of marketing skills will be productive because it addresses a basic characteristic of superproducers in the brokerage industry. Most important, brokers are extremely competitive. This holds true for young achievers as well as top-ranked, seasoned veterans. The greatest fear of brokers may be that their competitors will win a marketing enhancement contest. Most brokers can deal with the reality of not winning a sports car in the annual sales contest. However, few brokers will be able to stand on the sidelines and allow the competition to gain superior market skills and knowledge. Competition for marketing enhancement will be very keen.

The contest that I have described should include provisions for the recognition of the winners' achievement. Most ESPs have a constant need to be recognized as winners by their colleagues, managers, suppliers, family, and community. Your firm should make a special effort to ensure that the local, national, and trade press carry articles about the achievements of your best brokers.

Many top marketers suffer from a feeling of inferiority because their important contributions to our society are unrecognized. This is due, in part, to the ascribed social status that our culture typically associates with sales professionals.

Most top sales professionals in this country are married. A key element in developing a bond between your firm and the brokers of its mutual funds is to

involve the families of both parties. A stable and
supportive home life is a critical factor in achieving
ESP status. The contest that I have described provides
for the interaction of the families of your firm's
personnel (especially the wholesalers) and those of
the brokers. The transportation, lodging, and entertainment expenses for the spouses of both groups at
the trade association conferences should be fully ab-
sorbed by the company. Brokers will be more inclined
to market your funds when they realize that your employees, as well as their family members, benefit from
these sales.

"Sizzle" is another important factor that many
ESPs talk about when determining what products they
will endorse. Sizzle has many connotations, including unique selling points, strong relative advantage, and endorsements from highly credible sources.
The sizzle that you offer brokers is not only in the
form of the superior track records of your funds. The
fact that your firm manages the pension funds of a significant proportion of the top 100 firms in this country provides you with tremendous sizzle. Brokers are
always searching for weapons that they can use to market various types of investments. They are very supportive of funds that provide them with powerful
themes to use in prospecting. There are no more credible themes in this business than to be invited to become a fellow client with some of the most prestigious
firms in the United States.

What other factors influence a sales professional's decision to market your mutual funds? There are
several criteria beyond helping him find new prospects. These include: (1) the long-term track record
of each of the funds; (2) the longevity of key personnel, such as the fund managers and wholesalers; (3)
the availability of your researchers to answer the
questions of individual brokers (this is especially
important for small and medium-sized brokerages that
have no research department); (4) the customizing or
development of mutual fund products in response to the
requests your brokers make in light of their clients
changing needs; and (5) constant contact and promotional ideas and support from your wholesalers.

Your overall marketing program should include an orientation to mutual funds for selected brokers. Many sellers of securities do not understand the inherent benefits of pushing mutual funds. This is especially true among young sales professionals. Many extraordinary sales professionals in this industry achieved their status by focusing on the marketing of mutual funds. This directly relates to the concept of the deep and narrow. It is beneficial for brokers to develop marketing skills as early in their career as possible by selling a narrow line of offerings.

A cardinal error that many sales professionals make is attempting to master the marketing and investing disciplines simultaneously. Only a small minority of people in the brokerage industry have been able to master the skills of both the investment analyst and the marketing expert. Most successful sales professionals do not try to do someone else's job. They define the job of selling securities in terms of marketing and not of constantly analyzing hundreds and hundreds of offerings. Many sales professionals receive ego gratification from positioning themselves as investment experts. It would be ego deflating for these types to market mutual funds. Ego is often more important than income to these types of sales professionals. Most of those who are successful have a greater interest in their income than in enhancing their egos. Most ego enhancers never become extraordinary sales professionals.

This information should clarify some of the points that were made during my presentation of "Market Share Expansion: Targeting Investors or Marketers?"

Best wishes for continued success. I hope we will have an opportunity to share some more of our ideas.

Regards,

Thomas J. Stanley, Ph.D.
Chairman, Affluent Market Institute

CHAPTER 7

EXPERTISE

IS AN EXPERT AN EXPERT IF NO ONE KNOWS?

DR. STANLEY:
Who is your main adviser?
DECAMILLIONAIRE:
A security broker in California.
DR. STANLEY:
But didn't you tell me you're a resident of New York? Did you once live in California?
DECAMILLIONAIRE:
I'm a New York native—never lived in California.
DR. STANLEY:
Then tell me how you became a client of a stockbroker in California.
DECAMILLIONAIRE:
I read his articles on his investment strategy. I called him on the phone. He is quite famous. Perhaps you have heard of his work.

THREE WAYS TO BECOME A TOP PRODUCER[1]

There are many ways to become a top producer in the insurance industry. Let me reflect on three of them. These ways are not necessarily mutually exclusive.

---

[1] Recommendations given to the members of the Million Dollar Round Table at its 1986 international conference.

First, there is the *Traditional Way*. The agent sells to anyone and everyone he can—for example, friends, neighbors, relatives, strangers. The modus operandi: Just keep the pedal down to the floor. There may be no segmentation plan, no targeting, and no strategy—only very hard work and very long days and nights. Eventually, with courage, determination, energy, and discipline, the agent breaks the market crust. He has a customer base. He has created awareness and trust, but he has worn out three dozen pairs of shoes!

The second way is *Mentor Avenue*. Here, the successful agent shares his market secrets with you. (And, perhaps more importantly, his Rolodex.)

The third way is *Famous Lane*. In 1985, I was invited to the Heisman Trophy awards dinner. After the dinner, hundreds of people, myself included, stood in line waiting to get Bo Jackson's autograph. I heard people saying that Bo was going to be a great professional running back and a very wealthy man and thought to myself that Bo could become very wealthy, not as an athlete, but as a sales professional. Many people would buy insurance, securities, and real estate from a famous athlete. Some would even seek out the sales professional celebrity.

No, I cannot help you become Bo Jacksons. But I can tell you how to receive more visibility and enhance your image as an expert in your field. You do not have to be in the national press. Remember, your affluent targets are local. Thus, you should understand how to get the local press coverage that can precondition your affluent prospects.

I hope that my comments will also help you in obtaining a better focus on the *Traditional Way* of marketing. I cannot help you find a mentor, but I can help you find the affluent. I cannot provide you with a Rolodex of current customers, but I will suggest how you can develop affluent prospects into customers.

Finding Where and Who the Fish Are Is Not the Same As Attracting Them

Once we know where the fish are and who they are, we can make ourselves more attractive to them. How can we condition them to recognize us and to develop favorable images of us? The top producers in the insurance industry as well as related areas are often endorsed by the business media within their market territory. These top producers write articles about the insurance and financial problems of their target market. They appear on educational television programs that feature business topics and experts. They conduct seminars that attract not only prospective customers but also key influencers such as accountants and other trusted advisers.

You, too, must develop an appreciation for the benefits of being perceived primarily as an expert rather than as purely a marketer of insurance. Publicizing your expertise via highly credible channels of communication will enable you to reap handsome rewards. What is the ultimate method in marketing insurance? The answer is: To develop an image that causes affluent prospects to call and ask whether you have any time to counsel them about their insurance needs.

The ultimate marketing method is to assure that a growing proportion of your business is walk-in, call-in, or drive-in business. But you must make sure that hungry affluent prospects can find you. You must leave a scent, a trail of market clues. Those clues should be strategically placed so that the seekers have a trail to follow. How else will they find you?

The person that most people, including me, consider the best professional fisherman on Lake Lanier, one of Georgia's most popular lakes, is Bill Vanderford.

When I think of fishing on Lake Lanier and catching the big fish, I think about Mr. Vanderford's guide service. Bill is not only a true intellectual, an authority on fish and their habits; he is also considered the top expert on how to catch fish on Lake Lanier. In addition, no one knows more about how to market his services than Bill. All of those who wish to become more productive sales professionals can learn from him.

- Bill teaches a continuing education course at a local college on how to fish Lake Lanier.
- When the Atlanta and Georgia press want to do a story on Georgia fishing, they interview Bill.
- When the Atlanta and Georgia press want a story and picture about the big fish that are caught on Lake Lanier, they visit with Bill.

- Bill has a marketing personality; he has empathy for the needs of all types of customers. If the customers are rookies, he will teach them; if they are competitive, he will be sure to let them catch the big ones.
- Bill has state-of-the-art fishing equipment, including a high-performance bass boat, tackle, and clothing. (Bring your own lunch—he likes turkey sandwiches!)
- Bill has a delightful personality and is a wonderful story-teller.
- Bill is the author of *Everything You Ever Wanted to Know about Fishing Lake Lanier and More.*

What Bill has done is to stake out his claim to the Lake Lanier market. He has developed a marvelous method of simultaneously marketing himself and insulating himself from competition. Bill offers a service, and you cannot patent a service; you have to develop psychological barriers to protect your market for a service. The protection system that Bill has developed is as strong as any patent. His protection system is within the minds of the market. Lake Lanier is Vanderford territory.

Prospects are likely to feel more confident about hiring a fishing guide who has also written a book on fishing than about hiring one who has no written credentials. This is especially important if the prospect is an executive who hopes to entertain clients with a passion for catching fish.

Bill did not stop writing after his book was published; he is a frequent contributor to fishing publications. Nor did he shy away from reporters who wanted to write stories about him. Often, these stories feature Bill's wisdom and pictures of happy clients with their 35-pound striped bass.

Along these lines, allow me to relate another case history about how a top producer generates new customers. Just before I delivered a speech to a group of top producers in the securities and real estate industries, a distinguished-looking man approached me from the audience. He asked me what my definition of a "big hitter" was. I replied, "Someone who did a minimum of $200,000, $300,000, or $400,000 in commissions, depending on his trade area and experience." He asked, "What about someone who did $1.8 million?"

How did he accomplish this? He wrote articles about the financial and investment problems of entrepreneurs. The articles led to press interviews, and the press interviews led to a spot on regional television. This man receives at least 100 unsolicited calls a month from affluent prospects. He still makes sales calls, even some cold calls, but, in his own words, "Since I've been on television, few of my cold calls are really cold." Even in cold call situations, people often recognize him as an expert, an authority. Why else would he have been on television? Who but an expert would have been so highly endorsed by a television station with such high credibility?

And who calls this expert for advice? Many of the unsolicited inquiries that he receives are from people in or near the transition stage of their financial life cycle.

HOW IS YOUR TRANSITION GAME?

On February 25, 1986, the mail was delivered early to my office. In the middle of the pile of second-class mail was my March issue of *Georgia Trends,* the number one business magazine in Georgia. I noticed something on the cover about millionaires. I had completely forgotten that the editor had interviewed me on this subject and that this issue contained my comments. I was reading the article when Dillard Graham (pseudonym) telephoned. He had read the article and was in desperate need of advice. He faced a serious financial dilemma, the same dilemma that many affluent people in America will have to face. He had just sold his businesses and was trying to play the game called transition, but he had had little experience in this regard and he had no one he could call on for advice.

Most of the business owners in America will eventually have to play the transition game. The "in-between time" in a business owner's life, when he must move from an offensive financial lifestyle to a defensive or "golden years" lifestyle, provides a significant opportunity for the enlightened broker. The business owner does not learn how to play good transition in college. (By the way, Dillard had a ninth-grade education). However, even the school of hard knocks typically does not educate one for the transition game.

The business owner can be the best offensive player in the league and get badly beaten during this game.

There are basically three stages in an affluent business owner's financial life cycle.

Stage 1: The Career Commando

Aggressive wealth building is the theme of this stage. The business is the most important thing in life for many first-generation affluent prospects. This stage of the financial life cycle sometimes lasts until the prospect leaves the office in an oxygen tent.

Stage 2: The Transition Game

During this stage of his financial life cycle, the prospect must plan and execute a strategy to cash in his business chips, pension funds, partnership interests, and so on.

Most of the millionaires in America own a business and eventually sell that business. But many of these millionaires are not sure how to invest the proceeds of the biggest payday in their financial life cycle. Many are not even sure how to go about selling a business or how to determine its value.

So, let's look at the big picture. The needs of affluent business owners during transition provide a major market opportunity—an opportunity that the financial service industry has ignored. Most prospects are like Dillard; they don't know where to turn for advice. Dillard called me because he wanted to know whether I was aware of anyone who could help him play the transition game.

Dillard is like many of the affluent business owners I have encountered. During his salad years, he lost a good sum of money because of "bad advice." Since then, he has never used the services of an adviser. He has been completely invested in himself, his business, and traditional bank and government offerings. But now, at age 68, he realizes that he should no longer be invested in his own business.

Interestingly, in studying thousands of advertisements for products and services offered by brokerage firms, I have yet to encounter one that addresses the transition game. Therefore, how are affluent business owners who are in transition to know where to go for financial advice and investments? The securities industry has a product orientation, not a market orientation. Certainly, the industry already has the short-term and long-term investment offerings needed by those in transition. But this seems to be among the best-kept secrets on Wall Street!

Suggested advertisement for ESPs who wish to help prospects win the transition game:

Business Owners: How Good Is Your Tran$ition Game?
No one knows more about how to make money in your business than the owner.

You were wise to invest your money, talent, and time in your number one investment: your business.

You never thought that you needed a financial adviser, since no one knew as much as you did about maximizing returns on investment in yourself and your business.

You have succeeded in business, but now you wonder about your future. You are beginning to realize that you cannot operate a business forever.

During most of your business career, you have been successful in making your business prosper. You are a skilled and well-trained veteran in the school of practical business experience.

But you have had little or no experience in the game you are about to enter, the biggest game of your career. You are in between your offensive wealth-building years and your defensive wealth conservation years. You are in the *Transition Game.* For many business owners, this game is a brief one, but it includes the biggest payday of their lives: The day they sell their business.

Learning how to play the game can save you a considerable amount of frustration and can mean a significantly greater return on your most important investment.

You have given serious consideration to selling your business, but you are not sure:

How much the business is worth.
How to market the business.

> How to determine whether the prospective buyer has the dollars needed to consummate the deal.
>
> How to determine how serious the buyer is.
>
> How to negotiate the sale.
>
> How to provide the buyer with access to credit.
>
> How to take payments.
>
> How to invest the proceeds.
>
> Where to go for information to answer these questions.
>
> If you have given serious thought to these questions, you, like many other owners of small and medium-sized businesses, are probably entering the transition state of your career.
>
> One of our consultants offers a special transition package to those seriously considering the sale of their business—whether it be a sole proprietorship, a partnership, or a privately/closely held corporation—with a value in the $500,000 to $10 million range.
>
> For a free information booklet about how to play and win the Tran$ition Game, call or write us.

The Tran$ition Game is copyrighted by Dr. Thomas J. Stanley, Chairman, Affluent Market Institute, Atlanta, Georgia.

Stage 3: The Golden Years

Stage 3, when the prospect is "in his golden years," is often too late to establish a productive relationship. How should a broker capitalize on the transition game concept at that stage? In the case of current clients who are business owners, do not be afraid to ask whether they have ever considered playing the transition game. Develop a set of the right answers to questions that those entering Stage 3 may direct to you. Document your previous successes in helping clients win the transition game. Ask those clients for endorsements and referrals.

How should you relate to the Dillards of the affluent population—those who have no broker? Make it a rule that anytime you prospect a business owner you advise him of your knowledge and investment offerings with regard to the transition game. This is especially important when you prospect business owners who are over 50 years of age.

In addition, explore the marketing power of public relations. Write an article for a local business publication on the investment problems of business owners who are contemplating cashing in their chips. Be sure to include investment alternatives and successful case histories. Establish yourself in your market as the transition game expert. One of the most effective themes that a financial adviser can employ in a published article is his proven ability to help affluent business owners improve their transition game.

"Retirement Planning (The Decision You Will Need to Make)," a one-page article written by Michael Ringold, was published in the March–April 1987 *Gopher Oversea'r*. The *Gopher Oversea'r* is the official publication of the Department of Minnesota, Veterans of Foreign Wars, and is sent to more than 84,000 members. Ringold informed me that more than two dozen readers of this article solicited his advice about retirement/investment planning. These prospects were all nearing retirement. They had accumulated between $150,000 and $500,000 in their pension plans! I told Michael and many of his colleagues in the financial service industry:

> The affluent don't all read *Town and Country;* some are heavy consumers of advice given to them by articles in such publications as the *Gopher Oversea'r*. However, I have found that the heaviest consumers of published articles by writers like Mr. Ringold are other writers. Why do writers read other writers? To find ideas for their own writing and often to solicit the comments and articles of those who have demonstrated (via publishing) expertise in a specific subject area.

CREDIBILITY BY ASSOCIATION

Affluent prospects use proxies to evaluate the credibility of solicitations from sales professionals. These proxies may include word-of-mouth communication with accountants and attorneys as well as informal advisers. They may also include such other subjectives cues to credibility as a firm handshake and promotional brochures. Of the hundreds of millionaires that I have interviewed, only one reported using totally objective evidence to evaluate marketers of investment services. Whenever this millionaire receives solicitations, he asks to see the income tax returns of the sales professional who is prospecting for his business. He reasons, "If their income is higher than mine, I will pay attention to what they recommend." All the other millionaires relied at least in part on subjective criteria.

A sales professional can greatly enhance his marketing to the affluent if he is able to associate himself with highly credible symbols. Those symbols should communicate to prospects that the sales professional is truthworthy, has significant expertise, and is held in esteem by people who are knowledgeable in his field of endeavor. It is very important that the sales professional position himself as someone who is truly interested in the needs and well-being of his clients. This is not an easy task. Most affluent prospects view sales professionals as hawkers of products or services that have greater benefit for the seller than for the buyer. Hawkers retain clients for only a short period of time. They are constantly winning, exploiting, and alienating clients. A true sales professional must communicate that he is not a hawker.

Only a minority of sales professionals in the financial service arena have ever published evidence that they are truly professionals and not hawkers. These extraordinary sales professionals (ESPs) have developed a communications strategy that separates them from the crowd. Many of them have gained the endorsements of writers, reporters, and editors of highly credible publications. Some have aligned themselves with people and organizations that exude trust and credibility. As one ESP who markets management consulting services recently told me, "I can call anyone and they will talk to me. Being a senior official of United Way gives me instant credibility. People see my best side when I work with them in a charity. I associate with credible people, people who care. People who contribute are people to deal with."

Other ESPs as well as marketing organizations have successfully distinguished themselves from the ranks of the hawker population by making a major commitment to credibility enhancement. Here are some examples of the types of credible symbols with which ESPs have associated themselves:

1. Chairman—Heisman Awards Committee.
2. First woman president—local synagogue.
3. President—University of Alabama Alumni Association.
4. Vice president—local United Way.
5. Senior vice president—local Cystic Fibrosis Foundation.
6. Officer—regional venture capital association.
7. Supplier of direct investments to an agent of the Federal Bureau of Investigation.

Sales professionals who are on full commission often, by definition, receive little or no individual public relations, sales promotion, or advertising support from their employers. Thus, many ESPs are in fact their own advertising, public relations, and sales promotion professional. Take, for example, Michael Dieschbourg, a vice president of the PaineWebber Investment Consulting Group in New Orleans, Louisiana. Seven months after Michael received a recommendation from me to prospect attorneys by publishing articles in their journals, his article "Using Advisers to Help Invest a Firm's Cash" appeared in the *National Law Journal*. An editor's note described investment counselors such as Michael as "a new breed of securities brokers" and stated that the article could "aid in identifying the cream of the adviser crop." The *National Law Journal* is an ideal outlet since attorneys often have considerable influence on the investment of "other people's money" as well as the money of their own firms.

Dear Tom:

   Thank you for the opportunity to contribute to your book. Your work is excellent. I have enclosed some comments on our project to date, plus an introduction to our team. Three of us work together as one unit. David and I are both VPs, and Mike Jones will become one next year. Our team will do over $1.5 million in commissions this year. Not bad when you consider that our average age is 30. That puts David and me in the top 5 percent in production in PaineWebber, 10–15 years ahead of the rest of that group. We believe that our skills and your marketing ideas can double that number in three or four years.

Island Fever
"CATCH IT."

X
X X
X ✳ X X
✳ X
X
X X
X X

DQ
money
✳ = 40
X = 5
V = DQ

We are very proud of our team concept. The quality
of service we can provide to business, CPAs, and attorneys is the best on Wall Street.

Thanks,

Mike Dieschbourg
Vice President

Why Write Articles?*

We wanted to write articles to enhance our visibility in the local
community. It is great to become an expert in the field of providing financial services to businesses, but knowledge needs to be
put to work. We wanted the business community to know about
our expertise. We wanted to project a professional image so
that, as Dr. Stanley suggests, "the affluent prospects will call
and ask us whether we have the time to counsel them about
their financial needs." We also wanted the CPAs and attorneys
to know where we were and what services we offered.

We have found that the key to our success is to provide
quality financial services to our market. Now that we have developed the knowledge and services, we want the right prospects
to know that we have them. We want the community to view us
as experts in our field who, in a professional manner, educate
and service the community with state-of-the-art services. This
image will reinforce our relationship with our existing clients
and also establish us as experts to prospective clients and third-
party referral sources.

Using a Public Relations Firm

Define and understand your goals. Like a brochure, public
relations exposure, through local or national editorial place-
ment, speaking engagements, and so on is a sales tool. Although useful in prospecting, such exposure may not produce
clients immediately. However, the investment produces long-
range benefits. Articles may be leveraged by reprinting them and

using them in direct mail and as a sales tool, and in some cases they may be used for years.

Make a commitment to spend time with your public relations agency. To give you the best return on your investment, the agency needs to know what makes you unique and what story you want to tell. This doesn't just happen—the agency cannot read your mind. There are thousands of successful brokers in the United States. What makes you different? Take the time to share your ideas with the public relations people on a regular basis.

Understand what your fee will buy. Agency fees include a wide range of services—clerical, journalist, management, etc.—and a wide range of prices. What fee you pay determines how much service you will receive. If your budget is small, don't expect fast results. The agency is a business too, and cannot allocate more time to your account than you are paying for.

Check your company's policy toward the hiring of public relations or advertising firms by individual brokers. Many national firms have strict guidelines for individual brokers to follow and require that all information released be approved by a corporate office. Take the approval process into consideration, and understand that it may result in delays.

Set specific targets and goals for national and local articles, TV and radio appearances, appearances at organizations, and speaking engagements.

Identify who is going to write the articles. Set time schedules, and explain the subject matter.

Publishing Your Article

Local press is great. It provides immediate recognition and feedback. If another individual in your industry has that sewn up in your town, don't despair—it is just as easy, sometimes easier, to get articles printed in national publications and trade journals. Once your article appears in print, leverage it! Get reprints, and send them to third-party sources, hand them out to clients, give them to prospects. If you have trouble getting articles in your local paper, try to get the paper to quote you and ask the paper what types of stories it is looking for.

Don't Forget Your Home Office

If you work for a large firm, become friends with the advertising and public relations departments. Ask them to help you with your projects. They can kill the whole concept if you don't watch out.

Let these departments make the reprints for you. Have them print your name, address, and phone number in a box at the end of the article.

Reflections

The concept is right on target. Dr. Stanley is correct about the affluent market. The wealth of America is in the hands of the entrepreneurs. To reach them, you have to become the expert that they will trust and find.

Getting in press is effective but time consuming. You have to make a long-term commitment to build your business. We have worked with a public relations firm for 12 months to develop story ideas, solicit articles in magazines, and ghost-write the articles. It has been expensive. There are cheaper ways, however, such as hiring a writer, not a public relations firm.

The results we have obtained include several press clippings, a couple of speaking engagements, and two articles— one in a state business journal, the other in a national trade journal. Three more story lines have been accepted by national magazines but are still in production.

The immediate impact of our articles on business to date is minimal. Long range, we think they will have a very positive impact. Already, several CPAs and attorneys who in the past assumed that we were like all other brokers now realize that we are experts and want to know all about our services so that they can refer clients to us. Meetings with new prospects take on a whole new meaning when you hand the prospect a reprint of an article you wrote.

One big benefit of our articles is that they have given us the ability to shorten the sales process. In the past we might have spent 6–12 months educating a CPA or an attorney on our services. Now, we give them an article and the process is shortened immensely. In one case, I had been working on a CPA for two years—doing civic projects together and so on—and could not get him off center. Finally, I gave the CPA a reprint of my article and told him that I was an expert. Like magic, the relationship changed. The CPA is now asking me to provide education on our services. In another case, I gave the article to an attorney I barely knew and just told him that the article explained my expertise. He reviewed the article and asked whether he could have several copies for his clients.

In closing, getting in press is an excellent tool for developing your business. It complements knowledge. Be prepared to spend a good portion of your time on the project, and it will pay off!

˙This question is answered by David S. Thomas, Jr., Michael T. Dieschbourg, and Michael R. Jones of PaineWebber.

Publishing articles in targeted periodicals can be many times more effective than client referrals in generating new business. For most sales professionals, it seems that there are never enough clients to make such referrals. Although many prospects regard current clients as credible sources of information, typically these clients do not come into contact with large numbers of affluent people.

The real benefit of publishing articles is that this can communicate one's message to a great number of affluent readers. The communication process becomes geometric if the articles are published in media vehicles that influence high concentrations of patronage opinion leaders for the affluent—attorneys, CPAs, and so on. Published articles and referrals are inherently credible forms of communicating with prospects. Moreover, the publication of articles is in itself a form of referral—publishing one's thoughts is, in a sense, also endorsing those thoughts.

A LESSON FROM A MEMBER OF THE
YELLOW BRIGADE

People who attend my seminars on how to market oneself listen to me preach the value of writing, publishing, and relating to the press. Invariably, members of the audience will ask these questions: (1) Should I hire a public relations firm? (2) How can I publish when I hate to write? (3) Where do I go for advice? (4) What publications would be interested in what I have to say? and (5) How much exposure will I need to make my name known to targeted prospects?

While some ESPs have hired public relations firms, others have been successful in developing their own brand of self-promotion. However, only a small minority of sales professionals have the background and discipline needed to design and maintain their own public relations campaign. Writing and getting published are not easy tasks. They are very time consuming. Also, these tasks should never be viewed as stepchildren in one's overall marketing strategy. Therefore, I usually suggest to sales professionals that they consider hiring a professional to assist them with their public relations campaign. A public relations professional can help maximize the effects of publishing. He can also usually be more selective than sales professionals in the choice of vehicles.

Most public relations professionals will tell you that it is naive to think that one or two articles or news stories qualify as a true public relations campaign. My advice to sales professionals is that they set a minimum number of times to tell "their story" each year. There are no hard-and-fast rules concerning the amount of exposure, but a minimum of two publications per year for five years would probably provide a good foundation.

Two publications per year may appear to require a great deal of writing. This often frightens sales professionals who are concerned about their poverty of time. A public relations professional can facilitate the writing task by helping sales professionals to express their ideas. Many moonlighting English or journalism professors at a local college or university would also be delighted to help aspiring sales professionals in this way. However, the benefit of hiring a public relations professional for this purpose goes way beyond writing. Writing an article does not automatically assure its publication. The public relations professional that one selects should have important contacts among the editors at the targeted media. If he does, he should be able to translate the needs of those editors into acceptable articles.

The choice of media is a problem for many sales professionals—a problem that relates to the basic objective of "getting published." Obtaining exposure without targeting can have results that are more negative than positive. Without targeting, a high number of responses from people whom the sales professional cannot profitably service is a real possibility.

In addition to targeting, one must provide evidence of expertise. This can be done, for example, by publishing one's ideas about the problems and opportunities that affluent investors will encounter during the 1990s or about the effects of current monetary policy on the price of securities. Too often, however, the competitive instincts of even ESPs overwhelm their judgment about themes. This is evidenced by the fact that marketers of investments often publicize their sales production figures. I constantly have to remind sales professionals that they must view their audience as the affluent prospect and client, not as fellow sales professionals. The affluent are much more likely to respond favorably to solutions from someone who communicates investment expertise than from someone who is boasting about sales volume.

If sales professionals have already developed significant knowledge about a particular area of securities, insurance, real estate, or tangibles/collectibles, I recommend that they aim high when selecting media vehicles. This means targeting prestigious, widely circulated media vehicles. Such vehicles do not consist only of national publications that are read by the general affluent population. Many trade journals and even newsletters have credibility and prestige among affluent members of various industries.

Sales professionals who are still learning about the products and services they sell should develop more expertise about their offerings before attempting to penetrate any top-ranked media vehicle. However, this does not mean that they should not begin to write and publish. As they develop product expertise, they should acquire skills in public relations. Such aspiring ESPs will find that neighborhood publications and trade journals with a statewide circulation provide a proving ground for relating to the press. All aspiring ESPs should, in the words of one of the biggest producers in Canada, "trade up and trade out"—trade up each year in terms of the net worth of targets and trade out each year with the objective of moving from neighborhood publications and secondary trade journals to regional/national publications and primary trade publications that will expand their exposure. View the press as just another form of client. Members of the press are constantly seeking sources of information that can meet their objectives of reliability and expertise.

It has been my experience that the members of the business press are among the most ardent readers of news stories and articles that deal with various types of investment issues. Once a sales professional's articles, interviews, and news stories begin to appear in the press, an increasing number of writers, reporters, and editors will contact him for additional information and insight. Eventually, a considerable number of these players in the publishing game will regard the sales professional as a quality source of information. These players in the publishing game are constantly in need of new ideas and information that will enable them to deal with deadlines. Those sales professionals who help them meet these needs will be rewarded by "getting good press."

One of the main reasons that some sales professionals never have their story published is that they do not know how or where to begin. Having a "letter to the editor" appear in a credible publication is a great way to begin and the easiest way to get published. Yet this very valuable means for reaching affluent prospects is often overlooked.

On January 23, 1987, *The Wall Street Journal* (pp. 12–13) placed an interesting letter in its own publication. The letter bore this title: "A Word of Thanks to 10,000 Men and Women of Letters." Praising the people who wrote letters to the editor of *The Wall Street Journal,* it stated that 10,000 people wrote such letters during 1986, of which about one in six was published (1,671). Thus, if one were to write six letters to the editor of *The Wall Street Journal,* the chances are that one of them would be published.

Some might argue that prestigious/highly credible vehicles such as *The Wall Street Journal, Forbes,* or the *New York Times* would publish only letters from famous authors, statesmen, and the like. Although such people are well represented in the "Letters to the Editor" section, they do not monopolize it. Almost every weekday, a good number of little-known people with no title other than Mr. or Mrs. have their letters published. A well-written, provocative, timely letter stands a good chance of being published regardless of the author's credentials. So, the marketers who tell me that they do not write letters to the editor because only those of the "elite" get published are mistaken. I often use specific published letters to prove this.

Those who live by the "elite only" hypothesis find one of these letters particularly convincing. On July 12, 1986, the *New York Times* published a letter entitled, "Some Respect for the

Yellow Brigade, Please.'' The letter was written by Jere Van Dyk. Who is Jere Van Dyk? The *New York Times* described him in eight words: ''has been a taxi driver for three months.'' Yes, a cabdriver's letter covered a quarter page of one of the most prestigious, credible, and widely distributed publications in America. The elite hypothesis is refuted each day by the facts. People get published only if they try to get published. Those who get published write, and those who do not write do not get published.

What is the cost of a one-quarter page advertisement in the national edition of the *New York Times?* The answer as of fall 1987 is $1,291.50. But the value of having a letter published in the *New York Times* is far greater than that amount. The publication of such a letter can give instant credibility to its author.

Often, when I speak of the value of publishing a letter to the editor, a sales professional in the audience will ask, ''What good would it do to be published in *The Wall Street Journal,* the *New York Times,* or *Forbes?* Whoever reads letters to the editor? How many prospects will call me?'' It is true that a letter to the editor may not be read initially by a large number of affluent prospects. However, writing such letters is not intended to generate dozens of new clients immediately. Three valuable functions are served by a published letter. First, it is read by members of the financial press who may then view its author as a possible source for news reports and interviews. The sales professional can increase the chances that his letter will be read by important financial writers and editors by sending them reprints of the letter along with related materials. Remember that the press is a target of a long-term communications strategy.

Second, a letter to the editor is only one component of an entire campaign. It functions as a part of one's portfolio of credentials. Published materials in highly credible vehicles build the sales professional's confidence and self-esteem and also lower the defense barriers that many affluent people immediately conjure up when confronted with a solicitation from ''just another hawker.'' Publications often have their greatest impact on prospects and clients when they are used in the form of reprints. Some of the very best ESPs carry their reprints with them as others carry their business cards. Imagine how more credible you can be if you are in a position to ask a prospect this question: "Would you like to look over some of my ideas that were published in *The Wall Street Journal,* the *New York Times,* and *Forbes?*"

The third function of a published letter relates to the concept of other people's money. The professionals who influence the financial service patronage habits of the affluent are very careful about whom they endorse. In fact, it is often more difficult to influence the influencers of "other people's money" than the affluent themselves. Why should accountants or attorneys recommend a particular financial service provider to their clients? Much is at risk for these influencers. If the financial service provider fails to satisfy the clients, they stand to lose business. How do such influencers evaluate competing financial service providers? How much weight do they place on alternative sources of information? Third-party endorsements are very important to them. A letter published in a credible vehicle indicates that the editor considered the message of value to readers—that is, implies third-party endorsement.

What should the sales professional in letters to the editor write about? The letters most likely to be published are those that deal with important current issues in his area of expertise.

News stories, editorials, and letters to the editor published today provide an important base for comment in the form of a letter to the editor tomorrow. Rejoinder letters that express views different from those published in earlier letters are more likely to be published than many other types. Anytime one reads an article, editorial, or letter to the editor that deals with his area of expertise, he should immediately capitalize on it. For example, almost like clockwork, articles are published annually about how much it will cost to send one's children to college. Some marketers of securities, mutual funds, and insurance have spent considerable time developing alternative ways for parents to finance their children's education. Some have even developed their own estimates of college costs in the 1990s and beyond. In one case, a sales professional actually wrote a book about the quality/price trade-offs of various colleges and universities. In short, some sales professionals have acquired considerable knowledge about the topic of financing an education.

These experts will find that their views on this subject will probably be published if they are made available to editors during the "season for cost of college issues." Remember that, all else being equal, a well-targeted and well-timed letter is more likely to be published than one that reads like poetry but has no sizzle.

PUBLIC RELATIONS ACTIVITIES SHOULD BE BASED ON A CLEAR SET OF MARKETING OBJECTIVES

Dear Marketer:

A growing number of ESPs are self-directing and - financing public relations campaigns. This type of promotion is clearly reflected in the comments made by many ESP respondents to inquiries. However, I would predict that only a minority of all ESPs engage in some formal type of public relations strategy. Also, it would appear that the public relations programs developed by even some of the top sales professionals in this country are inefficient. While some respondents report having success in their promotional undertakings, others have had little or no success in generating new business via public relations campaigns.

It is unfortunate that many sales professionals have been turned off by what they believe to be counterproductive results of public relations programs. However, when properly designed, public relations programs have been highly productive in attracting and retaining important clients.

Before public relations success stories are discussed, it would be useful to consider the problems that some ESPs have encountered with public relations. These problems were disclosed during interviews with several groups of ESPs from the securities industry.

1. *Poor market targeting.* Most of the respondents who used public relations did not target it correctly. Articles, interviews, seminars, and television appearances will attract a broad audience. The responses from such an audience are often more of a head-

ache for a security broker than effective leads. Few ESPs target their public relations to specific industry groups in the market of affluent business owners. This can be partially explained by their lack of understanding of the types of media their prospects consume. A public relations effort that generates hundreds of prospects with little money to invest is counterproductive. Poor targeting is often the fault of the public relations firm. Many such firms are not conversant with the media consumption habits of specific affluent targets, such as wealthy business owners.

2. *Improper selection of a public relations firm.* The majority of public relations firms have little or no experience in dealing with the needs of financial service marketers. Only a small number have both experience in this area and experience in communicating with affluent business owners. Often, a public relations firm that represents a registered representative will get him "a lot of exposure" in media vehicles that the firm understands and with which it has contacts. Mass media vehicles are not necessarily the most suitable places to present one's story.

3. *Utilization of ineffective themes.* Too often, registered representatives are more interested in getting exposure than in getting business. The message that they often get across is that they are alive and intelligent. Other registered representatives are too interested in telling the technical side of the product, market, and so on. A minority of top producers present an image that reflects their knowledge and understanding of the major financial problems of the affluent and their ability to solve those problems.

4. *Failure to conduct autopsies.* Most of the respondents who had had unsuccessful public relations experiences were uncertain why these public relations undertakings had failed. For example, a respondent did not know why a very expensive breakfast seminar on financial planning failed to break even. Why not question the members of the audience?

5. *Lack of direction from the firm.* Many sales pro-

fessionals are unsure what their employers' policy is concerning public relations conducted by sales professionals. Even some of the most enlightened marketing firms do not take a proactive role in encouraging their sales professionals to try creative public relations and related promotion. Few firms have ever provided their brokers with advice concerning promotional targeting, the selection of communications consultants, audience receptivity to various themes, and cost/benefit trade-offs.

The following recommendations are presented to those marketers who seek to improve the efficacy of their promotional methods.

1. *Target affluent business owners.* Marketers who wish to reach affluent business owners should use a rifle approach. Successful business owners attribute much of their achievement to their understanding of industry changes. They obtain a lot of the information they value by reading related trade journals and by attending trade association meetings. The marketer must decide what industries he will attempt to penetrate. Then, he should work with his public relations professionals to identify the key media vehicles they wish to use. If a firm's objective is to have its sales professional service a variety of small businesses, other vehicles should be included. Local, state, and regional business publications should be exploited.

2. *How to select a public relations firm/communications consultant.* A public relations/communications firm should be selected only after communications objectives have been established. If the objective is to penetrate the market of heating and air-conditioning contractors, the public relations firm should have experience both in financial services and in industrial public relations. It should be able to place the broker's messages in the top media vehicles of the heating and air-conditioning industry. Ideally, its key personnel will have a close relationship with editors and writers who are connected with this industry. The public relations firm should also be able to set up speaking engagements for the sales professional and his firm's product experts.

These engagements should include top spots at the high-quality trade shows in the industry. In addition, the public relations firm should be proficient in arranging and setting up marketing booths at this industry's trade shows.

3. *Communication themes that attract affluent business owners.* The precise themes that should be used in communicating with business owners can only be hypothesized. Articles and interviews that are published in selected trade journals should emphasize how the sales professional solved the investment problems of the entrepreneur. The firm should study the effectiveness of various types of promotional themes. Data can be gathered from sales force members who have already undertaken their own communication activities. Future research should focus on the responses associated with different types of themes. Currently, no quality television program is oriented toward the financial service needs of the affluent business owner. Perhaps it is time that some firm took the initiative in developing its own message and media vehicle. This would be analogous to Procter & Gamble's solution to the problem of communicating with housewives. No media vehicle could provide Procter & Gamble with a rifle shot at this target. It therefore developed its own medium, the soap opera.

4. *Promotional methods for the affluent business market.* As with theme selection, the firm must determine the efficacy of different types of promotional methods. This information can be gathered by questioning its sales force about their experiences with alternative promotional methods. In the future, the firm should develop experiments that will test the net effect of variations in both promotional methods and themes. The promotional methods that should be tested include:

    a. Self-liquidating seminars.
    b. Appearances on educational TV.
    c. Published articles in trade journals.
    d. Marketing booths at trade association conventions.

e. Platform speaking at trade association conventions.
   f. Published interviews.

The firm should consider developing its own television program for cable or educational stations. This
program would address the major financial problems of
affluent business owners. The format would include
dialogue and a question and answer period. The program
would showcase the firm's selected sales professionals who are experts in small-business investment. Entrepreneurs and "friendly" financial experts would
also be invited to participate.
   5. *How to use the firm's communications expertise
in marketing to small-business owners.* The firm
should produce a handbook of information sources on
methods for communicating with small business. Also,
the firm's policy concerning the use of various promotional methods and themes would be presented in this
handbook. The "resources" section would include:
(*a*) the names of the firm's internal small-business
communications experts, (*b*) discussion of who should
and who should not undertake communications strategy, (*c*) information on how to get a promotional campaign approved, (*d*) the names of sales professionals
who have had experience in developing their own promotional programs, and (*e*) the costs typically associated with such programs.
   I hope this information will be helpful to you and
your firm.

Sincerely,

Thomas J. Stanley, Ph.D.
Chairman, Affluent Market Institute

TJS: SW

SOME EXTRAORDINARY MARKETING ORGANIZATIONS AND THEIR PEOPLE

Not all of the great marketers are part of a traditionally defined
sales force. Some are employed as senior marketing executives for
corporations. Also, it is not unusual for the best "sales profession-

als" to be the chief executive officers of well-run market-oriented firms.

Two exceptionally well-managed market-oriented organizations in the financial service industry are a bank, the U.S. Trust Company of New York, and a security brokerage firm, Edward J. Jones & Co. These organizations offer different products and have different affluent targets. However, both organizations provide pro forma examples of how to effectively and efficiently communicate with and influence targets via public relations. Much can be learned by examining the methods they employ. Sales professionals and other marketing professionals will benefit greatly from studying the outstanding marketing standards that these organizations have established in the financial service industry.

Interestingly, neither of these organizations is the biggest in its industry, and neither can be accused of having overspent on its advertising. On the contrary, both the U.S. Trust Company and Edward D. Jones & Co. have relatively modest promotional budgets. But despite this, or perhaps because of this, they have generated considerable media coverage through their public relations efforts.

ONLY A FEW HAVE EXTINGUISHED THE FIRE SALE IMAGE

One of the major objections that the affluent have to appointing a bank trust department executor relates to the concept I call the fire sale. Many affluent respondents have told me that they are reluctant to have a bank act as the executor of their estate because "the bank will liquidate everything at fire sale prices." This is a particularly sensitive issue with wealthy business owners. These business owners often feel that a business is of more value to their heirs when it is operating than when it is sold at depression prices.

A millionaire respondent recently said to me:

> A [bank] executor will simply say get rid of it all, sell it, convert to cash, and chop it up. . . . An executor who has some personal feelings for the estate will sit down with the family . . . and work it out. A bank could do it, but you don't know if it would.

Many affluent individuals feel that the objective and impersonal bank/trust entity will not be sensitive to the subjective needs of the heirs or the true wishes of the testator. Most of my affluent respondents have indicated that they want subjectivity from the executor even if this causes a time delay in liquidating assets. Many of the affluent believe that "objective executors" are insensitive to the amount of money that can be generated from the sale of the assets in an estate—that is, "the fire sale objection."

Recently, a decamillionaire had this to say about the problem with fire sales:

> The co-op market is very tight. It is very hard to find apartments. I know two people who have been looking for a while, and they both say that they pray that they can get an estate for which a bank is the executor. Because a bank will just sell it. It won't wait for the highest amount that the apartment will bring.

This statement is indicative of a major obstacle that trust organizations have in marketing their estate services. However, some trust organizations have used credible themes and vehicles to overcome the fire sale. The quality image of U.S. Trust Company among the affluent has been enhanced by favorable news stories and articles published in credible vehicles. On August 24, 1987, for example, Meg Cox wrote a front-page article for *The Wall Street Journal* entitled, "Star Salesman: Top Art Auctioneer Needs Much Ingenuity to Keep Bids Climbing." This article focused on the ability of John L. Marion, Sotheby's auctioneer, to get consistently top prices for items being sold. The article stated: "When U.S. Trust decides to sell a big estate at Sotheby's, Chairman Daniel Davison demands that Mr. Marion preside. 'It's a bottom-line thing,' says Mr. Davison. 'He gets the best prices.' "

Statements of this type in highly credible vehicles have considerable influence on the affluent and their advisers. Such statements create the impression that U.S. Trust understands the needs of the affluent. They also make it clear that policies and methods concerning the sales of estate items are mandated by the chairman of U.S. Trust.

No other organization in this country has come close to generating as much quality press as U.S. Trust. In fact, U.S. Trust's recent achievements could fill a textbook for a college course on how to use public relations as a marketing weapon. Of all the news stories and articles written during the 1980s about upscale banks, one in particular stands out—a 10-page article featuring U.S. Trust that appeared in the award-winning, upscale magazine *Manhattan, Inc.* (Patricia O'Toole, "The Upper Crust at U.S. Trust," *Manhattan, Inc.,* May 1985, pp. 90–99).

In a content analysis of my interviews with the wealthy, I worked up a list of the dimensions that they consider important in developing and maintaining bank/trust patronage habits. (These dimensions are italicized in the discussion below.) The *Manhattan, Inc.* article indicates that U.S. Trust possesses these dimensions. The article also clearly demonstrates that U.S. Trust has adopted the ideal strategy for relating to the affluent market, namely, a deep *commitment* to a narrowly defined segment of the population whose members are very sensitive to variations in service quality and less sensitive to variations in fees.

All too often, public relations–type publications intended for the affluent stimulate responses from individuals who are not affluent. However, the "textbook article" in *Manhattan, Inc.* makes such responses unlikely. "Fees are stiff, a fact the company flaunts in order to discourage all but the seven-figure set. 'When you do something very well,' the ads sniff, 'you simply cannot do it for everyone.' "

The *Manhattan, Inc.* article is jam-packed with praise for U.S. Trust's *rapid approval of loan requests* and for the *certainty of the supply of credit* at U.S. Trust. O'Toole states that "it often takes about 15 minutes to borrow a hundred grand. More than half of the loans are unsecured" (ibid., p. 93). As evidence, she quotes a bank client whom she interviewed:

> They'll tide you over if you get caught short. . . . When I was selling one apartment and buying another, I needed several hundred thousand for a few months. In three hours, I had an okay. (ibid., p. 93)

The *empathy, flexibility,* and *resourcefulness* of their key bank contact are critical dimensions for most affluent individuals. O'Toole's article provides credible evidence that U.S. Trust personnel possess these qualities. She quotes a credit-prone client:

> When you tell U.S. Trust what you need, they don't tell you why it can't be done, they figure out how to do it. Then, poof, poof, it's done. (ibid., p. 95)

But the empathy, flexibility, and resourcefulness displayed at U.Ş. Trust go beyond selling money, beyond even financial services. A *human element* is also clearly communicated to clients and prospects.

> There seems to be nothing (at least nothing legal) that a trust officer will not do for a U.S. Trust customer. Anyone who has ever heard of the bank knows the story about the trust officer who even walked a customer's dog. Dogless clients are just as pampered. Problems getting into a co-op? Need a good yacht broker? Finding it hard to sell the Ivy League on your academically recalcitrant offspring? U.S. Trust can help. (ibid., p. 92)

I have often found during interviews that many of the heirs to fortunes are less self-sufficient than the relatives/spouses who generated those fortunes. It is not unusual for a strong-willed, domineering self-made millionaire to keep his wife totally ignorant of his business and family financial situation and to discourage his wife from making even household decisions. Typically, if the wives of such millionaires outlive their husbands, they feel alone, abandoned, and frightened. This is especially true if they also outlive their friends and relatives. Thus, there are subsegments of the affluent population that have a strong need for *emotional support* and even *companionship*. Many readers of the *Manhattan, Inc.* article may have felt that U.S. Trust could satisfy that need.

> Vice President Mary B. Lehman, who heads financial counseling, has located housekeepers, made hospital visits, and found drug-abuse treatment programs for clients. "Every Friday I get a call from a client who is in ill health and thinks he's going to die," she says. "He wants to know where I can be reached over the weekend." She always tells him. (ibid., p. 92)

Confidentiality is also a very important determinant of the bank patronage decisions made by the affluent.

> The privacy of those who bank at U.S. Trust is guarded ferociously, but the list of clients would be part *Social Register* and part *Who's Who* . . . and top officers of other banks, who don't want their own employees to know about their borrowing or spending. (ibid., p. 96)

Having top executives from the financial community as clients serves as an important cue to other clients and prospects. This cue effect is an example of what I call the *patronage opinion leadership* phenomenon. The affluent are more likely to patronize an institution that satisfies the needs of financial experts—that is, opinion leaders. They feel that such people are well equipped to judge the quality and service offerings of financial institutions.

Other important attributes and dimensions of financial institutions that are important to the affluent include the *expertise, track record, tenure,* and *authority* of contact personnel and specialists. What credible evidence suggests that U.S. Trust is strong in these dimensions? O'Toole's article addresses these matters.

> Our best people manage personal money. And that, say bank analysts and consultants, explains why a small outfit like U.S. Trust can clobber financial giants in the competition for well-heeled clients. For the past five years, U.S. Trust's asset managers have outperformed the Standard & Poor's 500. (ibid., p. 96)

A major problem that the affluent have in dealing with banks in general is turnover among key contact personnel. O'Toole's article relieves whatever doubts they may have on that score.

> The rich dislike dealing with inexperienced junior officers who don't have adequate lending authority and who are often promoted to other departments. . . . Officers in [personal banking] have a median of 16 years in banking, 6 at U.S. Trust. The average age, a reassuring 43. (ibid., p. 97)

Articles like the one discussed above can have an enormous impact, can influence influencers, solidify relationships with current clients, and stimulate new business from prospects. A public relations article of this kind is worth many times more than the same amount of advertising space. Paid advertising often lacks credibility. What one says about oneself carries much less weight among the affluent than what objective reporters and writers publish.

In addition to its impact on influencers, clients, and prospects, an article like the one discussed above can have an even greater impact on the morale and productivity of an organization's personnel.

Exceptionally talented people prefer to associate themselves with exceptional organizations and to work with other winners. It is very important that such employees be reminded about the quality of the organization that employs them and about their high caliber and that of their coworkers.

Winners want to be viewed as winners. When a highly credible article describes them as winners and praises their organization, the psychological bonding between them and their organization is enhanced. People perform at a high level of productivity for reasons that are often independent of money. They want to be admired by their peers in their industry because of their own image and that of the organization that employs them. Such recognition is critical for high-performance employees.

The most productive people typically set their sights on eventually working for the most admired organization in their industry, and the most admired organization achieves that status by documenting its image via credible articles and news reports. Recruiting the cream of the industry's crop is much easier if the best seek you out. Winners are also much more reluctant to change employers when they view their current employer as the best organization in their industry.

The pride and high performance of employees are readily communicated to affluent current clients and affluent prospects.

"GETTING GOOD PRESS"

When writers and reporters approach an organization with the proposal to publish an article about its operation, they are often turned off. People in the business of reporting must be assured that their target will provide a rapid response to their requests for information. They also like to feel that the targeted organization and its personnel will be very candid about all aspects of the operation. The major reasons that many financial service organizations do not receive "good press" include (1) not responding to requests for information from the press, (2) taking too long to respond/to approve requests, and (3) grossly limiting the information that they make available to writers and reporters.

U.S. Trust has a reputation among business writers for being very responsive to requests for information. In addition, this organization has often given writers and reporters complete access to all of its key personnel. Empathy for the needs of the press is the hallmark of U.S. Trust's communications strategy. A high-quality organization that is candid and responsive to writers and reporters is likely to "get good press."

In any organization, an effective communications strategy designed to influence the affluent market must have the strong support of top management. Rodney Woods, the senior marketing officer for U.S. Trust from 1978 to 1987, provides some insight into the priority that U.S. Trust's management places on marketing. Woods resigned from U.S. Trust in 1987 to accept a similar position with Merrill Lynch.

DR. STANLEY:

[Referring to the proposed article in *Manhattan, Inc.*] Did you have to go to the management committee to get approval for the story?

MR. WOODS:

Well, at that time I reported to one member of the management committee—and Mr. Davison obviously had a proprietary interest in the whole undertaking, because he put so much into the house [the branch office on 54th Street]. It was in that forum that I said we really ought to do it because it's going to involve each one of you guys [management committee] being a participant. I had to convince them it was in the firm's interest to do it. We went ahead and did it.

Even after all the interviewing was completed, I still wasn't sure exactly how the story was going to come out. We had to sweat until the issue came out to find out what it was going to say. And I think the upshot was obviously well written.

We actually took that as a definitive story—used reprints of that article liberally. I think, frankly, that the Trust continues to use it until this day.

DR. STANLEY:

Rodney, what I was impressed with were two things. First, your willingness to deal with the press in the whole banking environment. Second, I spoke to a woman several years ago from a publication called *Ultra Magazine* in Texas. She said that you were one of the few upscale banks that would talk to her. How does that work?

MR. WOODS:

We got into it originally probably because it was a sincere effort when we did it—but we published that millionaires' survey. We didn't intend to publish it. We had produced a report—an algorithm really—that projected some of the growth in income, together with our state [tax] return experience. We worked out this fairly complicated mathematical projection which was claimed to be statistically, deadly accurate, but we felt it was probably a better measure than just about anything else.

I don't remember who got hold of it first. I seem to remember somebody in the trade press got wind of it and published it. All of a sudden, we had just a phenomenal public interest in the shape of *Time* magazine and I think the *London Daily Telegraph*. There was a paper in Hong Kong—every daily across the country. Radio stations were calling up live. Some of them would say, "Hi, I'm Bill Potts from WPITZ in Amarillo, Texas—you're apparently the authority on millionaires in this country."

The reporters' appetite for this stuff was insatiable. And we were sort of bemused by the whole thing, but we actually used it—we published this thing for a couple of years, I guess. We felt there had been enough interest and it was obviously good to broaden the awareness of our name, and we had a national franchise. Although clearly not very dense. It certainly didn't hurt to have our name associated with stories of that nature. The great thing we did was build an offshoot to the original calculation. We did a little subset that was the population density of these guys. There was enough in the major cities like New York, Chicago, and Los Angeles because in absolute numbers they had the most to talk about. Some of these little states could claim to have the highest density per thousand, relevant to their size.

That was probably the starting point. That was around the first phase of our more aggressive campaign—they were concurrent. And I think the two together made us somewhat of a phenomenon in the fact that we were willing to talk about handling the affairs of the rich, although we never gave away clients' names. No effect on the confidentiality or discretion.

But we became known as "the private bank." There was a story in the *New York Times* on the same subject, where I think we talked about there always being a carriage trade in every business. That wasn't normally thought of in terms of the banking industry. We were beneficiaries of being the first. We were a private bank and had been a private bank for 125 years or so. We had the authenticity to talk about it.

DR. STANLEY:

Rodney, was the whole idea when you put out some of that information about millionaires—that you really cultivated a whole new clientele in the sense of the press itself?

MR. WOODS:

We didn't start out that way. That was actually one of the by-products that we benefited from. One of the side effects that we didn't care for, however, was the endless succession of people that called thinking that we had a list of millionaires. This could include everybody from a Beverly Hills Rolls-Royce salesman to a Palm Beach real estate guy.

DR. STANLEY:

It was my impression that you really handled the public relations, and not a public relations firm.

MR. WOODS:

We did.

DR. STANLEY:

In other words, you had an advertising agency, but you did the public relations internally?

MR. WOODS:

Well, the thing is that we had a small public relations department that was pretty good. There was an ex-Thompson guy who really had come up with the idea of the wealth survey. When this thing took off, he did a lot of work to build its awareness. We felt it was important to respond directly to these inquiries because they were coming straight from reporters. There was not any need for an intermediary—that would just slow the thing down. I couldn't do that.

DR. STANLEY:

In terms of the ad agency, your approach, your public relations and everything else—my speculation is that you got more mileage per dollar than anybody else I know in the industry. Was it planned that way—was it a matter of it being the essential ingredient in that they [management] said they were not going to give you a lot of money to work with?

MR. WOODS:

We never did have much of a budget. Obviously, the problem we had back in the Ogilvy days was that the amount of money we had to spend on media was somewhat limited. Clearly, we were outspent 20 to 1. Plus, we operate in the most competitive marketplace in the country. The intent in trying to harness public relations at the same time we were running a new ad campaign was to try to get a little more mileage out of it. Using all of the disciplines that we could muster within the marketing mix, we thought we got more bang for the buck. We probably got a little bit more mileage out of it than the norm simply because it was so different in tone and appearance and unexpected from such an organization. So, there was the shock value. Plus, we did some different things in terms of media scheduling. One of the very early users of *Town and Country*—now used widely for financial services advertising. There was a sort of an interruptive effect, if you will. You flick through the jewelry and the clothing ads and suddenly hit on a banker leaning against a mantlepiece in Manhattan. It has more of an impact.

Town and Country wrote a couple of articles about us. We got some real additional mileage from that limited budget. The notoriety factor was certainly one aspect of the campaign that we had not calculated and couldn't possibly gauge, but we were very happy at the impact we received.

DR. STANLEY:

Rodney, tell me what impact your communications campaign had on what we would call the influencers—the accountants, the attorneys—who were pondering whether or not to recommend that this widow talk to you folks or someone else.

MR. WOODS:

That's a little difficult to speculate about. But I would say some. One of the biggest audiences (and I think this is where Mr. Davison was enormously shrewd—he endorsed the campaign from the word go)—the internal effect on the troops was phenomenal.

DR. STANLEY:

The troops?

MR. WOODS:

Yes, the troops had had a tough time at the end of the "nifty 50s," and they suffered from all those stories about how the Trust could make you a small fortune, provided you bring them a big one. You know, that sort of thing. It was a real shot in the arm, I think, for the working staff, and the morale was improved immeasurably. They liked the fact that their clients talked about the campaign, and they liked seeing things in *Time* magazine and stuff like that—it really helped.

As far as the bar and other people that could refer people to us, I think it didn't hurt. It was evident that attorneys noticed we were standing up claiming to be not only back in business, but business in a big way. There certainly were instances where they brought business.

DR. STANLEY:

I guess the whole gist of this thing is what I would call an enlightened approach to dealing with the media. How did that take place? Mr. Davison was there, and yourself. But without trying to make you feel good, most banks view public relations as a way to tell people who left and who died. Where did this come from, Rodney?

MR WOODS:

Really, I don't think it's more than a willingness to. Let's start with one premise, and that is we knew people were going to write about us. It makes good copy.

We felt for the same reason that if we had a story to tell about the wealthy, it would have a fair amount of interest to a lot of people because, simply, it was good copy, and we thought we'd develop it into a story that would certainly be carried by some of the local papers. Mr. Davison never envisioned that we would get the coverage nationally or even internationally—and that was a very important element because, although he's modest by nature and certainly in my book the epitome of the prudent and well-balanced chairman of the bank, he clearly saw the need for competitive reasons to tell the bank's story in the best light. His willingness to be the spokesman both in the advertisements and with the press, to talk to them when encouraged to do so, was really the critical difference.

When a writer wanted to do the story, he was willing to take some time to sit down and talk freely to the reporter and to tell him why U.S. Trust was such a gem of an organization. He believed it. He's highly credible, because he believes it. We stopped using Mr. Davison as a spokesman for the same reason we stopped using symbolic art. Once it became copied, we decided there were too many chairmen as spokespeople, so we then moved to the third phase of the program where, to really talk about performance, we used client testimonials. We felt there was nothing more credible than having the clients talk about their experience—the performance not only in numbers but in terms of what we had done for them and for their family.

DR. STANLEY:

The other thing I wanted to ask is about your apparent ability to generate interest from other parts of the country where people have substantial wealth or at least intermediate size—who really seek an institution outside of their own trade area. Is it maybe the allure of New York, is it the image itself . . . ?

MR. WOODS:

Well, we had a couple of occasions where we planned that one fairly carefully and felt that our location on Wall Street plus the one midtown office was, again, distinctly different from the norm. It enables us to, if you like, equate ourselves to a private equivalent of a Zurich banking house. We feel that there are a lot of rich people across the country who don't want to keep all of their assets in local banks. They don't like to have their macro affairs handled at the local level. They obviously want some housekeeping funds, and their immediate needs are satisfied at the local bank. But they'd rather have their broader issues and the overall estate planning function somewhere else where there is a certain amount of confidentiality. We found that there was a great deal of interest in a money center bank that was still small enough to have a personality.

AN EXCEPTIONAL ADVERTISEMENT FOR TRUST SERVICES: THE MESSAGE FROM THE CITIZENS AND SOUTHERN NATIONAL BANK

Dear Marketer:

Many affluent entrepreneurs fear that if they die or become disabled, their organization will quickly become unproductive. Some are strong believers in the hypothesis that their business has value only if they personally manage it. These types of affluent business owners are reluctant to establish relationships with trust organizations that offer estate-related services. They fear that a trust organization will immediately sell the business at a "fire sale" price upon their death.

How can the affluent business owner be certain that his business will continue to operate profitably after his death or at least until a suitable buyer is found and a top price is paid to his estate? This question is being asked by affluent entrepreneurs throughout this country. In response to this problem, the Citizens and Southern National Bank developed an advertisement that documented its ability to help a business survive the loss of its owner/manager. Here is the text of this advertisement.

The Nursery That Survived a Loss

Nothing could put back into this business what Henry Williams took with him when he died.

He started with one small greenhouse behind his house, and in 20 years expanded to five retail outlets and a growing farm.

He planned the expansion himself, managed the shops virtually single-handedly, and never hired a successor, even when Mrs. Williams thought he should. When he passed on, she felt that she couldn't handle it alone.

But Henry Williams had planned his estate as prudently as he managed the business.

In association with a C&S Trust Officer he'd known for years, he had arranged for the bank to step in and pick up the reins.

The business was managed, supervised, and operated at a profit for five years, at which time it went to the three Williams grandchildren. So, Mrs. Williams was able to retain the business and watch a third generation become a part of it. Most important, it continued intact, and it prospered.

Thanks to years of experience in small business management, the C&S Trust Officer didn't have to learn vital details from scratch. He knew what had to be done, who should do it, and he personally watched over the family's affairs for five years. More than an advisor, he was a friend. A dependable ally.

If you feel the need to reorganize your affairs (or review your estate in light of changes in the estate and gift tax laws) please feel free to talk with a C&S Personal Trust Officer. We're always here to help you with your estate, investments, and other financial arrangements.

We're ready, whenever you are, to attend to the smallest detail. Ask for one of us when you stop by. And ask about our experience in small business management.[1]

Despite the fact that this message is in the form of a paid advertisement, it is much more credible than typical chest-thumping themes too often employed in this industry. Credibility is enhanced when information is presented in a case history format. Many business owners and their families are concerned today about the continuity of the enterprise once the founder has passed away. This advertisement demonstrates that the C&S Bank can operate a business, assure continuity, and ultimately fulfill the wishes of its founder and his family. Any organization can sell a business at fire sale prices. However, few have the image and demonstrated ability to make certain that its heirs will receive the maximum benefit from their inheritance. There are many other organizations in this country that have a history of "helping a business survive a loss." However, as I have stated on numerous occasions, most of these organizations never communicate this ability. They are overly cautious and still operate upon ancient rules of secrecy about clients. However, some satisfied clients would gladly

[1] Published with permission of the Citizens and Southern National Bank.

tell in print media the story of how such an organization helped them "survive a loss." This would not
alienate current clients or prospective clients. On
the contrary, messages of this type go to the heart of
the dilemma faced by the families of affluent entrepreneurs.

Sincerely,

Thomas J. Stanley, Ph.D
Chairman, The Affluent Market Institute

TJS:sw

FROM TOWNHOUSE TO FARMHOUSE

In 1979, I delivered a speech at the Fall Marketing Conference of
the Securities Industry Association. Excerpts from the speech,
"Market Segmentation: Utilizing Investment Determinants," are
given below.

> The truly innovative brokerage firm of the 1980s will not attempt
> to cater to all market segments with a single strategy. Instead, it will
> employ a variation in strategy focusing on one or more specific
> targets.
> . . . clients in the penetrated segments mentioned have some
> similar characteristics. . . .
> This evidence suggests that competing houses have all attempted
> to market to these upscale consumers while ignoring other prospec-
> tive segments.
> However, it is not wise for all firms to concentrate on only these
> [upscale] segments.
> The marketing mix variables associated with the vast majority of
> brokers are focused, whether by design or accident, upon the up-
> scale/upper-middle-class values and symbols. Choice of a broker is
> in fact a matching of self-concepts. The self-image of brokers, as
> well as account executives, is almost totally upper middle class.
> Also, it is not surprising that consumers, many of whom have high
> discretionary dollars, are turned off by the symbols and information
> publicized by most brokerage firms.

Opportunities exist in segments that the industry has ignored for years. The very cautious achievers, solid breadwinners, financial dreamers, investment-oriented novices, and optimistic novice groups combine into what can be referred to as the "really big segment" in terms of population and long-run potential.

The profile of this composite segment is *blue collar/lower middle class*. However, many members of the "really big segment" have very significant discretionary incomes. These *wealthy blue-collar prospects* do not need to puchase the expensive artifacts that are part of the white-collar worker's status knapsack.

[What are the] barriers that have separated brokers from the wealthy blue-collar prospect?

The securities industry has, in reality, demarketed its service offerings to all but upscale segments, discouraging, perhaps unknowingly, all but the upper-middle and upper class from participating. (But social status and wealth are not the same measures.)

The barriers of inaccessibility. . . . brokers are perceived . . . as being inaccessible in terms of location convenience. Never underestimate the importance of location in explaining professional service patronage. This is especially true in cases where the potential client is in the early stages of the investment learning curve. Remember . . . a significant portion of the life insurance sold in this nation is literally marketed in the privacy of the prospect's home.

Symbolic barriers. The symbols that are associated with most brokerage firms are indicative of the upper-middle and upper classes. The language, cues, atmospherics, architectural style, advertising, and dress may indicate that the broker is not interested in their [the blue-collar workers'] financial service needs.

The barriers of self-image. Closely associated with the symbolic barriers are the barriers of self-image. We have found in our studies of the personalities of account executives a modal personality type. Most account executives interviewed have a strong need to associate with higher-class clients. Their ideal self-concept is one that dictates rubbing shoulders with and being part of the upscale segments. . . . They do not feel comfortable working with blue-collar, working-class prospects. . . .

The barriers of fear and ignorance. . . . people innately dislike and distrust things they are not familiar with. "In many cases, the public exhibits massive ignorance of brokerage products" (*Public Attitudes toward Investing,* New York: New York Stock Exchange, 1979, p. 5).

Recommendations. The barriers . . . must be penetrated. The "market" must become more accessible. We must learn to move closer to the client and not be wary of bringing the market into the prospect's home. Firms must learn to communicate with the symbols that have meaning to the target segments. The needs and wants of segments differ; thus, variations in advertising themes must reflect this. Not all segments are interested in the rate-of-return numbers. Some . . . are interested in security. The brokerage industry must . . . [simplify] its explanations of the market, service offerings, pricing, and risk. Firms that wish to attract prospective clients from new segments must be willing to improve the matching of the personalities of their account executives with those of the prospects. Penetration of the barriers of fear and ignorance may be the most difficult task to achieve. This ignorance translates into fear of the market and brokers. A brokerage firm can educate prospective clients about the market. In turn, a favorable image can be established. Such persuasion should center on personalities with high credibility.

The Gauntlet of 1,000

Immediately after my presentation, a fellow approached me and commented on my discussion of the realities of the affluent market. He told me that his firm had developed a success formula that was very effective in overcoming the barriers I had discussed. I found out later that this gentleman was John W. Bachman, a managing partner of Edward D. Jones & Co. Edward D. Jones is one of the most profitable brokerage firms in the United States. It also has the largest number of offices. However, those offices are unique. The typical Edward D. Jones office is staffed by one registered representative and one assistant. Traditionally, all of the company's offices were strategically located in small towns. Its strategy of becoming the dominant supplier of investment products within a narrowly defined geographic area proved extremely successful.

The driving force behind the company's marketing philosophy is to view its registered representatives as clients. The company reasoned that if its brokers were given every opportunity and support, they would become very productive. However, all of its brokers are required to test their mettle by passing the "gauntlet of 1,000." Each broker must personally introduce himself to at least 1,000 prospects within his trade area before he is considered a viable candidate with Edward D. Jones & Co. Personally visiting

1,000 homes or businesses is not an easy task, especially if none of these prospects has ever heard of Edward D. Jones!

It might be easier for its representatives to prospect if Edward D. Jones were promoting itself on national television and in such prestige publications as *The Wall Street Journal* and *Forbes*. However, given the traditional company strategy of dominating smaller towns, the cost of national advertising is prohibitively expensive. There is no sense in advertising nationally or even regionally if only a fraction of the audience lives within the company's small-town trade areas.

The communications dilemma that Edward D. Jones faced was solved, at least in part, by a brilliant public relations strategy. The strategy was based on the company's need to favorably influence the members of the "gauntlet of 1,000." That need was met through articles that appeared in some of the most credible and prestigious print vehicles. As the company will attest, the best things in life and communications are often free.

John W. Bachman provided some interesting details about his firm's recent public relations successes. He also elaborated on the role that public relations plays in his firm's overall marketing strategy.

DR. STANLEY:

John, the first thing I want to ask is for you to give me some idea of how you view your major marketing goal for the firm.

MR. BACHMAN:

Our major goal is quite simple because we have such a sharply defined niche. Our basic goal is to expand our system of offices. The way we do it is with one registered representative and one branch support person. Then, we surround them with as much technology as necessary to enable them to provide the same services as any other investment firm in the country. Basically, we focus on increasing the productivity, the profitability, and the effectiveness of each location. In other words, you add locations and then make each location more effective.

DR. STANLEY:

John, in terms of that, you purposely picked towns [with populations] under 50,000 or 25,000.

MR. BACHMAN:

Not any more. We are finding great receptivity in the urban markets. The most successful market we've ever entered is Chicago.

DR. STANLEY:

Why do you think that's the case, when you do so well and some other people don't?

MR. BACHMAN:

It's basically a very personal, one-on-one business. If you live in a small community, in order to survive you've got to know the people in town and know their wives' names and be familiar with the community. You take that for granted when you go into the dry cleaner's and the filling station. You go to Chicago, it's different—you've got the finest shopping malls in the world with the greatest choices in the world, and it is totally impersonal. The people in the urban markets are starved for those kinds of face-to-face personal relationships.

DR. STANLEY:

Is your approach—the idea of passing out 1,000 cards, meeting 1,000 people in a small town—the same in a big town?

MR. BACHMAN:

Oh, yes, the same way.

DR. STANLEY:

Even door-to-door? Is this business door or house door?

MR. BACHMAN:

Both.

DR. STANLEY:

How does the public relations—for example, your article in *The Wall Street Journal*—fit into your overall goal and strategy for expansion?

MR. BACHMAN:

Our approach to public relations, quite simply—we know that in a free, private enterprise economy we are going to have a certain number of things go wrong. That's just the nature of products. Consequently, if the only thing that the customer or prospect knows about us is where we stubbed our toe, then we may not be terribly well thought of. So, what we try to do is tell our story as straightforwardly as possible. We know it's an attractive story. It's an all-American story, so we try to tell the story in a way that people understand who we are and what we are about, so that when we make a mistake, they can balance the pluses and the minuses.

DR. STANLEY:

What kind of response did you get when you were on the front page of *The Wall Street Journal?* From your clients and your sales force? Can you give me some idea of your gut feel, data, or what you heard from people?

MR. BACHMAN:

I can't give you a technical/statistics answer. But our people certainly felt good about it. Many customers mentioned it, and we inevitably get some applications for positions with the firm that will come out of an article like that. You'll get some people that will write from different parts of the country and say they'd like to do business with us.

DR. STANLEY:

So, do they [prospects] say, "How come you haven't called me yet?" I get calls from people that are millionaires that say, "How come you haven't interviewed me?" Is this what happens—are people waiting to hear from you?

MR. BACHMAN:

They wonder why we're not in western Pennsylvania or in upstate New York. One of the interesting and kind of amusing things isn't really tied to this point, but we've talked about the 1,000 cold calls. I was down in Kernersville, North Carolina, speaking at the Chamber of Commerce annual dinner, and a couple of people came up to me, very proud of the fact that they were among those 1,000 people that Jim Barrett chose to call on. It's interesting how it almost has an element of fashion about it now that it's well known that we do it and we're successful and we're decent people.

DR. STANLEY:

It would seem to me that it would be difficult for you to use a major promotional vehicle in the sense that you couldn't sponsor, obviously, the SuperBowl, because you're going to hit a lot of people where you don't have locations. Do you see this as really a substitute, to get into a prestige vehicle and tell your story—as with *The Wall Street Journal* article?

MR. BACHMAN:

Well, it certainly validates our story, because you don't tell *The Wall Street Journal* what to write. So, if they say something about you, it has a certain validation to it.

DR. STANLEY:

Are you finding now that there is a greater following in the press?

MR. BACHMAN:

I think you do. Certainly, the biggest piece we ever got, as far as getting a direct response in some areas, was the piece that *Time* magazine did recently. Frankly, that triggered some network videos.

DR. STANLEY:

Beyond that, did you find, for example, your sales force personnel were telling you, "Now when I make a cold call, it's not so cold anymore—I feel more comfortable and proud going out there"? Is that typical?

MR. BACHMAN:

I don't think there's any question that that kind of article reinforces, and it does give people a certain pride.

DR STANLEY:

The actual sales force people who are doing cold calls—would they keep that article in a packet with them?

MR. BACHMAN:

Yes, certainly. It tells you something about the firm and, once again, it's just third-party endorsement.

DR. STANLEY:

What about other kinds of public relations? Do you see anything coming up in the future?

MR. BACHMAN:

I think that with public relations per se, you really don't have much control over it. I think that it's on its own course. There are some things that we do have control over that we work on. We have, for example, Founder's Day, where we try to stage an event in our communities where we can underscore the roots, the history of our firm, where we can thank our customers, where there's no commercial or financial tie-in. And we find that those are well received.

DR. STANLEY:

Founder's Day—is it like a picnic?

MR. BACHMAN:

It's different things. It's an open house. In Stephenville, Texas, Barb Gillman donated a flagpole. They didn't have one. There are many things—planting trees, doing community service things, things just to be able to thank the community for receiving us warmly.

DR. STANLEY:

Do reporters pick up the phone and say, "John, I want to interview you"?

MR. BACHMAN:

The process sometimes will come through our public relations firm and sometimes directly to us.

DR. STANLEY:

What's your policy on dealing with these guys?

MR. BACHMAN:

I'm always accessible. You'll find that my name is in the phonebook. That's really what I'd like—for it to stay in the phonebook.

DR. STANLEY:

If they call you, what do you do? You must get a lot of calls from people—local press, medium sized, big sized—how do you deal with them? What do you do with these people?

MR. BACHMAN:

We have a public relations person—a partner in our firm who came to us right out of journalism school and does a superb job of keeping things going at our end. She tells me very often who to call and what the subject will be. I'm one of those who writes my own speeches, so I'm not much good at you telling me exactly what to say.

DR. STANLEY:

Do you have any kind of training program to help your sales force do some of their own public relations locally?

MR. BACHMAN:

We haven't done much. Most of what we do is mailing things, which somtimes we mail directly to the local press, sometimes they will hand-deliver them, depending on circumstances. I would say that is an area, if you were looking for areas, where over the next few years we are going to have to do a better job. I think it's clearly one of those areas.

One of the problems we have, and the reason that public relations is so important to us—another reason—is that we are not of a size where we can do national advertising. We would be buying these huge urban markets, eastern markets, and California markets that we couldn't serve even if the people were eager to do business with us. Soon, we will be. If you give us another five to seven years, I think you will see us involved in those kinds of things. Until we are able to be meaningfully represented in every major market, the cost is prohibitive.

DR. STANLEY:

Can you give me some idea of your success in the last year in terms of offices?

MR. BACHMAN:

I can give you some numbers that I just happen to have. These numbers are pretty good if you look at us today compared to the beginning of 1980. We have 1,298 representatives. Our key measure of growth is the number of representatives. We don't look at revenue or earnings; we look at number of reps. That is the critical number. Certainly, we pay attention to the others, but the driving number for us—1,298. At the beginning of the decade, we had 307. We expect our revenues at the end of this year to be between 280 and 300 million. And as we went into the decade, they were $25 million.

DR. STANLEY:

When I first ran into you, one of the things you were very proud of was the fact that you really look at your reps as the consumer or the priority—do everything that you can do to support them. How does that relate to some of the communications that you've been doing? I know that you have state-of-the-art interaction on wire to people, but talk also about the public relations factor.

MR. BACHMAN:

We think the most important thing that happens at Jones—the one that drives everything—is what takes place between our investment representatives and the customer. Therefore, we want to focus everything we can on enriching that encounter or that transaction so that it has the highest possible value added for the customer over the longer term.

Frankly, we're more concerned about the longer term than we are about the shorter term. We're concerned that we do things that wear well. We would see our role as being akin to that of the merchant we would define as the informed buyer for the customer.

DR. STANLEY:

How do you think public relations interacts with your goals?

MR. BACHMAN:

I think that what you've seen really reinforces the public—in a way it does, and in a way it doesn't. In the way it does, it focuses on that individual relationship which we think is what distinguishes Jones from every other financial institution. Ours is built on an individual as an entrepreneur—a badly overused term—but nevertheless, a strongly entrepreneurial individual. The frustration of those articles—to make them charming, they always focus on our rural markets, which is no longer the direction in which the firm is going. We certainly continue to open in smaller communities, but the fact of the matter is that people are in the city. That's where our market is.

If you read Tom Watson's article—a fascinating story, I thought—in the August 31 *Fortune,* he talks about their markets and the constraint on IBM. I confess to you, we study companies that may be a little fanciful, but we study them carefully. At IBM, he said (and I quote—it's really two quotes that I've run together), "We felt if we didn't grab the business, someone else would and we'd never have that kind of opportunity again." Then he goes on to say: "So we decided to push the company as fast as the market would permit."

You see, his constraint was that only so many people could afford to buy a computer. We don't see that constraint. We think our constraint is tied to our ability to manage as opposed to the size of the market.

DR. STANLEY:

How did this affect marketing training? I know you have the training center where you have the Country Kitchen and the Country Store and those kinds of things. Can you give me any insight? Are there any differences in training people for an urban environment?

MR. BACHMAN:

There really are none. There are subtleties. You may make your calls at a different time during the day, you may have to shift them more toward evening, or you may have some of those kinds of subtleties, but it's basically just doing the work.

DR. STANLEY:

In other words, in urban areas like Chicago, your people actually are knocking on doors? Can you give me some examples of how it's worked for you?

MR. BACHMAN:

The only thing I can relate is that it's the most successful region we've ever started.

DR. STANLEY:

But John, in terms of prospecting, is it the same format? Are they walking into stores and businesses? into houses?

MR. BACHMAN:

Yes, they are going in and meeting people face-to-face to talk about investing. And they are in the community. This is not a disembodied voice in some tower on LaSalle Street calling out to the suburbs. This is somebody who is a member of the same chamber of commerce, who sends his kids to the same school and is a part of the community paying taxes there.

DR. STANLEY:

John, you'll be interested to know that I interviewed one of the very top real estate persons in the United States, Holly Boyett. She started her career knocking on doors, and she still knocks on doors.

She still calls people who have houses for sale "by owner". I hope to put all of you together in my book.

Edward D. Jones & Co. understands the needs of investors as well as the needs of writers and reporters. Members of the press are in constant need of fresh information, and many of the finest marketing organizations and their ESPs instinctively capitalize on that need. They view the press as a marketing resource and as a vehicle that, given the proper attention, responsiveness, and candor, will provide credible third-party endorsements.

"Getting good press" is not something that happens overnight. Nor is it ever likely to happen if the organization or its ESPs do not have a high level of intellect. Although intellect takes a long time to acquire, it often takes much longer for the affluent population to recognize that someone has intellect and to label him an expert.

The press cannot increase one's knowledge of product and service offerings. "Good press" can greatly reduce the lag time that traditionally exists between the acquisition of intellect and the recognition of intellect, that is, expertise. Even those with considerable intellect often go unrecognized as experts. Some of them are not recognized as experts until after they retire. Most ESPs should not wait that long.

TECHNICAL
APPENDIXES

Technical Appendix 1

THE RESPONSE OF AFFLUENT CONSUMERS TO MAIL SURVEYS*

SURVEYING THE AFFLUENT

Few articles address the questionnaire response behavior of the affluent. Because less than two percent of all U.S. households have annual incomes of $100,000 or more, the primary survey design issue is developing a mailing list that contains a high concentration of upper-income households. A second issue is whether questionnaire recipients will be motivated to complete and return the survey.

Sample Design

Popular wisdom suggests that the affluent can be surveyed by obtaining a list of owners of expensive automobiles, yachts, and other affluent artifacts. There are major problems with this approach. Owners of expensive durables are not all affluent, and lists of this type may not be representative of the total affluent population. One recent survey of affluent consumers found that most of them do not own luxury automobiles; the most widely owned car brand was Chevrolet (Lehner 1984).

An alternative to ownership lists is the neighborhood income statis-

* The original version of this paper was published in the *Journal of Advertising Research*, June–July 1986 pp. 55-58. The paper was written by Dr. Thomas J. Stanley and Murphy A. Sewall.

tics published by the U.S. Census. Each of these neighborhood areas, "block groups," contains approximately 280 households. Research has shown that families within a particular block group are fairly homogeneous in terms of income (Claritas Corporation 1983).

Block groups with average incomes of at least $50,000 can be selected from census data purchased on computer tape by state from the U.S. Census Bureau. Of the 48 contiguous states, 24 contain only 11.8 percent of the households in this country with incomes of $50,000 or more (U.S. Bureau of the Census 1984). An economically efficient sample of upper-income block groups can be obtained by sampling from the remaining states.

Incentive to Respond

In several surveys of the general population, a monetary inducement has been reported as improving the response rate in mail surveys (Armstrong and Overton 1975; Furse and Stewart 1982; Linskey 1975; McDaniel and Rao 1980; Schewe and Cournoyer 1976; Tedin and Hofstetter 1982). In a survey of "elites," that is, government ministers, corporation directors, and so forth, Godwin (1979) found that both the promise of a monetary incentive and its size significantly increased the number of questionnaire items completed and the number of accurate responses. He also observed that larger incentives produced a higher probability of respondents taking the time to provide additional, clarifying information. The size of the incentive had a greater effect on the completeness and accuracy of responses than on the response rate.

The relationship that exists between the size of an incentive and the response rate is not clear. Armstrong and Overton (1975) suggest a nearly proportional reduction in nonresponses for increases in small incentives. However, Linskey (1975) and Kanuk and Berenson (1975) concluded in their reviews that 25 cents is the most productive incentive to mail survey response literature.

The effects of questionnaire length on response rates for surveys of the general population have been examined in several studies (Berdie 1973; Champion and Sear 1969; Childers and Ferrell 1979; Kanuk and Berenson 1975; Roscoe, Lang, and Sheth 1975). Only Champion and Sear (1969) present a statistically significant relationship; they found that more nine-page than three-page questionnaires were returned. Whether affluent respondents would be more likely to return long questionnaires has not been addressed by previous studies.

Study Design

A random sample of 800 block groups was selected from a listing of neighborhoods with average incomes exceeding $50,000 in the states ranked in the top half by income according to 1980 census data (U.S. Bureau of the Census 1981). Commercial list organizations were able to supply head of household names and addresses for approximately 95 percent of the census-tabulated homes in these 800 block groups. The commercial lists included telephone numbers for 77 percent of the homes. Addresses with more than three lines and with more than one name at the same phone number were purged because of the high probability that these were the addresses of commercial organizations. Nine thousand households were selected at random for use in surveys from the enumerated households (approximately 213,000 names and addresses) in the 800 block groups. A random sample of 396 households was drawn from the list of 9,000 for an analysis of the effects of questionnaire length and magnitude of incentive on survey response rate.

The levels for questionnaire length were 300 versus 500 choice scale questions about consumer attitudes toward financial services and investments. The offered incentives were pocket calculators; the less expensive model had a retail value of $7, and the more expensive model had a retail value of $12. The sampled households were randomly assigned to four groups of 99 each and mailed questionnaires and cover letters offering a calculator.

All of the letters that accompanied the questionnaires were personalized. Each letter was individually typed, hand-signed and personally addressed. All of the letters were sent by first-class mail, and a single, follow-up reminder was also mailed.

RESULTS

A total of 144 of the 396 (36.4 percent) selected respondents returned usable questionnaires. Table 1 presents the response rates for each experimental condition. Table 2 contains the results of an analysis of variance of the treatment effect (following the same procedure as Childers and Ferrell 1979). Only the main effect for the magnitude of the incentive qualified as statistically significant.

Sampling from high-income block groups was an effective means of assuring a high concentration of affluent respondents. Table 3 presents

TABLE 1
Response Rate by Experimental Condition

Experimental Condition	Mailed	Responses	Response (Percent)
Number of scale-type items			
300	198	75	37.9
500	198	69	34.8
Value of incentive			
$7	198	60	30.3
$12	198	84	42.4
Combinations			
300 items × $7 incentive	99	32	32.3
300 items × $12 incentive	99	43	43.4
500 items × $7 incentive	99	28	28.3
500 items × $12 incentive	99	41	41.4

the income distribution for those households that returned the completed questionnaires.

CONCLUSIONS

The findings of this study have three practical implications for obtaining information about affluent households.

1. Surveys of the affluent may be targeted efficiently using census data.

TABLE 2
Analysis of Variance of Experimental Conditions

Source of Variation	Squares	D.F.	F	Significance of F
Main effects				
Value of incentive	1.46	1	6.33	.012
Number of items	.091	1	.40	.53
Interactive effect				
Value of incentive × number of items	.01	1	.04	.83
Error	90.08	392		
Total	91.60	395		

TABLE 3
Income Distribution of
Respondents

Total Annual Household Income	Percent
Less than $40,000	16.7
$40,000–$59,999	28.2
$60,000–$79,999	19.2
$80,000–$99,999	13.0
$100,000 and over	23.0
	100.0

2. The rate of mail survey response is positively related to variation in the value of an incentive, but a larger initial mailing may be a more cost-effective means of obtaining a desired number of completed questionnaires.
3. The response rate for mailings to affluent households does not appear sensitive to the number of response items included in the questionnaire.

Household income distributions at the neighborhood level provide and important base for surveys of the affluent market. These statistics may also be useful for defining other survey target segments. Census data at the block group level provides statistics on many characteristics, including age, education, race, value of home, and source and amount of income. The growing cost of mailings and the continuing fragmentation of consumer markets place increasing importance on more objective and productive methods of targeting survey research.

Although response rates may be increased by offering respondents a larger reward, the incremental cost of a more expensive incentive must be compared with the expected increase in the number of responses. In this study, an incentive that cost $4 more (at wholesale) increased the response rate from just over 30 percent to just over 42 percent. A mailing of 1,000 questionnaires offering the more costly incentive can be expected to return 424 completed surveys. A mailing of 1,400 offering the less costly one can be expected to yield the same number of usable returns (30.3 percent of 1,400 = 424.2). The incremental cost of printing, stuffing, addressing, and stamping 400 more questionnaires would be less than $1,000. The incremental cost of the more expensive incentive would be $1,696 ($4 × 424).

Lowering the nonresponse rate from nearly 70 percent to just under

60 percent is not likely to have much effect on nonresponse bias as a threat to validity. The findings of this study suggest that obtaining the desired number of completed questionnaires by increasing the initial mailing would be more economical than offering a more valuable reward.

This study found no evidence that longer questionnaires discourage returns from affluent households. There may be some upper limit beyond a 500-item instrument that will reduce the response rate, but a great deal of data can be gathered with 500 or fewer questions. It is possible that a survey asking fewer than 300 questions would generate a higher response rate, but the implication in this study that little change is likely is consistent with most of the other research reported in the literature. The evidence suggests that any gains in response that might be associated with short questionnaires are likely to be offset by the inherent limitations on the amount of information that such questionnaires can collect.

Armstrong, J. Scott, and Terry S. Overton (1975). "Monetary Incentives in Mail Surveys." *Public Opinion Quarterly* 39 (Spring), pp. 111–16.

Berdie, Douglas R. (1973). "Questionnaire Length and Response Rate." *Journal of Applied Psychology* 58 (October), pp. 278–80.

Champion, D., and A. Sear (1969). "Questionnaire Response Rate: A Methodological Analysis." *Social Forces* 47, pp. 335–39.

Childers, Terry L., and O. C. Ferrell (1979). "Response Rate and Perceived Questionnaire Length in Mail Surveys." *Journal of Marketing Research* 16 (August), pp. 429–31.

Claritas Corporation (1983). *Geo-Demographic Data*. Arlington, Virginia.

Furse, David H., and David W. Stewart (1982). "Monetary Incentives versus Promised Contribution to Charity: New Evidence on Mail Survey Response." *Journal of Marketing Research* 19 (August), pp. 375–80.

Godwin, Kenneth R. (1979). "The Consequence of Large Monetary Incentives in Mail Surveys of Elites." *Public Opinion Quarterly* 43, pp. 378–87.

Kanuk, Leslie, and Conrad Berenson (1975). "Mail Surveys and Response Rates: A Literature Review." *Journal of Marketing Research* 12 (November), pp. 440–53.

Lehner, Urban C. (1984). "Affluent Buyers Want Value as Much as Luxury in New Cars." *The Wall Street Journal,* July 5, 1984, p. 17.

Linskey, Arnold S. (1975). "Stimulating Responses to Mailed Questionnaires: A Review." *Public Opinion Quarterly* 39, pp. 82–101.

McDaniel, Stephen W., and C. P. Rao (1980). "Effect of Monetary Inducement on Mailed Questionnaire Response Quality." *Journal of Marketing Research* 17 (May), pp. 265–68.

Roscoe, A. Marvin; Dorothy Lang; and Jagdish N. Sheth (1975). "Follow-Up Methods, Questionnaire Length, and Market Differences in Mail Surveys." *Journal of Marketing* 39 (April), pp. 20–27.

Schewe, Charles D., and Normal G. Cournoyer (1976). "Prepaid versus Promised Monetary Incentives to Questionnaire Response: Further Evidence." *Public Opinion Quarterly* 40, pp. 105–7.

Tedin, Kent L., and Richard C. Hofstetter (1982). "The Effect of Cost and Importance Factors on the Return for Single and Multiple Mailings." *Public Opinion Quarterly* 46, pp. 122–28.

U.S. Bureau of the Census (1981). *1980 Population Census*. Washington, D.C.: U.S. Government Printing Office.

Technical Appendix 2

THE FINANCIAL LIFESTYLES OF AMERICAN MILLIONAIRES

The number of millionaires in this country has been growing rapidly. Millionaires are typically the heaviest users of financial services and account for a disproportionate share of the profits made by security brokers, banks, and financial managers. Yet little or no published objective research exists about the financial lifestyles of American millionaires. This study provides an objective analysis of these lifestyles. The 16 financial lifestyles examined are based on a series of analyses of qualitative/focus group studies. Several contrasts are made regarding hypothesized relationships among financial lifestyles, demographics, and need characteristics, and a financial lifestyle segmentation model is proposed. The results of this study provide objective insights into the motives and opinions of millionaires.

BACKGROUND

This study profiles the financial lifestyles of American millionaires. Despite the importance of the millionaire market, very little empirical information has been published about that market. Marketers of financial services would be wise to take note of the importance of the millionaire population—that is, of those households whose net worth exceeds $1 million. Millionaires are potentially the most profitable segment of the population for such marketers.

According to this author's most recent estimates, more than 1 in 100 households in the United States has a net worth of at least $1 million, and such households account for 11 percent of U.S. income. Financial service organizations are becoming more interested in addressing the needs of this market.

The Internal Revenue Service estimated that millionaires own 65.9 percent of the corporate stock, 68.8 percent of the bonds, 40.1 percent of the debt instruments, and 39.3 percent of the real estate in this nation (U.S. Internal Revenue Service, *Statistics of Income Bulletin,* Winter, 1984–85, Washington, D.C.). The author's research also suggests that nearly 65 percent of a security brokerage firm's commissions is generated by 10 percent of its clients.

The millionaire who realizes a seven-figure annual income spends, on average, nearly $100,000 annually for interest on personal loans. The average American household, in contrast, spends about $700 annually for interest on the money it borrows from various types of business organizations. Thus, as with investment services, a very clear positive relationship exists between wealth and the use of credit.

The number of millionaire households in this country has been growing at an unprecedented rate. The U.S. Trust Company estimated that there were 574,324 millionaires in this country in 1980. The author estimated that there were 832,602 U.S. millionaires in 1985 and over 1.2 million by 1987.

Although the millionaire population is a very important one for many marketers of financial services, no objective research has been published about its financial lifestyles. Lifestyle research is especially appropriate to the study of consumer financial and related activities, interests, and opinions (W. D. Wells, "Comment on the Meaning of Lifestyle," in *Advances in Consumer Research,* vol. 3, *Proceedings of the Association for Consumer Research, Sixth Annual Conference, 1976,* ed. B. B. Anderson, Chicago). Lifestyle studies are designed to uncover the motivations behind behavior. Without understanding the motives behind the financial behavior of millionaires, productive marketing to millionaires is not possible (J. Plummer, "The Concept and Application of Lifestyle Segmentation," *Journal of Marketing,* January 1974, pp. 33–37). The development or modification of marketing programs and services directed to millionaires should be based on an objective assessment of their financial lifestyles.

Profiles of these financial lifestyles will enhance the media choices of marketers and the efforts of marketers to design productive promotional themes. Since no objective empirical research on the financial lifestyles of millionaires exists, an alternative to the traditional literature review was utilized in developing the hypotheses of this study. Instead, an analysis of a series of focus group interviews of millionaires was undertaken. The results of these interviews, which are not projectable, provide the base on which this research was developed.

Based on qualitative (focus group) studies, one may speculate that American millionaires in reality differ from the perception that some financial service providers have of them. Most financial planners and personal trust departments assume, for example, that American millionaires are net users, as opposed to net providers, of financial advice. The focus group results suggest that for some categories of millionaires the opposite is true—that is, some categories of millionaires give more advice about investments than they receive. Along these lines, it should be noted that many American millionaires appear to be more interested in wealth enhancement than in wealth protection, as may be seen in their negative view of many investments that offer very little risk. More often than not, millionaires will say that they have created their wealth without the help of so-called investment advisers. Millionaires often prefer to deal with investments directly, not through an intermediary. This is a major reason why most millionaires invest directly in real estate and various types of closely held businesses. This study hypothesizes that only a minority of millionaires have a defensive posture, though millionaire widows, divorcées, and children of self-made millionaires are more likely than other millionaires to adopt a defensive strategy. If these hypotheses are confirmed, the financial services industry in this country will need to reorient itself in its dealings with offensive-minded American millionaires.

PURPOSE OF THE RESEARCH

In reviewing the literature, several facts emerge as important in the context of understanding the affluent market for financial services:

1. The millionaire population will probably grow at an unprecedented rate through the next century.
2. This population is a heavy consumer market for a wide variety of financial services.
3. No objective empirical research has been published about how financial lifestyles vary within the millionaire population.

The purpose of this study is to determine the relationships among millionaires' financial lifestyles and their demographic and need characteristics. The study is intended to determine (1) what financial lifestyle segments exist among the millionaire population, (2) how large those segments are, (3) the profile of each segment, and (4) how to develop strategic recommendations for marketers that are making changes in their service offerings. The study is also intended to provide an important base of knowledge for researchers on the behavior of the millionaire market. Since such research is especially important in light of the growth of that market, it is the author's hope that this study will encourage other researchers to expand upon that base of knowledge.

Sample and Survey Design

A two-stage survey design was employed in this study. First, potential respondents were contacted by mail. Second, those who qualified as millionaires and responded to the invitation (screener) were interviewed.

The potential respondents were identified by means of a geodemographic-based method. Census block groups (neighborhoods) were selected from a listing of neighborhoods that contained high concentrations of households in the highest income category. (Income was used as a proxy for net worth because the census data did not include an actual wealth measure.) The neighborhoods selected were located in the 11 states that accounted for over 50 percent of all the millionaire households in America. The number of households selected in each state was in direct proportion to the relative size of the millionaire population in that state.

Independent estimates of the millionaire population within the targeted block groups indicated that about 12 percent of the selected households would meet the $1 million or more net worth parameter. Of the 8,500 households selected, it was estimated that about 1,020 were in the millionaire category. Of these millionaires, 215 responded (a response rate of 21.1 percent). These respondents were interviewed in person at their primary residence.

RESULTS

Profile of the Sample

The characteristics of the millionaire sample are given in Table 1. The typical respondent's household had a net worth of $3.4 million. All of the respondents represented households that had at least $1 million in net worth. Net worth is defined as the current dollar value of all assets owned by household members minus the current dollar value of all their liabilities.

More than 8 out of 10 respondents (84.3 percent) indicated that they were self-made affluent. Correspondingly, only 12.7 percent of the respondents households' net worth came from inheritance and/or gifts. The

TABLE 1
Characteristics of the Sample of Millionaires (n = 215)

Net worth of household	
Mean net worth (millions)	$3.4
Net worth $1 million or more	100.0%
Households' net worth inherited	12.7%
Wealth-to-inheritance ratio	7.9
Households received no inheritance	51.0%
Respondents self-designated as self-made affluent	84.3%
Income of household	
Mean realized pretax annual income (000s)	$301.5
Mean income as a percentage of mean net worth	8.9%
Sex of respondent	
Male	94.1%
Marital status of respondent	
Married (first marriage)	78.4%
Education of respondent	
Attended college but never received degree	12.8%
College graduates	84.7%
Age of respondent	
Mean age in years	56.4
Age less than 50 years	30.6%
Occupation of respondent	
Professional	21.5%
Entrepreneur	21.9%
Executive	29.1%
Retiree	21.1%
All other categories	6.4%
Business owners	60.7%

typical respondent reported that for every inherited dollar, 7.9 dollars were self-generated. Slightly more than one half of the respondents received no inheritance. The mean realized pretax annual income reported by the respondents was $301,500. This mean income represented 8.9 percent of the mean net worth of the sample. A typical result found by the author in other studies of the affluent is that income as a percentage of net worth declines at the upper levels of net worth. Millionaires and especially multimillionaires often achieve their status by minimizing their realized income and maximizing their unrealized income. The data obtained from this study are in harmony with the data obtained from previous studies undertaken by the author.

Nearly all of the respondents (94.1 percent) were male, and most of the respondents (78.4 percent) were currently married and never divorced/remarried and so on. These results are indicative of a very traditional lifestyle. The male head of household was designated by the family unit as the main financial/investment decision maker in more than 90 percent of the cases.

Most of the respondents (84.7 percent) were college graduates. Only 12.8 percent attended college but never received a degree. The millionaire population in general exhibits a considerable degree of discipline, as is evidenced by its propensity for completing college, remaining married to the same spouse, and achieving its investment goals.

The average age of the sample was 56.4 years. About 3 respondents in 10 were under 50 years of age, while slightly more than 1 in 4 (25.4 percent) was 65 years of age or older.

About one respondent in five (21.1 percent) was retired. Nearly the same percentage of respondents (21.5) were classified as professionals, such as physicians, attorneys, and accountants. About 1 in 10 respondents was an attorney. Twenty-nine percent of the respondents classified themselves as executives, and 21.9 percent considered themselves to be entrepreneurs.

It is important to note that 6 out of 10 respondents indicated that they owned their businesses. Affluent respondents who self-designate themselves as executives or professionals are often really entrepreneurs.

The distinction between working exclusively for oneself as opposed to being a hired employee has major implications for financial service marketers. Millionaires who are business owners have complex financial service needs, some of which are personal, while others can be classified as commercial. Most of the respondents in this study have both personal and commercial service requirements, though it should be noted that many millionaire business owners make little or no distinction between their business-related wealth and their personal wealth.

Dimensions of Financial Lifestyle

The factor analysis of the responses to the 66 lifestyle items revealed 16 factors. These factors were classified into four major categories (see Table 2): (1) investment orientations, (2) components of influence, (3) financial service patronage orientations, and (4) traditional patterns.

The 16 hypothesized lifestyle scales and the corresponding Likert items were developed by analyzing the contents of a series of focus groups and in-depth interviews. These interviews were conducted prior to the development of the survey instrument and served as a base for the hypothesized Likert items and financial lifestyle scales. Also, an a priori

TABLE 2
Profiling the Financial Lifestyle Segments* (n = 215)

Financial Life Cycle Domain "Scale/Sample Items"	Parochial Wealth in Transition (22.8%)	Active Investor (27.0%)	Loan-Prone Shopper (31.6%)	Inheritor/ Achiever (9.8%)	Inheritor/ Underachiever (8.8%)	Number of Statements	Factor Loading
		Investment Orientations					
Offensive risk-oriented investor "To make money, I will take substantial risks when investing."	Low (5)	High (1)	High (2)	Average (3)	Low (4)	7	.62
Inflation protection "Real estate investments are my major defense against inflation."	High (1)	Average (2)	Average (3)	Low (5)	Low (4)	4	.77
Tax reduction orientation "Minimizing my income taxes is a major consideration that is closely reflected in my investment decisions."	Average (3)	High (1)	High (2)	Low (5)	Low (4)	3	.61
Doomsayer "Given the future of our economy, it is wise for investors in this country to keep at least part of their financial assets in a foreign bank."	Low (4)	Average (3)	Average (2)	Low (5)	High (1)	4	.43

Components of Influence

Investment/patronage opinion leadership	Average (4)	High (1)	High (2)	Average (3)	Low (5)	5	.71
"I influence my friends when they are choosing financial institutions to deal with."							
Influence expectation	High (1)	Average (2)	Low (5)	Low (4)	Average (3)	6	.57
"I expect the officers of the bank I deal with to introduce me to influential people."							

Financial Service Patronage Orientations

Officer proneness	Average (2)	Average (4)	High (1)	Average (3)	Low (5)	4	.76
"It is important to know personally the senior officers of the bank with which I deal."							
Parochialism	High (1)	Average (3)	Average (4)	Low (5)	Average (2)	4	.82
"I prefer to deal with banks that are owned and operated by local people."							

TABLE 2 (concluded)

Financial Life Cycle Domain "Scale/Sample Items"	Parochial Wealth in Transition (22.8%)	Active Investor (27.0%)	Loan-Prone Shopper (31.6%)	Inheritor/ Achiever (9.8%)	Inheritor/ Underachiever (8.8%)	Number of Statements	Factor Loading
Anti-large institutions "Large financial institutions are too big to devote much attention to my financial needs."	High (2)	Low (4)	Average (3)	High (1)	Low (5)	6	.79
Quality orientation "I am always willing to pay a premium price for first-quality financial services."	Average (2)	Low (4)	Average (3)	High (1)	Low (5)	2	.83
Investment time "Usually, I have sufficient time to handle my investment properly."	High (1)	Average (4)	Low (5)	High (2)	High (3)	4	.77
One-stop financial patronage "It would be desirable for me to have one main financial adviser."	High (1)	Low (4)	High (2)	Low (5)	Average (3)	5	.76
Financial service bargain shopping "I shop around for the lowest interest rates on loans."	High (1)	Low (5)	High (2)	Low (4)	Average (3)	4	.78

Traditional Patterns

Inherited wealth "Much of my wealth is inherited."	Low (4)	Low (5)	Low (3)	High (2)	High (1)	3	.89
Chauvinism "Men make better financial decisions than women do."	Average (4)	High (2)	Average (3)	High (1)	Low (5)	2	.74
Philanthropic orientation "I have given substantial amounts of my wealth to charitable organizations."	Low (4)	High (1)	Low (5)	High (2)	Average (3)	3	.84

* Ranks were computed from each of the segment means for each financial life-cycle scale. Designations of high, average, and low refer to significantly above average, average, and significantly below average in regard to the net sample mean values.

examination of service offerings, marketing methods and themes, and related promotional literature provided additional foundation material for hypotheses about the major dimensions of the financial lifestyles of millionaires.

The respondents were asked to indicate agreement with 66 statements for 16 financial lifestyles. The 16 scales contained multiple Likert-type items that requested levels of agreement on a six-point scale ranging from "strongly agree" to "strongly disagree." The scales were investigated in terms of stability and construct validity. Each of the scales selected had a strong conceptual base from previous studies of the affluent that had been conducted by the author.

In order to construct several continuous variables, the item values were summed across subjects in the traditional Likert fashion. The scale names, sample statements, and factor loadings are given in Table 2. The 16 scales used in the study demonstrated high reliability and stable factor structures.

In an effort to categorize respondents into homogeneous groups according to their financial lifestyles, a cluster analysis was undertaken. Cluster analysis is a technique that places individuals into groups possessing similar responses. The clusters were arrived at by grouping the two individuals who were closest in their lifestyles along the 16 scales, then the next closest, and so forth, until all of the respondents had been clustered. The goal is to obtain groups with maximum intergroup differences and minimum intragroup differences (J. Veldman, *Programming for the Behavioral Sciences* [New York: Holt, Rinehart and Winston, 1976]). This approach is particularly attractive for marketers of financial services who are attempting to identify affluent segments.

As an initial step, respondents were clustered according to their respective positions on the lifestyle scales. After each respondent had been categorized, an analysis of differences among the clusters in terms of demographic and need variables was undertaken.

Veldman's H Group hierarchical cluster program was used to generate the five-group solution illustrated in Table 2. The five-group solution was appropriate because the margin of error increased significantly when a four-group solution was examined. Also, the test of significance across the group in regard to the 16 variables provided additional support for the five-group solution. All among-group univariate F-ratios for the 16 desirability dimensions were significant at the $<.001$ level.

Table 2 also indicates that each of the five clusters has a unique financial lifestyle. Ranks were assigned to each cluster along each financial lifestyle scale. A rank of one indicated the highest scale values, and a rank of five, the lowest. Designations of high, average, and low referred to significantly above average, average, and significantly below average in contrast to the entire holdout samples' usage mean values. Names were given to the clusters based on their respective financial lifestyle and other correlates (see Tables 3 and 4).

FINANCIAL LIFESTYLE SEGMENTS

The financial lifestyle, demographic, and need characteristics of the five segments are illustrated in Tables 2, 3, and 4. Names were given to each of these segments based on their most distinctive characteristics.

Segment 1—Parochial Wealth in Transition (PWT)

More than one respondent in five (22.8 percent) was classified as a member of this segment. The PWT segment had a number of distinctive characteristics. It ranked first on six of the financial lifestyle dimensions: inflation protection, influence expectation, parochialism, investment time, one-stop financial patronage, and financial service bargain shopping. It ranked last on the offensive risk-oriented investor scale.

The PWT segment had a slightly lower average income than the mean income for the sample ($297,700 versus $301,500). Its mean net worth of $2,900,000 was below the overall average ($3,400,000). It inherited only $1 for every $22.7 of its net worth.

The PWT segment is the oldest of the five segments and has the largest number of retirees. However, 56.6 percent of the respondents in this segment still own businesses. Age in this study appears to be related to several of the financial lifestyle scales and to the needs of the respondents. For example, the PWT segment had the lowest scale value for the offensive risk-oriented investor measure and it also appears to be more concerned about protection from inflation than are other segments.

Interestingly, the PWT segment appears to have more time to "handle investments properly." This is likely to be a function of the higher than average retired proportion of the segment. At the same time, however, this segment has an indicated propensity to deal with "one main financial adviser" and to "shop for the lowest interest rates on loans." Obviously, this segment is willing to patronize a more narrowly defined set of financial advisers than of lending institutions.

But the relationship between advice and credit may also be interpreted in terms of the lifestyle hypothesis. As affluent consumers, most of whom are credit-prone business owners, reach retirement, they have less

TABLE 3
Demographic Correlates of Financial Lifestyles of Millionaire Segments (n = 215)

Demographic Correlate	Parochial Wealth in Transition (22.8%)	Active Investor (27.0%)	Loan-Prone Shopper (31.6%)	Inheritor/ Achiever (9.8%)	Inheritor/ Underachiever (8.8%)
Net worth of household					
Mean net worth (millions)	$2.9	$3.5	$3.4	$4.6	$2.9
Inherited wealth	4.4%	5.7%	10.2%	24.0%	50.3%
Self-designated as self-made affluent	92.5%	98.4%	89.5%	72.7%	18.2%
Wealth-to-inheritance ratio	22.7	17.5	9.8	4.2	1.9
Income of household					
Mean realized pretax annual income (000s)	$297.7	$320.1	$293.3	$396.4	$191.7
Income as a percentage of net worth	9.4%	10.3%	10.6%	11.6%	6.6%
Sex of respondent					
Male	92.6%	96.8%	97.4%	95.5%	77.3%
Marital status of respondent					
Married (first marriage)	84.9%	75.8%	77.9%	81.8%	68.2%
Education of respondent					
Attended college but never received degree	15.1%	12.9%	9.2%	4.5%	27.3%
College	79.2%	82.3%	90.1%	95.5%	72.7%
Age of respondent					
Mean age in years	61.8	54.4	52.6	57.6	57.8
65 or older	43.4%	22.6%	11.7%	31.8%	31.8%
Business ownership by respondent					
Own a business	56.6%	59.0%	63.6%	76.2%	50.0%
Occupation of respondent					
Higher proportion of	Retirees	Professionals (especially attorneys) and executives	Entrepreneurs	Executives/entrepreneurs and professionals	Executives

TABLE 4
Need Correlates of Financial Lifestyles of Millionaire Segments (n = 215)

Need Correlate	Parochial Wealth in Transition (22.8%)	Active Investor (27.0%)	Loan-Prone Shopper (31.6%)	Inheritor/ Achiever (9.8%)	Inheritor/ Underachiever (8.8%)
Financial goals					
More important	Minimize financial risk Liquidity of assets	Long-term capital appreciation Minimize taxes Enjoyment of challenge of investing Use money for personal enjoyment	Long-term capital appreciation Minimize taxes	Long-term capital appreciation Finance business ventures	Guaranteed, fixed return on investments Keep up with inflation
Less important	Long-term capital appreciation Finance business ventures	Guaranteed, fixed return on investments	Guaranteed, fixed return on investments Minimize financial risk	Guaranteed, fixed return on investments Use money for personal enjoyment	Finance business ventures
Assets/investments in meeting financial goals					
More important	Large interest-bearing deposits Cash management/cash trust account Utility stock Real estate/residential	Commercial real estate/rental property Employee retirement program Listed common stock Closely held stock/partnership interest	Listed common stock Closely held stock Commercial real estate/rental property	Closely held stock/partnership interest Listed common stock Tax-free municipal bonds/mutual funds	Listed common stock Cash management/cash trust account Real estate/residential Tax-free municipal bonds/mutual funds Trust accounts

273

TABLE 4 (concluded)

Need Correlate	Parochial Wealth in Transition (22.8%)	Active Investor (27.0%)	Loan-Prone Shopper (31.6%)	Inheritor/ Achiever (9.8%)	Inheritor/ Underachiever (8.8%)
Less important	Closely held stock Stock options Commodity contracts Securities traded on foreign exchanges	Utility stock Large interest-bearing deposits	Large interest-bearing deposits Tax-free municipal bonds/mutual funds Trust accounts	Commercial real estate/rental property Real estate/residential Trust accounts	Commercial real estate/rental property Employee retirement program Employee profit sharing plan
Financial service offerings					
More desirable	Tax planning Investment advice/ management Asset appraisal Offices near home	Line of credit Loans for major personal assets	Line of credit Loans to purchase securities Bank transactions by phone No-service-charge checking	Custody service for securities Asset appraisal Liberal overdraft/ line of credit	Investment advice/ management Bank credit cards Trust services Estate planning Location close to home
Less desirable	Life insurance Loans to purchase securities	Asset appraisal Estate planning Treasury bills	Custody service for securities Trust services Offices near place of business	Tax planning Investment advice/ management Real estate investment advice Loan to purchase securities Estate planning	Line of credit Loans for major personal assets Custody service for securities

Images and behavior regarding financial institutions

Image	High number of "don't knows" and "no opinions" about major money center commercial banks and brokerage firms	Significantly more knowledge of most major financial service organizations. More favorable image of the quality of personnel at commercial banks	Commercial banks a source of loans but not advice ("The best investment advice is one's own"). Has a low regard for the quality of bank personnel	Strong, favorable image of "upscale" money center–based commercial banks	Significantly less knowledgeable about specific financial institutions
Behavior	Current and past patrons of small and medium-sized commercial banks	More likely to be "patronage loyal" than other groups	"A former customer" of more large commercial banks than any other segment	Very cosmopolitan in regard to bank patronage. Bank at high quality/"upscale" specialty banks, independent of physical location	Has a history of changing financial institutions more often than average

need for credit and more need for financial advice. Given their demographic and need characteristics, one may hypothesize that a high proportion of the members of this segment are in transition, that is, in between being an active business owner/manager and a retiree.

The respondents in the PWT segment indicated a greater-than-average need to "minimize financial risk" and have "liquidity of assets" (see Table 4). These goals are not in sync with the large portion of business owners in this segment. Along these lines, "closely held stock" was rated as being less important by this segment in meeting its financial goals.

Transition needs are also reflected in the financial service offering considered desirable by this segment. For instance, asset appraisal was rated as desirable by a significant portion of the segment. What assets will be appraised, and why will they be appraised? In light of the age and need characteristics of this segment, one may hypothesize that its business assets will be appraised and liquidated.

The transition hypothesis is also supported by the segment's desire for investment advice/management, tax planning, and "offices near home." Transition-type services may not be provided by the commercial banks that PWT members currently patronize.

The data in this study indicated that the PWT segment patronizes small and medium-sized "local" banks. It is not at all unusual for wealthy individuals to patronize banks that are not major national institutions. Millionaire business owners often suggest that they patronize a smaller bank because they wish to be the "biggest fish" among the bank's customers. They feel that this gives them significant leverage with the bank's loan committee.

But what happens when the business owner's demand for credit diminishes and his need for transition services emerges? Very often, his suppliers of credit have little or nothing to offer him in the way of investment and other transition services.

One might expect that the major trust institutions in this country would be well known to most American millionaires. But an obvious conclusion of this research is that a significant number of these millionaires have little or no knowledge about many of the major trust organizations in this country.

Aggressive marketers will certainly view this as an opportunity. But how can they capitalize on the presence of PWT millionaires? There are many ways in which marketers can address this issue. One of the most compelling ways centers on marketing to so-called small and medium-sized banks.

Several top brokers in the securities industry view such banks as clients. They provide investment services for banks that have little or no investment expertise and make loan referrals among their clients on behalf of such banks. The officers of these banks often reciprocate by referring customers in transition to security brokers who are "friends" of the bank.

Bankers are not the only professionals who can provide information about the PWT segment. In fact, some bankers never realize that clients are in transition until after many of the critical financial events have taken place. Accountants and lawyers in private practice are also excellent sources of information about parochial wealth in transition. Land surveyors can also be important sources of such information. Often, affluent business owners own commercial property/land. Those who contemplate liquidation have their commercial landholdings surveyed as part of the initial stage of transition.

The members of the PWT segment are often owners of businesses that are not mentioned in *The Wall Street Journal* or *Fortune*. They are often the owners of small and medium-sized businesses, such as beer distributorships, printing companies, and wholesale tool and hardware organizations. Most of them will never be well known to the financial press. Many of them are millionaires but are reluctant to communicate their success. Nevertheless, marketers can find members of the PWT segment if they take the time and effort needed to do so.

Segment 2—Active Investor (AI)

Twenty-seven percent of the sample members were categorized into the AI segment. This segment had several distinctive characteristics. It had the highest scale value on the following financial lifestyle dimensions: (1) offensive risk-oriented investor, (2) tax reduction orientation, (3) investment/patronage opinion leadership, and (4) philanthropic orientation. It also had significantly lower-than-average scale values on these financial lifestyle measures: (1) anti–large institution, (2) quality orientation, (3) one-stop financial patronage, (4) financial service bargain shopping, and (5) inherited wealth.

Although the AI segment is similar to the LPS segment with regard to several lifestyle dimensions, there are notable differences. The AI segment is much less likely to bargain-shop for financial services, especially for the lowest interest rates on loans. This difference in financial lifestyle is indicative of the fact that the AI segment contains fewer entrepreneurs than the LPS segment. However, the AI segment appears to have used credit to enhance its investments and, ultimately, its net worth. This segment contains a higher-than-average proportion of attorneys and executives. It has a history of investing in emerging companies. However, it is less likely than the LPS segment to have hands-on, day-to-day managerial responsibility for such undertakings.

The AI segment's important financial goals include the enjoyment of the challenge of investing and the use of money for personal enjoyment. Financial risk appears to be motivated by factors that go beyond economic gain. This is counter to conventional economic theory, which suggests people invest purely for monetary return. To many members of the AI segment, return on investment is a useful report card on the quality of their judgment. However, challenge and excitement are also salient factors in their investment behavior. A guaranteed fixed return on investments is the least important goal for this segment. The segment is heavily invested in closely held stock, listed common stock, and commercial real estate. Many of its members are in positions of strategic importance to entrepreneurs who are creating new business concepts. These members are the attorneys, financial advisers, and, in some cases, the accountants for many of the entrepreneurial loan-prone shoppers of Segment 3. Many of the professionals in the AI segment invest their own money in what some people would consider high-risk entrepreneurial ventures. Members of this segment have a desire for lines of credit that can be used to invest in such undertakings.

Borrowing for investment purposes is not this segment's only use of credit. Its members also rated loans for major personal assets as very desirable. This relates to their goal of using money "for personal enjoyment."

Financial institutions should pay particular attention to the ability of this segment to influence others. Its members have the highest scale values for investment/patronage opinion leadership. This means that they strongly influence friends and associates who are in the process of choosing investments and financial service providers. Successful attorneys should be a prime target for every financial institution that wishes to cater to the affluent. They are among the most affluent occupational groups in this country, and they are often heavy borrowers as well as investors. They are also perhaps the most important source of patronage referrals for many other affluent occupational groups.

Segment 3—Loan-Prone Shopper (LPS)

The LPS segment had the largest number of respondents (31.6 percent). It was given the title "loan-prone shopper" because its members' financial lifestyles, demographic characteristics, and needs closely related to a central dimension of credit shopping. The LPS segment's financial lifestyle scale values were the highest of all the segments for officer proneness (see Table 2). The segment was also significantly above average in its reported propensity to bargain-shop for "the lowest interest rates on loans."

The results in Table 3 show that the LPS segment, on average, was the youngest segment, with a mean age of 52.6. Although younger than the typical respondent, the LPS segment had an average net worth of $3.4 million. Such wealth accumulation among relatively young millionaires is often a direct result of aggressive credit-based investing.

The LPS segment was much more interested in maximizing long-term capital appreciation than in minimizing financial risk (see Table 4). Its most important investments included listed common stock and closely held stock/partnership interests. It rated large interest-bearing deposits as being least important in meeting its financial goals.

What additional evidence is there to support the hypothesis that this segment engaged heavily in leveraged investing? The LPS segment rated loans for the purchase of securities and liberal overdraft/line of credit as more desirable service offerings than did any of the other segments. The other behavioral component of the LPS label, namely "shopping," is also demonstrated by measures independent of the financial lifestyle dimensions. The LPS segment reported actively "shopping banks" and had the highest number of "former customer" responses to the question regarding their patronage of specific commercial banks.

Why do the members of the LPS segment change their patronage habits so frequently? This question is central to understanding its motives. The LPS segment has the highest concentration of entrepreneurs/owners and managers of business ventures. These people have a great deal of ego involvement in their entrepreneurial undertakings. While members of other segments often have equity positions in small and medium-sized, privately/closely held businesses, they are less likely than members of the LPS segment to have managerial responsibilities. Thus, the members of the LPS segment tend to relate to their entrepreneurial undertakings as an overprotective parent would relate to his children.

When members of this segment are confronted with commercial lending officers who are cold to their business proposals, they often become emotional and immediately seek new sources of credit. They are especially annoyed when such lending officers are relatively young, inexperienced, and egocentric. Many of these millionaires complained to the author that commercial banks renege on promises that their key lending contacts will be seasoned professionals with significant lending authority and the intellect to understand the value of unique business ventures. Some of these millionaires have been forced to deal with constant changes in the key contact personnel and to reeducate new credit officers every time there was a change.

Clearly, not all of the business concepts proposed by members of the LPS segment have value. However, there are alternative ways of informing entrepreneurs in this segment that their loan application has been denied. Most of these entrepreneurs believe that there is nothing worse than being denied credit by a junior credit officer who has no empathy for hands-on entrepreneurial methods. As one multimillionaire/entrepreneur recently told this author, "My credit officer spent 30 minutes telling me about his ski trip to Colorado while I had 12 hours to make payroll for my workers. These MBAs have absolutely no idea of what it means to be in business."

But even financial institutions with quality contact officers wonder why they have a difficult time convincing members of the LPS segment to avail themselves of bank services other than credit. Two major issues relate to this question. First, financial institutions often fail to leverage credit in order to assure the adoption of other services by their clients. Many millionaire entrepreneurs have told this author that financial institutions were unwilling to lower their interest rates even when offered valuable pension and profit sharing plans in exchange. Such entrepreneurs also complained that they were constantly being evaluated as though they were "rookies." Financial institutions should place considerable weight on the lifetime batting average of members of the LPS segment. Most of them complained that their track record of success meant very little to such institutions. But that track record is one of the most cherished possessions of the self-made millionaire/entrepreneur.

The second issue that financial institutions should consider relates to the nature of the entrepreneur. Most entrepreneurs live by the principle "*Never have a single source of credit.*" Entrepreneurs are also reluctant to share information with financial organizations. That reluctance is directly related to the failure of many credit organizations to market financial planning, for example, to their LPS-type customers. A statement made by one affluent entrepreneur illustrates the problem: "If they ever had any idea about how highly leveraged I really am, they would call all the loans right now . . . shut me down in an instant. . . . I have to borrow money from my workers to purchase lunch. I would never purchase a financial plan from my bank because it would kill my credit deals."

The quality of the credit organization's key contact is the critical dimension in maintaining stable patronage relationships with members of the LPS segment. Financial organizations should experiment with the concept of industry experts/credit officers. In nearly every major market in the United States, there is a unique taxonomy of entrepreneurial categories. Northern California has a high concentration of entrepreneurs in the farming, wine, and high-tech industries, and New York has a high concentration of affluent apparel manufacturers. There are a disproportionate number of real estate developers in Atlanta and a large number of heat exchanger manufacturers in Tulsa. In each of these markets, it would be productive for financial organizations to encourage credit officers to become "industry experts." Such commitment would demonstrate to many members of the LPS segment that these organizations are truly empathetic to the entrepreneur's goals.

The LPS segment is especially important to financial organizations not only because of its size but also because its members are patronage and investment opinion leaders for many other individuals in the community. One such member can be the source of many important affluent prospects. Financial institutions can benefit from placing selected members of the LPS segment on their marketing advisory task forces.

Segment 4—Inheritor/Achiever (IA)

Nearly 1 in 10 respondents (9.8 percent) were classified as an IA. This segment was labeled IA because its members, on the average, received significantly more of their wealth from inheritance than did the sample's mean (24.0 percent versus 12.7 percent). In this respect, the IA segment was similar to Segment 5 (Inheritor/Underachiever), discussed below. But the IA segment differed significantly from Segment 5 in many other respects. Its members had a far higher mean income ($396,000) and a far higher mean net worth ($4,600,000) than the members of Segment 5—in fact, the highest mean income and mean net worth of all the segments studied (see Table 3). They generated $4.2 of net worth for every dollar inherited, or twice the ratio for Segment 5.

The financial lifestyles of the members of the IA segment closely corresponded to their demographic and need profiles. The results illustrated in Table 2 indicate that this segment had the highest scale values on both the anti–large institution and quality orientation dimensions. Correspondingly, this most affluent segment had a strongly favorable image of "upscale" specialty banks that were based in money centers. These results are also reflected in the fact that the segment had the lowest mean value on the parochialism financial lifestyle scale. The IA segment was the most cosmopolitan in its orientation toward banks. It appeared to be more sensitive to variations in the quality of services than to either variations in the price of services or the physical locations of service providers. This insensitivity to price relates to the lower than average position of the IA segment on the financial service bargain shopping dimension. The results suggest, however, that the IA segment is prone to rely for financial advice on a set of specialists rather than a single generalist.

Of the members of the IA segment, 95.5 percent were males. This was slightly more than the percentage for the entire sample (94.1). However, the IA segment occupied the top position along the chauvinism scale. Often, chauvinist husbands do not educate their wives about business and financial matters. Then, if they die before their wives do, as is typical, their widows have to seek financial guidance from other parties. A significant group of such widows are likely to be found in Segment 5 (Inheritor/Underachiever). The IA segment comprises some of the most successful sons of America's millionaires. These men are often the opinion leaders and financial advisers for their more passive brothers and sisters. They may act to protect their relatives from overly aggressive financial service providers.

The IA segment has a stated preference for achieving long-term capital appreciation and financing business ventures. Its members often provide venture capital to entrepreneurs. They do this directly in some cases and through specialty organizations in other cases. Among this segment's important assets are closely held stock and listed common stock of organizations that have gone public. This segment places a priority on such financial services as custody services for securities, asset appraisal, and liberal overdraft/line of credit. Custody of securities is often important to its members because they deal with a variety of specialists from the securities industry. Custody at one institution enables them to minimize the confusion and errors typically associated with active trading with multiple sources.

Although the IA segment is the most affluent of the five segments, it is not necessarily the most viable target for marketers. Not only do its members deal with a variety of financial service providers; they also seem to be rather satisfied with the services that are being provided to them. Also, since this segment is more easily identified than other segments because of its members' legacy of wealth and publicized philanthropic activities, it has already been heavily targeted by marketers. People who market to this segment must make quality of service their strongest selling point. In addition, since members of the IA segment appear to be enamored with the idea of providing seed capital for emerging companies, financial institutions may find it valuable to provide them with quality opportunities for their venture capital interests. These "qualified investors" often look beyond conventional equity offerings and seek direct participation in exciting ventures.

Segment 5–Inheritor/Underachiever (IU)

The members of this smallest segment (8.8 percent) were the most un-usual in their financial lifestyles, demographics, and need characteristics. According to the results given in Table 2, the IU segment had the highest scale values on the doomsayer and inherited wealth financial lifestyle dimensions and the lowest scale values on the investment/patronage opin-ion leadership, officer proneness, anti–large institution, quality orienta-tion, and chauvinism dimensions. The segment had a significantly lower scale value than the average for the sample on the offensive risk-oriented investor, inflation protection, and tax reduction orientation continuum.

Several demographic differences between this segment and other segments were also noted (see Table 3). The IU segment had a signifi-cantly lower net worth and income than the sample as a whole. While 12.7 percent of the entire sample's net worth came from inherited sources, 50.3 percent of this segment's wealth was inherited. The members of the segment had, on average, only $1.9 in net worth for every dollar they inherited. This was considerably less than the ratio for the entire sample, which was $7.9 in net worth for every dollar inherited.

The segment also differed from the norm in the relatively high per-centage of women that it contained. While about 1 in 20 of all the respon-dents to this study was a woman, nearly 1 in 4 of the respondents in this segment was female. The members of this segment were also more likely to have been divorced or to have married more than one time than the members of the sample as a whole. The members of this segment were more than twice as likely to have been college dropouts than the members of the sample as a whole.

The financial service needs of the IU segment (see Table 4) are cor-related with its financial lifestyles and demographics. The segment's im-portant financial goals include receiving a guaranteed fixed return on in-vestment, keeping up with inflation, and long-term capital appreciation. Financing business ventures was significantly less important for this seg-ment. The assets/investments that this segment favors for achieving its goals include listed common stocks, cash management services, residen-tial real estate, tax-free municipal bonds/mutual funds, and trust ac-counts. The financial service offerings that it rates as desirable include investment and advice/management, bank credit cards, trust services, estate planning, and offices close to home. Less desirable financial service offerings are lines of credit, loans for major personal assets, and custody services for securities. The segment is significantly less knowledgeable than other segments about specific financial institutions in this country despite the fact that it changes financial institutions more often than the average for the sample as a whole.

How should marketers of financial services relate to the IU segment? What major opportunities are associated with it? The segment as a whole was unwilling to take even moderate financial risk, as demonstrated by its significant cash holdings. While 50 percent of its members indicated that they owned a business, clearly many of them were not entrepreneurs. They merely inherited stock in the "family business."

Often, wealthy individuals in this country place a priority on dealing with senior officers at the banks they patronize. The IU segment, however, may feel intimidated by authority figures. Consequently, many of its members are turned off—and some are actually frightened—by the prospect of a so-called business lunch with senior officers. Many of the commercial banks in this country have alienated members of the IU segment by assigning them to an authority figure. It would be more productive to allow members of this segment to select their own key contact from a wide variety of choices. This holds true especially for the female members, who often complain of the blatantly chauvinistic attitude of many financial service providers. Lack of empathy for the feelings and needs of this segment appears to translate into a high frequency of changes in the financial institutions used by its members.

The members of the IU segment place heavy reliance on the financial advice and wisdom of relatives and friends. Who are these opinion leaders? The answer to this question is complex because the IU segment comprises several subsegments. Sons and daughters who inherit the fortunes of their parents often rely on the financial advice of their most successful sibling (see Segment 4, above). The IA segment (Segment 4) occupies a significantly higher position than the IU segment on the investment/patronage opinion leadership scale. Widows and affluent divorcées also rely on enlightened relatives and family financial advisers. Attorneys, whether or not they are relatives, are a very important source of financial and patronage advice. Marketers who wish to target the IU segment should place a strong priority on aligning themselves with attorneys who specialize in estate law or domestic specialties.

The IU segment is important for financial service markets for a reason that goes beyond the recorded data. It has been this author's experience that members of the IU segment are less likely to respond to surveys than members of any of the other segments. It is therefore quite plausible to conclude that this segment accounts for a significantly larger portion of the millionaire market than 8.8 percent. That figure may understate the size of this segment by at least 25 percent.

Technical Appendix 3

MARKETING TAX-ADVANTAGED INVESTMENTS: THE INVESTOR'S PERSPECTIVE*

I am often asked what effect the proposed tax law changes will have on the market for securities and related offerings. Overall, these changes will provide some excellent opportunities for those who market such offerings. But in order to capitalize on these changes, their major implications must be understood.

One major implication of the new tax law is that the greatest tax-advantaged investment of all times will lose some of its appeal. At present, the average U.S. corporation pays approximately $30,000 in federal tax per year and only about 45 percent of all active corporations in this country pay any federal tax. About 90 percent of the approximately 3 million U.S. corporations are quite small (have annual sales of $2 million or less), and the managers and owners of these corporations are often one and the same. There are also almost 12 million sole proprietorships and 1½ million partnerships, many of which have little or no taxable income. The new tax law's most compelling feature is that these businesses will pay more tax.

Many lawmakers are also saying that the new law will result in significant tax reductions for most households. My opinion is somewhat different. The new law will not only demand more tax from business, it will, in reality, mean that many affluent individuals, including many of your top clients, will be facing substantial increases in their tax liability. But how can this be the case when both the Senate and House bills stipulate a

* Keynote speech, Security Industry Association, Limited Partnership and Direct Investment Conference, New York City, February 6, 1986.

lower tax for most households, including upper-income households? The highly publicized tax rate reduction has been one of the greatest promotional campaigns of all time. On the surface, the bills being considered suggest that most high-income households will pay less tax. In reality, this will hold true for only a minority of affluent households.

I have stated many times that the affluent market has two faces. Most millionaires acquired this financial status by successfully operating their own sole proprietorship, partnership, and/or privately/closely held corporation. Most affluent business owners have a simple financial objective— to maximize their unrealized income and minimize their realized personal income. Thus, they often increase their wealth substantially each year without having significant personal realized or taxable income.

It is not unusual for an affluent household in the $5 million net worth category to realize (in annual personal income) less than 2 or 3 percent of its wealth. But how can such a household maintain its socially defined economic position with only moderate realized income? By driving company autos, exploiting company entertainment allowances, borrowing from the company at special rates, and playing golf via company-paid country club dues. It has also been well established that many owners of cash-type businesses understate their realized income. (This does not include the growing underground economy, which reflects an almost total disregard for the government's definition of taxable income.)

The game of income and tax is about to change. The traditional ability of a business to act as a tax shelter for its owner will be lessened considerably by the new tax law. Although our lawmakers speak of lowering corporate tax rates, the intent of the new tax law is to have business pay more tax. Redefining how income for businesses is computed is one of the ways in which that intent will be realized. Consider what effect the following proposed changes will have on the definition of business income:

1. A minimum tax for all corporations.
2. Possible repeal of the investment tax credit.
3. A significant reduction of depreciation write-offs.

The proposed tax law sponsored by the Senate also establishes a new system of funding to underwrite the cost of significantly increasing the Internal Revenue Service's ability to assure compliance with the tax laws. Strengthening the IRS will result in a shift of income from the unreported to the reported category. Many cash businesses will probably become more candid about their income, and a larger portion of the sale of real estate, timber, and energy-related property will be reported and consequentially taxed.

The new tax law will have a dramatic effect on how affluent households balance their personal and business income objectives. I believe that most affluent households will decide to take more money out of their businesses, to significantly increase their realizable income in an effort to reduce the tax liability facing their businesses.

But the proposed tax law also has some interesting provisions that will affect affluent households. Slightly more than one half of households with annual incomes of over $250,000 use special provisions of the current tax law that the new tax law will probably remove. It has been proposed, for example, that interest paid on loans for investment purchases be deductible only up to the level of investment income and that interest on many other types of loans no longer be deductible. At present, the more affluent the household, the more likely it is to borrow large sums of money. It is not unusual for a household with a million-dollar annual income to pay over $100,000 a year for personal loans. What influence will the proposed tax law changes have on the borrowing, investing, and spending of the affluent?

A crude answer to this question can be given by explaining the probable influence of the pending tax legislation on three segments of the affluent population. These segments do not account for all of the affluent households in America. However, they illustrate the opportunities that the new tax law will present to enlightened marketers of financial services. The first segment is represented by Don Vi-Vant.

THE DON VI-VANT SEGMENT

Don Vi-Vant is a 46-year-old sales professional. His income has averaged $260,000 a year for the past five years. His only real shelter from tax is the amount of money he spends on interest. Last year, he spent over $40,000 for interest on personal loans. The loans included a mortgage on his primary residence and his vacation home, loans on two European luxury autos, and a loan on a boat. Don paid over $80,000 on federal income tax in 1985.

Who are Don's financial advisers? He has an unimaginative CPA who has never approved of any limited partnership and who believes that income should be spent for interest on loans and that, where possible, assets should be depreciated rapidly. Don's financial advisers also include a BMW sales professional who sells customers on the theme of sending checks either to the government for tax payments or to the bank for BMW payments.

Don does have a broker, Bobby, but Bobby is at best a marginal producer. Don is by far his most affluent client. Like many of his colleagues, Bobby is a specialist. He loves equity investing and recommends such investments to all of his clients. Bobby has yet to sell a limited partnership or a financial planning package. But Don likes Bobby. After all, Bobby was his big brother in his college fraternity. Don thinks Bobby is doing a fine job in helping him with his financial lifestyle.

In reality, however, Don has little to invest. His lifestyle is one of heavy consumption spending. Interestingly, although he has a net worth of less than $500,000, he believes that he is very well off. If the current tax proposals are enacted, he will probably pay between $30,000 and $45,000 per year less in taxes. Will Don spend this part of his discretionary income, or will he invest it?

But the Affluent Market Must Be Fully Penetrated

One may rightfully ask this basic marketing question: Are there really any Don Vi-Vants in America? Many marketers of investments, especially of tax-advantaged investments, have the perception that the affluent market has been deeply penetrated and that the prototypical Don Vi-Vant is a fantasy. However, the empirical evidence does not support that perception. According to the IRS,

> nearly half of the high-income taxpayers for 1983 reported a substantial share of their income in taxes—47.0 percent reported taxes of at least 20.0 percent of their (total) positive income. These high-income taxpayers made hardly any more use of special provisions of the tax code for reducing tax liability than did typical upper middle-income ($30,000–$75,000 total positive income) taxpayers. (IRS Statistics, Statistics of Income Bulletin, IRS, Washington, D.C., Fall 1985).

What effect will the proposed tax law changes have on the unsheltered minority of the affluent, the Don Vi-Vants who have been paying substantial amounts of their income in tax? These affluent taxpayers will pay far fewer dollars in tax, whereas the affluent who have been heavy adopters of tax-advantaged investments are very likely to face significant increases in their tax liability.

Can Don be convinced to (1) invest the money he will have discretion over and (2) deal with a more enlightened broker? Before these questions are addressed, a more compelling one should be answered. Why was Bobby the only broker who noticed and solicited Don?

Often, registered representatives overlook people with money to invest because these people do not have the occupational prestige of a lawyer, physician, or senior corporate executive. One of the most overlooked groups in the high-income, moderate-prestige category is the high-performance sales professionals, such as Don Vi-Vant. Even the top sales professionals have nowhere near the occupational status of a physician. However, there are more affluent sales/marketing professionals in this country than affluent physicians (affluent being defined as having an annual income of $100,000 or more). In fact, sales/marketing occupations account for about one half of the affluent prospects in the top 10 affluent occupation categories. Given the proposed changes in the tax law, thousands of sales professionals like Don Vi-Vant will have many more dollars to invest. They may also be less likely to continue their heavy borrowing/consumption lifestyle since it is very probable that interest on loans for luxury goods will no longer be deductible.

You're Right—You Will Never Discover All the Don Vi-Vants

Not all of the affluent sales professionals are identifiable. Often, these sales professionals are employed in small, even offbeat types of organizations. Therefore, in cases where you cannot locate the prospect, develop a system for ferreting out the yet undiscovered Don Vi-Vant. How? Develop your public relations skills. When properly employed, public relations can be a very powerful offensive tool.

Allow me to share with you an example of how this weapon can be used by marketers. Recently, I was asked by a trade organization to address the issue of marketing to the affluent. During my presentation, a member of the audience reflected on his marketing dilemma. He had only a small advertising budget to open a new branch "in a town not served by any major airlines." I advised him that small advertising budgets were often blessings in disguise. I gave him my boilerplate lecture on how to get into the press—with one exception: I advised him to write a press release about the branch opening that emphasized his firm's commitment to affluent clients, including *wealthy sales professionals.* Within two days after the branch opened, eight affluent walk-in or call-in prospects emerged including four Don Vi-Vant sales professionals with annual incomes in excess of $200,000. *For every 20 lunches you purchase for an affluent prospect, treat one hungry business reporter or writer to food, beverage, and your story.*

Will Don Vi-Vant Ever Change Brokers and His Consumption Habits?

My research documents that people who deal with enlightened brokers have more wealth than people who deal with brokers for reasons other than expertise. But how can Don Vi-Vant ever be made to realize that his current broker (and fraternity brother) is not providing him with the proper advice and guidance? And how can Don be convinced that he should spend less and invest more of his income?

Often, the Don Vi-Vants of America feel that, in terms of wealth accumulation, they are very well off. For they are not very different from many highly paid professional athletes. More often than not, when a professional athlete is asked whether he is financially well off, he will respond somewhat as follows: "I have three homes, two swimming pools, a Rolls-Royce, a Porsche, six Great Danes . . ." Like Don, such professional athletes really do not know the proper way to assess (1) their net worth, (2) where they stand in relationship to other "affluent" people, and (3) whether their favorite financial adviser is a winner.

Often, prospects producing even the highest incomes have to be shocked in order to understand that wealth is difficult to achieve without a sound investment strategy. But what credible statistical evidence is there that would change the investing and patronage habits of such prospects? What the industry needs is an affluent index that provides a report card telling the affluent investor what he is *expected* to do in terms of wealth accumulation. An index of this type may be compared to a weight chart that tells you what you are *supposed* to weigh given your sex, height, and age.

What is the normal, expected net worth of an individual given his age and income? I have asked myself and my research assistants this question many times over the past few years. I have concluded that no statistical model will fully explain all of the variations in wealth among the affluent. There are a great many expectations and unknowns. However, I have developed an Affluent Index that I employ to judge my own relative financial position.

Age and income are highly significant predictors of wealth accumulation. There is a distribution of levels of net worth that corresponds to the age and income characteristics of affluent households. Wise investors are those who have above-average wealth accumulation given their age and income characteristics. Conversely, imprudent investors, such as Don Vi-Vant, probably have a significantly lower net worth than would be expected from their income and age characteristics.

What value can the Affluent Index have for marketers of investments? The best way to answer this question is to provide some pro forma case examples. Having evaluated his level of wealth accumulation and broker's performance on the basis of a personal/nominal view of achievement, Don Vi-Vant is satisfied with himself. It is time to break his bubble. Tell him what the normal expected net worth is for a 46-year-old who is making $260,000 annually. Point out that according to the formula Expected net worth = 0.1(age) × Annual realized income, the average investor with his characteristics is expected to have at least a net worth of $1.2 million. Where does Don stand on the Affluent Index Report? With a net worth of $500,000, he is near the bottom of the scale. His worth is that of a person 10 years younger than he is and with an income of approximately $132,000. Once you have enlightened Don in this way, he may be receptive to information about your offerings, including a model portfolio and comprehensive financial planning.

Far too often, affluent consumers view their economic position on their own nominal scale. Interestingly, affluent consumers who have accumulated a below-average level of wealth tend to overestimate their positions on the wealth continuum. Conversely, those who are above average on this scale tend to underestimate their positions.

If Don is still skeptical, show him the Affluent Index Report on one of your best clients. Max, a prudent user of your offerings and a prototypical example of the intelligent/aggressive investor, is 58 and has an annual realized income of $610,000. Given these characteristics, his expected net worth is approximately $3.6 million. Thus, his actual net worth of at least $20 million places him "significantly" above average on the Affluent Index. In fact, Max has the net worth characteristics of someone over 60 years of age with an average annual income of approximately $3.3 million. Obviously, not all of his success can be attributed to his broker's input. However, Max may be more appreciative of his broker after he looks at his scorecard. Don, on the other hand, has never felt a need to develop a relationship with anyone but his broker/fraternity brother, and this is reflected in his wealth position.

The Affluent Index is valuable in dealing with both Max and Don. Max, based on his standing, should be more appreciative of his broker, which hopefully will translate into more loyalty and more activity. Don and others in the bottom of their affluent class standing are likely to be more sensitive to your message.

The Affluent Index is not yet stable enough for commercial use. However, someday it might be used in concert with promotional strategies. Advertisements placed in print media might contain a form on which the prospect would indicate his age, income, and net worth characteristics. The prospect would mail the completed form to the firm for analysis and would receive his Affluent Index Report by return mail. Prospects who receive bad news about their wealth accumulation characteristics are likely to be very receptive to marketing messages that tell them about possible solutions to the problem of wealth accumulation. *Encourage prospects to view their level of wealth accumulation on a relative scale as opposed to a nominal scale.*

Care must be exercised in employing any index of this type. Obviously, luck and source of wealth have something to do with wealth appreciation. Thus, the model does not fully explain all of the variations in wealth. Also, some clients who are not at the top of the affluent scale may blame their favorite broker and everyone else but themselves for this.

THE DUNCAN R. CASH SEGMENT

Duncan R. Cash is the owner of a small chain of service retail stores. Last year, his salary from his family-owned corporation was $82,000. His adjusted gross income totaled $56,581 for 1985. His business had reported sales of $1.5 million for the 1985 fiscal year. Over 90 percent of the corporation's sales volume in 1985 was in cash. The corporation paid less than $3,000 in federal tax on a net income of approximately $20,000.

Security brokers have called on Duncan from time to time. To date, however, he has not been sold by any of them. Why? He insists that he does not need a broker. He tells every registered representative the same story: "I invest where I get the greatest return—in myself, in my business. I always beat the stock market's performance with my own business performance. Besides, I really don't have a very big income anyway."

Duncan and his corporation have always taken full advantage of the tax-advantaged elements of the current tax code, including (1) investment tax credits for new equipment, (2) short-term depreciation of equipment and vehicles, (3) entertainment allowances, (4) pension provisions, and (5) deferred income savings plans. Perhaps Duncan did not need a security broker in the past. But what will his needs be if the proposed tax law is adopted?

Helping Duncan Deal with the Cold Turkey of the New Tax Proposals

In reflecting on the tax liability of Duncan's corporation under the current and proposed tax laws, one notes dramatic differences. Under the current tax law, the corporation pays approximately $3,000 annually in federal income tax. Under the worst of the proposed tax laws, within the next five years its annual income would be redefined from the current $20,000 to nearly $300,000 and it might be taxed at double the current 18 percent tax rate. The effects of these changes would be magnified by the IRS's commitment to enhance compliance with the tax law and increased accuracy in the reporting of income.

In addition, the self-directed pension plan of Duncan's corporation would probably also be affected by the new tax law. Currently, the plan calls for vesting at the tenth year. However, 90 percent or more of the corporations' employees leave before their pensions vest, so that Duncan and his family of executives are in reality the pension plan. It is possible, however, that the new tax law will include a five-year vesting mandate. This would probably triple the number of vested employees within the next seven or eight years.

Duncan is genuinely confused about the course of action he should take in light of the proposed tax changes. He is giving serious consideration to increasing his salary and thereby reducing his corporation's tax liability. It is conceivable that his personal income will double in the next year or two. Like most of the latent affluent, he has never been and probably never will be a conspicuous consumer. He feels that he needs advice about how to invest his personal income.

Duncan needs someone who will help him minimize the cold turkey symptoms of paying big corporate tax dollars for the first time. He needs someone to sort out his financial alternatives. He perceives a need for professional advice, but he has always been price sensitive. Who will develop a fully integrated financial plan for Duncan R. Cash?

A Relationship Account for Duncan

All too often, marketers of investment services have failed to understand the importance of building relationships with clients. Integrated financial planning holds promise for the development of longer-lasting client relationships. In the past, the offerings of such marketers, especially the expensive offerings, have sometimes been difficult to market as "first contact" items. Under the new tax law, however, financial planning may assume an entirely different marketing posture. Even price-sensitive and traditionally do-it-yourself investors such as Duncan are beginning to recognize the need for quality financial planning.

Usually affluent business owners become sensitive to the need for various financial services only when a personal or business event takes place. Rarely is there a major situation to which the affluent business owners become sensitive at the same time. The new tax law is certainly such a situation. It will provide the proactive marketer with a great deal of revenue—revenue that will come both from current clients and from the latent affluent Duncans.

Our Duncan, however, will be more easily sold on the benefits of financial planning than on the fees associated with it. Yet Duncan has never complained about his medical bills. Why not? Because his corporation pays all of them! Well, many senior corporate executives are given allowances for financial advisory fees. Why not encourage Duncan to have his corporation pay for his financial planning fees?

Recently, I developed an asset management package for a large commercial bank. During this assignment, I interviewed groups of senior corporate officers. Several mentioned that their employers reimbursed them up to $6,000 a year for financial advice, planning, and the like. I have also found that a growing number of privately/closely held corporations have been including such provisions in their fringe benefit programs for senior officers. Incidentally, none of the executives I spoke to had ever spent a dime of their $6,000 fringe benefit. Why? The usual answer, of course—they were too busy with their careers, and no financial service provider had ever asked whether this benefit existed! My probing of this topic made it evident to me that these executives would welcome a financial planning solicitation. But their brokers had never asked them for this business.

How can firms that market financial planning capitalize on such fringe benefit programs? Clearly, anyone who spends anywhere near $6,000 each and every year for financial planning with your firm should be given special consideration, such as lower rates on transactions. Segmentation of this kind is especially valuable in encouraging the Duncan types to develop strong financial service patronage habits.

Some of the very best marketers of financial planning packages are quite creative in their approach. They call on the top two or three executives/owners of a private corporation with a rather persuasive theme. They establish a need for planning in the minds of these prospects and provide a step-by-step method for developing a financial planning fringe benefit option in the prospects' corporation. The corporation pays the full costs of that option. Some marketers even provide the prospects with a suggested dialogue to follow in presenting this fringe benefit to the board of directors.

THE MAX PROVISION SEGMENT

Max Provision is a 58-year-old attorney whose profit from his law practice has exceeded $500,000 annually for the past seven years. In addition, he is the major shareholder in three privately held corporations. Since Max has taken full advantage of the special provisions in the current tax law, none of these organizations have demonstrated net income under the current tax law. As an officer of these organizations, he has taken only a token salary while paying handsome salaries to his hired professional managers.

Max's net worth has doubled in four years primarily because of the appreciated value of his privately held corporations and because he has minimized his taxable income. His net worth is estimated to be between $20 million and $35 million. This estimate excludes his large farm and two apartment complexes that have provided him with significant tax-advantaged opportunities.

In addition to being your client with regard to his "personal" tax-advantaged investments, Max is one of your very best limited partnership clients. For more than 10 years, he has used your advice and products to minimize his realized income. Although his total income for the past five years has averaged over $600,000, he has rarely paid more than 5 percent of that income in federal tax. Despite his very high total income, Max's realized income is well under $200,000, so that his total personal federal income tax is less than $35,000. Of the taxpayers with such a high total income, only about one in eight has been able to pay this low rate.

How You Are Perceived by Max

As Max's broker, you are very proud of your role in having helped him reach his investment goals—to minimize his taxable income and to maximize his long-term wealth appreciation. But Max has always viewed your expertise as limited to products and information related to tax-advantaged investments. This is unfortunate because he is seriously thinking of going into the transition stage of his financial life cycle. That is, he is about to move from an offensive wealth-building philosophy to a defensive one, namely liquidating much of his current investment holdings.

Max has often stated that if the current tax proposals are enacted, "It will take 5 times more paperwork and 10 times more tax. I would rather cash in my chips than send $200,000 or $300,000 a year to Washington." Thus, he wants to bail out of one of his corporations (perhaps go public) and eventually sell all of his private business holdings. "I will just put it all into munis if they are still tax free."

Unfortunately, Max does not view you as someone who can help him play the transition game. During your relationship, you have never suggested to him that he go public and you have never mentioned your experience in helping clients play transition. This is unfortunate since several aggressive financial planners have been starting to hit him with a proposed five-year transition plan. He is unaware that you and your firm offer better transition planning. In making proposals to him, several of these financial planners have referred to you as someone who has just a product but not a fully integrated investment banking/planning orientation!

Time to Play Hard Ball

It is not too early to tell Max and your other clients with similar problems that you play the best transition game in America. Talk to the home office. Put together a transition task force. Provide Max with your task force's track record and with the credentials of its members. Gain the support of Max's accountant and other noncompeting financial advisers.

The new tax law will precipitate the sale of many privately held businesses. Thus, it is important that you not let yourself be left out in the cold when a client goes into transition. In several recent cases, affluent individuals have gone public with the help of firms that they never dealt with prior to transition. These same individuals had a long term relationship with full-service firms that they viewed as marketers of products but not of privately held companies, farms, apartment complexes, and so on.

Technical Appendix 4

A STRATEGY FOR TARGETING BY GEODEMOGRAPHY

WHAT IS GEODEMOGRAPHY?

In one afternoon, he may sell over $1,000 worth of magazine subscriptions by knocking on the doors of single-family homes. He only prospects in upscale neighborhoods because "that's where the subscribers and readers are." It's not unusual for this sales professional to sell over $200 worth of magazine subscriptions to one prospect. Much of his success is based on geodemography.

Recently, I was asked to address a group of security brokers at a seminar on marketing municipal bonds. Several top producers discussed their methods of marketing these investment vehicles. All of them presented innovative ideas on prospecting, and one of them had an unusually productive method. He often identified affluent prospects by the mailbox method. What is the mailbox method?

This young top producer and his wife often drive through some of the most affluent neighborhoods near his office. When he finds a cluster of very expensive homes, he writes down their street addresses. As a next step, he obtains the names and telephone numbers of their occupants from an address directory.

This method of prospecting is of particular interest. Essentially, this young man is utilizing geodemographic marketing. Geodemography can be defined as relating household characteristics, such as the income and net worth of households, with neighborhoods and their propensity to buy, invest, borrow, and so one.

Geodemography is one of the ways in which I locate the affluent in America in order to survey them. Yes, the tasks involved in my survey business and in marketing to the affluent are very similar. In order to interview affluent Americans, I must be able to identify them. Once I have identified these wealthy prospective respondents, I must make certain that a significant portion will complete a survey and/or subject themselves to a personal interview.

There are about 250,000 neighborhoods in America. The census refers to these small areas as block groups or enumeration districts. Each of these areas contains about 280 households. The 250,000 neighborhoods in America can be ranked by income. Obviously, the top-ranked neighborhoods, those with the largest proportion of households with the highest incomes, are the ones that I have the greatest interest in surveying and that many marketers have the greatest interest in penetrating.

Once the top-ranked neighborhoods have been identified, some fine tuning may be in order. For example, one may wish to focus on areas with the highest concentrations of the older affluent or in areas with significant numbers of the younger affluent who have very high incomes. The younger affluent are often prime candidates for life insurance and tax planning products, while the older affluent have a propensity for purchasing municipals.

After an affluent area that will be surveyed has been identified via data from the U.S. Census Bureau, the names, addresses, and telephone numbers of the heads of households within that area can be hired from a list company. Not all of the households in the area will have listed phone numbers, but a large majority of the telephone numbers will be available.

The natural question at this point is: How should these affluent be contacted? I found out long ago that trying to survey the affluent by telephone is a nightmare. The hit rate is very low, especially when the number of mid-interview hang-ups is taken into consideration. But many top producers have been very successful in marketing municipals by telephone.

Many people who sell to the affluent are completely turned off by the concept of marketing by direct mail. Some of them have told me that the response to this type of solicitation is so low that it is not worth the effort. Friends of mine in the direct mail business have informed me that a 4 percent response rate is in the good range (even when a sale is not being proposed initially).

The response rates to my surveys of the affluent have ranged from 40 percent to 82 percent, though I ask the most personal and detailed financial questions imaginable. Picture the type of investment planning that could be carried out with the responses to 100, 200, and even 300 financial lifestyle questions.

Why do so many wealthy individuals complete my surveys? One reason may be that they find the surveys interesting. Beyond this, all of the surveys are personalized. A higher response rate is achieved if the letters are individually typed on high-quality bond paper. All too often, direct mail campaigns fail to generate a high response rate because the same message is sent to all households. More interest is generated if both the message and the questions are fine-tuned to the unique character of each neighborhood area.

But one word of caution. It is unconscionable to tell a potential respondent that you are conducting marketing research when you are actually marketing a product or service. Make it clear that you are in the marketing business. Professional marketers never try to deceive a prospect by pretending to be in the marketing research business.

DEVELOPING A GEODEMOGRAPHICALLY BASED AFFLUENT MARKET STRATEGY

The development of a marketing strategy for a firm that wishes to target the affluent often requires research. In typical assignments of this type, the objectives proposed include:

1. Estimating the size and composition of the affluent market for financial services within targeted trade areas.
2. Determining the penetration that the firm has in this market with regard to several affluent products and services.
3. Developing a multidimensional segmentation model of the affluent market based on wage and salary income, age, occupation, and income-producing assets.
4. Relating these geodemographic segments to financial service needs.
5. Developing a need/opportunity analysis for each geodemographic segment.

Table 1 illustrates the four dimensions and the corresponding codes of a geodemographically based affluent market segmentation matrix. All of the affluent area block groups are classified in up to 81 market cells or segments. These cells, in turn, are related to financial service usage (see Table 2, for example). The greatest opportunities for many organizations lie within the three most affluent block group segments: 1 1 1 1, 1 2 1 1, and 1 3 1 1. The financial service needs of the households within these segments are discussed in detail. The financial service needs of the households within other segments are presented in outline form in Tables 3, 4, and 5.

TABLE 1
Dimensions and Codes for Affluent
Market Segmentation Matrix

Dimension 1 (column 1): Average wage
and salary income
1. Top group $150,000–50,001
2. Middle   50,000–40,001
3. Bottom   40,000–30,000

Dimension 2 (column 2): Percentage of
households with householder 65 years
of age or older
1. Top group   60.0–20.1%
2. Middle   20.0–10.1
3. Bottom   10.0– 0.0

Dimension 3 (column 3): Percentage of
population employed as executives,
managers, administrators
1. Top group   75.0–25.1%
2. Middle   25.0–15.1
3. Bottom   15.0– 0.0

Dimension 4 (column 4): Percentage of
households with assets of $1 million or
more
1. Top group   20.0–5.1%
2. Middle   5.0–2.1%
3. Bottom   2.0–0.0%

TABLE 2
Financial Product and Service Offerings

1. *Passive wealth and/or golden years offerings*
    a. Investment management services
    b. Custody of securities
    c. Estate planning services/executor
    d. Traditional trust services (testamentary)
    e. Comprehensive financial planning
    f. Direct investment advice and offerings
    g. Jumbo term investments
    h. Auxiliary insurance on deposits
    i. Private bank services—deposit and/or investment oriented
    j. Nonbusiness asset appraisal service
    k. Collection of interest, dividend, or rental income
    l. Living trust services

TABLE 2 *(concluded)*

2. *Personal credit services*
   a. Personal loan
   b. Auto loan with balloon
   c. Overdraft/line of credit
   d. Conventional mortgage
   e. Mortgage for out-of-state purchase
   f. Loans for purchase of personal investments
   g. Loan approvals by telephone
   h. Loans for purchase of major tangibles/collectibles
   i. Private bank services—credit oriented
   j. Travel/entertainment cards
   k. Prestige credit cards
   l. Bridge/swing loans

3. *Active investor services*
   a. Tax-advantaged financial planning and direct investments in oil, gas, etc.
   b. Discount brokerage
   c. Margin loans
   d. Stock options
   e. Commodity contracts

4. *Business financial services*
   a. Fringe benefit fund management
   b. Business investment management
   c. Corporate money market account
   d. Small business loans
   e. Account receivable loans
   f. Group insurance products
   g. Buy-sell agreement insurance

5. *Transition game services*
   a. Business valuation
   b. Business brokerage
   c. Investment advice regarding business liquidation
   d. Prospect evaluation
   e. Financing for purchase of business
   f. Investment products—short-term
   g. "How to" seminars: how to play to win the transition game
   h. Business for sale listing service
   i. Bridge loans in anticipation of business liquidation

6. *Traditional banking services*
   a. Checking account
   b. Money market account
   c. Safe-deposit box
   d. Etc.

7. *Nontraditional financial services*
   a. Mutual funds marketed by direct mail
   b. Life insurance marketed by direct mail
   c. Prepaid legal services marketed by direct mail

Segment 1 1 1 1

In this pro forma example, Segment 1 1 1 1 contains over 50 block groups and nearly 30,000 households (see Table 3). The block groups in this segment have the highest average wage and salary income; the highest percentage of households with householders 65 years of age or older; the highest percentage of population employed as executives, managers, and administrators; and the highest percentage of households with income-producing assets of $1 million or more. Net worth can be computed by capitalizing the interest and dividend income reported by the census. The other components of the model can be taken directly from census data.

Thus, this segment contains a high concentration of very affluent block groups. The high average wage and salary income of these block groups indicates a situation in which a large portion of the population is employed despite having accumulated a considerable amount of income-producing assets. The high proportion of household heads in the executive, manager, and administrator category suggests a different quality. Respondents to census questionnaires (the base on which these data are generated) who give their occupation as executive, manager, or administrator can actually be more finely categorized into subsegments. Typically, more than one half of the respondents at these high income and net worth levels are really managers/owners of their own businesses. The other half comprises professional managers of businesses.

Neighborhood Typology and Financial Service Needs

What financial service needs are required by households contained in the block groups designated as 1 1 1 1? Such households, because of their income, net worth, age, and occupational status characteristics, are heavy users of a wide variety of financial services.

Although these households are likely to be heavy adopters of a wide variety of financial services, their needs in this regard can be prioritized. A significant portion of them are in or near the transition stage of their financial life cycle. During this stage, the affluent business owner plans a strategy to cash in his business chips and the affluent professional business manager plans the consolidation/reinvestment of dollars from his pension plan.

A high concentration of the millionaires in the 1 1 1 1 segment own their own businesses. The value of these businesses is usually less than $10 million. Most of the 1 1 1 1 business owners will eventually sell their businesses. They are not sure how to go about doing so or what to do with the proceeds of the biggest payday in their financial life cycle. Many are not even sure how to go about determining the value of a business.

TABLE 3

Affluent Segment 1 1 1 1 and Related Segments: Characteristics and Opportunities

Key (Related) Block Group Segment	Number of Households (000s) and Percent of Total	Salient Financial Service Needs	Level of Market Opportunity	Recommended Marketing Methods
1 1 1 1 (1 1 2 1) (1 1 3 1) (2 1 1 1) (2 1 2 1) (2 1 3 1)	28.0 (8.0)	Transition game leading into golden years offerings. Transition especially significant in 1 1 1 1 because of the high concentration of entrepreneurs.	*Very high.* Large, very affluent segment. The 1 1 1 1 segment is very important because of the high number of entrepreneurs it contains.	Cross-sell via private banking relationship. Utilize all methods, both traditional (e. g., referrals) and nontraditional (e.g., public relations, seminars, multistage direct mail)
3 1 1 1 (3 1 2 1) (3 1 3 1)		Golden years offerings. Some transition game needs. Transition of business assets less important in 3 1 2 1 and 3 1 3 1 than in 3 1 1 1 because these segments comprise fewer entrepreneurs than 3 1 1 1.	*Moderate.* Demographics indicate that many households already in golden years stage.	Same as above, except more emphasis on personal referrals. Also, cross-sell via current private banking relationship.
1 1 1 2 (1 1 2 2) (1 1 3 2) (2 1 3 2) (2 1 2 2) (2 1 1 2)		Transition game leading into golden years offerings. Also, some need for personal credit, active investor, and business financial services.	*Moderate.* Segment includes several small subsegments with somewhat diffused needs. However, growth projections are high.	Nontraditional marketing, such as multistage direct mail with emphasis on menu offerings. Use public relations to encourage the more valuable prospects to self-designate their needs by making inquiries.

303

TABLE 3 (concluded)

Key (Related) Block Group Segment	Number of Households (000s) and Percent of Total	Salient Financial Service Needs	Level of Market Opportunity	Recommended Marketing Methods
3 1 3 2 (3 1 2 2) (3 1 1 2)		Golden years offerings. Some transition game needs.	*Moderate.* Households with high net worth diffused within block groups. However, two very large subsegments. Middle level affluent. Many likely to be in golden years.	Public relations publications to encourage "diamonds in rough" to self-designate their needs by making inquiries. Also, *if* direct mail is employed, adoption of the menu approach is a necessity.
2 1 1 3 (2 1 2 3) (2 1 3 3)		Limited needs, such as traditional financial services and perhaps mutual funds.	*Low.* Older, lower-level affluent. A small, well-diffused affluent group does exist within these block groups.	Indirect/self-selection marketing with the objective of extracting "gold from a sea of saltwater." Cross-classify business list with home addresses of affluent entrepreneurs.
3 1 1 3 (3 1 2 3) (3 1 3 3)		Given low ability to pay, most of the households in these segments are limited to traditional banking services.	*Low.* Most households do not have income/net worth levels high enough to be of interest. However, small minority are millionaires.	Indirect/self-selection marketing with the objective of extracting "gold from a pile of dirt." Cross-classify business list with addresses of affluent entrepreneurs.

Interestingly, in studying thousands of advertisements for upscale financial products and services offered by financial service marketers, I have found that few, if any, address transition needs. Therefore, how are affluent business owners who are in transition to know where to go for related financial services? In this regard, most marketers have a product mentality, not a market orientation. Certainly, most financial service organizations have many of the services and products needed by those in transition (see "transition game services" listed in Table 2). But this seems to be among the best-kept secrets in America.

Why do so many organizations wait until Stage 3 of the affluent prospect's life cycle to establish a "long-term relationship"? By the time an affluent prospect reaches his "golden years," it is often too late to establish a productive relationship. The organization that assists the affluent business owner during his transition stage is in a strategically superior position to provide products and services that fit the needs associated with the golden years phase of the financial life cycle. These are listed in Table 2 under the heading "Passive wealth and/or golden years offerings."

Too often, upscale marketers ignore the transition needs of affluent households. Typically, the trust departments of banks are given control of the golden years products and services. Ideally, these departments want to manage assets that are in liquid form—for example, securities of public corporations. They should understand that the total dollar value of all the shares listed on the New York Stock Exchange is about the same as the dollar investments in equity in noncorporate businesses by households, as estimated by the Federal Reserve System. Despite these facts, the financial service industry has done little to meet the transition needs of the affluent business owner.

Market Strategy

Despite the accuracy with which geodemography can identify affluent block groups, this system does not provide the complete answer to the problem of marketing upscale financial services to the affluent. Households within any given block group are not identical in terms of wealth-related variables, and not all of the households in affluent neighborhoods are wealthy. For example, even in some of the wealthiest block groups, fewer than one in four households has a net worth of $1 million or more. Moreover, not all of the households within the 1 1 1 1 segment will be in or near transition. Thus, the geodemographic system must be supplemented with other innovative marketing tools and tactics.

Strategy by Geodemography

The marketer should consider generating a list of the names, addresses, and telephone numbers of those living within block groups in the 1 1 1 1 segment. Lists of this kind can be purchased from commercial list/directory organizations. Two-stage direct mail marketing can be carried out after the list has been compiled. The first stage presents the prospect with a menu of the services that the marketer offers. The menu would list a variety of needs that reflect the predicted character of the households defined by the block group segment. Corresponding to those needs are such generic product categories as "transition game services" and "passive wealth and/or golden years offerings." The prospect is asked to specify his current and future financial situations by return mail. Those situations may range from a routine CD rollover to an extraordinary event such as the sale of capital assets—for example, a privately held business. The effectiveness of marketing tactics hinges to a large extent on how well the offer of services is timed with the prospect's key situations and on how congruent the product offerings are with the prospect's need.

In the second stage, the prospect who self-designates his needs in Stage 1 receives information tailored to those needs by mail and/or by telephone or a personal visit. The marketer's mailings should be made according to marginal response analysis. The first mailings should be made to the block groups within the 1 1 1 1 segment that have the highest concentrations of the four characteristics used to define their areas. The value of the response to mailings is expected to be a direct function of the concentration of affluence within a neighborhood.

Segment 1 2 1 1

In this example, nearly 1 in 20 (4.8 percent) of the households in affluent areas is in the 1 2 1 1 segment (see Table 4). This translates into nearly 17,000 households.

The 1 2 1 1 segment comprises the block groups that have the highest average wage and salary income; a midrange percentage of households with householders 65 years of age or older; the highest percentage of population employed as executives, managers, and administrators; and the highest percentage of households with income-producing assets of $1 million or more. This segment differs from the two other very affluent segments (1 1 1 1 and 1 3 1 1) only in regard to the age dimension. It is composed of block groups that contain between 20 percent and 10.1 percent older householders—that is, householders 65 years of age or older. Thus, many of the needs of the households in this segment are similar to

TABLE 4
Affluent Segment 1 2 1 1 and Related Segments: Characteristics and Opportunities

Key (Related) Block Group Segment	Number of Households (000s) and Percent of Total	Salient Financial Service Needs	Level of Market Opportunity	Recommended Marketing Methods
1 2 1 1 (1 2 2 1) (1 2 3 1)	16.8 (4.8)	A very wide variety. Business financial services are needed by the entrepreneurs, 1 2 1 1, and the professionals, 1 2 2 1 and 1 2 3 1. Other important offerings include personal credit services, active investor services, transition game services, and some passive wealth services, especially asset management.	*Very high.* The 1 2 1 1 segment is quite large and contains a significant number of very affluent entrepreneurs and senior corporate executives. This segment is growing rapidly.	All methods must be capitalized on, including multistage mail with menu, simultaneous public relations articles, personal follow-up of inquiries and referrals, and cross-classification of business and professional owners with home addresses.
(2 2 1 1) (2 2 2 1) (2 2 3 1) (3 2 3 1)		Similar to 1 2 1 1.	*Moderate.* Small segments.	Similar to 1 2 1 1, with more emphasis on indirect marketing methods.
1 2 2 2 (1 2 3 2) (1 2 1 2)		Similar to 1 2 1 1, except that 1 2 2 2 and 1 2 3 2 contain a high proportion of professionals and sales representatives. Thus, more emphasis should be given to the personal side of financial needs.	*Moderate.* Middle-range net worth but high income. Credit prone.	Same as 2 2 1 1.

307

TABLE 4 (concluded)

Key (Related) Block Group Segment	Number of Households (000s) and Percent of Total	Salient Financial Service Needs	Level of Market Opportunity	Recommended Marketing Methods
2 2 2 (2 2 3 2) (2 2 1 2)		A very wide variety. These segments contain almost equal portions of entrepreneurs, executives, professionals, and sales persons. Needs range from business financial services to transition game and golden years offerings.	*Moderate.* Only middle-range affluent, but in considerable numbers and with high expected growth. Some significant opportunities if high-grade affluent can be extracted from these areas.	Marketing methods should be based on the objective of servicing subsegments of these segments. Direct marketing via multistage systems with menu is advised. The very affluent can be extracted by encouraging inquiries and referrals.
3 2 3 2 (3 2 2 2) (3 2 1 2)		Needs reflect the relatively low income of these households. Also, a high portion are in the sales representatives area and lower-paid professional groups. This suggests lower-grade loans. Perhaps some opportunity for nontraditional financial services.	*Low.* Moderate-sized segments with moderate to low growth. Few of the households in this segment will generate significant credit, transition, or even golden years business.	Indirect marketing may be more productive than direct approaches. This segment may be sensitive, however, to lower-priced, nontraditional services. As in other low-grade situations, use the extraction methods that are least costly.

Segment	Needs	Rating	Marketing approach
(1 2 2 3) (1 2 3 3)	Credit.	*Very low.* Segment too small to warrant special programs.	If any special marketing is to be used, perhaps a menu of credit via direct mail would be useful.
3 2 3 3 (3 2 2 3) (3 2 1 3) (2 2 1 3) (2 2 2 3) (2 2 3 3)	Below-average needs. The people in these segments are affluent more by occupational title than by dollars. Needs include nontraditional and traditional financial services and personal credit.	*Low.* Although 3 2 3 3 is a large segment, it contains very few really affluent households.	Public relations methods should be used to extract the small quantities of millionaires from these segments. In addition to this "inquiry" method, referral and business cross-classification methods may be productive.

those of the households in Segments 1 1 1 1 and 1 3 1 1 (see Tables 3 and 5).

Neighborhood Typology and Financial Service Needs

Of the three most affluent segments, Segment 1 2 1 1 has the most varied financial service needs. This is because households are more widely distributed along the age continuum in this segment than in the two other segments. The 1 2 1 1 segment contains a substantial portion of successful entrepreneurs, while its closely related segments contain high portions of professionals and sales representatives. Within these segments, however, the use of financial services is difficult to predict with high precision.

Obviously, affluent business owners are in need of business financial services, especially high-yielding, corporate cash management accounts. But, it may be difficult to get entrepreneurs who are middle-aged and older to give up their credit relationship with the institution with which they currently deal. Thus, their needs, in terms of changing their patronage habits, may be stronger on the personal side.

Some members of Segment 1 2 1 1 are likely to want to enter the transition phase early. Therefore, there is some opportunity for marketing transition game services within this segment. Marketing of this kind is more fully detailed in the discussion of Segment 1 1 1 1 given above.

Early transition in Segment 1 2 1 1 comes in two forms. First, business owners sell their firms and have a need for business liquidation and related services. Second, senior executives of public corporations "retire" early in light of current mergers, takeovers, and buyouts.

Another interesting need is associated with this segment. A significant portion of its members are in the age category at which they will inherit wealth from their parents or other relatives. Only about 20 percent of the millionaires in America have inherited most of their wealth. However, this percentage is likely to be significantly higher within neighborhoods of the 1 2 1 1 type. What will the affluent household in this segment do with the proceeds of an estate? What are its needs with regard to the dollars generated from the sale of a business? Such problems would suggest opportunities for generating significant fee revenues from financial planning and investment management services.

The members of Segment 1 2 1 1 will probably include a bumper crop of wealthy widows. (Females typically live longer than males, and affluent males tend to marry younger women.) Such widows, only about 20 percent of whom have their own career/work full-time, may not be able to manage their investments effectively without the assistance of outside service providers. This provides an opportunity for investment management services and investment-oriented private banking services. Wealthy widows are also interested in purchasing auxiliary insurance on their jumbo term investments, such as $100,000 CDs.

Naturally, a good portion of the 1 2 1 1 and related segments will need personal credit services—large overdrafts, bridge loans, and so on. As with Segment 1 3 1 1, many members of Segment 1 2 1 1 and its related segments need tax-advantaged financial planning.

Market Strategy

It is difficult to develop a single market strategy for the 1 2 1 1 segment and its related segments. The diversity of age in these segments is reflected in the diversity of the financial services they use. Therefore, several subsegments and their needs are dealt with in this discussion.

Early retirement by some executives and business owners should be addressed in any marketing plan. Executives, even those associated with public corporations, often own considerable stock in their organizations. Alternatively, many will want to remove/reinvest their entire pension fund. Often balances in these funds are in the seven-figure range. Entrepreneurs who wish to cash in their business chips early are likely candidates for transition game products and services.

In direct mail promotions, the same multistage methods outlined for Segments 1 1 1 1 and 1 3 1 1 apply to this segment. The menu for Segment 1 2 1 1 should include (1) tax-advantaged financial planning/direct investment, (2) corporate high-yield money management, (3) early transition for both business owners and executives, (4) products and services for the "inherited wealth event," (5) trust services that assure the client that his estate will go to his grandchildren and bypass his children, (6) business management for the affluent entrepreneur who becomes disabled, and (7) asset management in the context of significant windfall gains.

Segment 1 3 1 1

This affluent segment contains 30 block groups and approximately 12,000 households. The block groups in this segment have the following characteristics: (1) the highest average wage and salary income; (2) the lowest percentage of households with householders 65 years of age or older; (3) the highest percentage of population employed as executives, managers, and administrators, and (4) the highest percentage of households with income-producing assets of $1 million or more (see Table 5).

The 1 3 1 1 segment represents the most affluent segment within the youngest age category. It constitutes a unique category of fast-track, young achievers. High economic achievement levels at a relatively young

TABLE 5
Affluent Segment 1 3 1 1 and Related Segments: Characteristics and Opportunities

Key (Related) Block Group Segment	Number of Households (000s) and Percent of Total	Salient Financial Service Needs	Level of Market Opportunity	Recommended Marketing Methods
1 3 1 1 (1 3 2 1) (1 3 3 1) (2 3 2 1)	12.0 (3.4)	Primary needs include business credit services (especially in block groups in the 1 3 1 1 segment), personal credit services, active investor services, and some transition and golden years services. Strong need for credit-oriented private banking.	*Very high.* Younger, very affluent subsegments, high growth, large size, and users of a wide variety of financial services. May provide the other side of the business broker opportunity (buyers).	Utilize all methods, both traditional (e.g., referrals from professionals) and nontraditional (e.g., multi-stage direct mail with personal follow-up and public relations articles in sequence with direct mail and personal contact). Credit-oriented private banking may be an excellent introductory service.
(3 3 3 1)		Undefined.	*Very low.* Segment too small to be of special interest.	Special marketing program not warranted.
1 3 1 2 (1 3 2 2) (1 3 3 2)		Similar to those of 1 3 1 1, except that the needs are somewhat more on the personal side as opposed to the business side. Moderately wealthy segment in terms of net worth.	*High* for key segment. See details for 1 3 1 1.	See recommendations for 1 3 1 1.
2 3 1 2 (2 3 2 2) (2 3 3 2) (3 3 2 2)		Similar to those listed for 1 3 1 1, except that 2 3 3 2 contains a large concentration of affluent professionals and sales	*Moderate* compared to 1 3 1 1. However, the size and growth of the 2 3 3 2 segment provide significant opportunity. Few banks have	For 2 3 1 2, use methods outlined under 1 3 1 1. For 2 3 3 2 and 2 3 3 2, focus on trade and lists. For example, secure lists of top

	reps, groups that are typically heavy users of personal credit services and active investor services (especially tax shelters).	ever catered to high-performance sales professionals.	sales professionals in the real estate, life insurance, and high-tech areas.
1 3 1 3 (1 3 2 3) (1 3 3 3)	Personal credit and business financial services and active investor services for 1 3 1 3, the entrepreneur segment. Similar needs for 1 3 2 3, the professional segment. Personal credit and active investor services for 1 3 3 3, the sales representative segment.	*Moderate.* Overall, these segments are small, but they are likely to be heavy users of credit.	Use multistage direct mail with service menu. Emphasize credit.
2 3 2 3 (2 3 1 3) (2 3 3 3)	Personal credit services, traditional banking services, nontraditional financial services, and active investor services.	*Moderate.* Key segment is very large. However, net worth levels are in low category for a majority of the population. "A middle-class credit type neighborhood" with some highly diffused affluent households.	Market methods should reflect the objective of extraction of "gold from a large quantity of dirt." Primary method should include public relations, trade journal promotion, and cross-classification of business owners with residential addresses. Any direct mail should be done with menu only.
3 3 1 3 (3 3 2 3) (3 3 3 3)	Nontraditional financial services, traditional banking services, personal credit services. Some need by subsegments for business financial services.	*Moderate to low.* Only positive feature is the large size of these subsegments. These segments can provide a "farm team."	Offer nontraditional financial services by direct mailing of menu offers. Attempt to mine the minority (the affluent) by referrals, response generation from public relations articles, and trade journals advertisements.

age are an excellent indication of future wealth accumulation. The 1 3 1 1 segment is not only an important market today; it represents a future market of seven-, eight-, and even nine-figure asset management accounts and related business.

Neighborhood Typology and Financial Service Needs
Given the characteristics of the households in this segment, what financial services are its members likely to adopt? Many of them have two financial lifestyles. First, a significant portion own a business and/or a professional practice and therefore need business financial services. Second, given their age, income, and net worth figures, they are likely to need a wide variety of personal financial services.

Business financial services are likely to be adopted heavily by many of these households. Business credit may be the most important of these services. The 1311 segment contains affluent prospects for the "other side" of transition game services, that is, the purchase of businesses via the financial service firm's business brokering service. As a natural consequence of facilitating the sales of businesses, a financial service firm would be in an advantageous position to provide credit to purchase those businesses. In addition, it would be able to leverage the relationships established in this way, into more personal and commercial financial service business, such as fund management, corporate money market accounts, and investment management.

What are the personal credit needs of the 1 3 1 1 segment likely to be? Given its wealth, income, and age characteristics, it is likely to need large credit lines, loans for the purchase of personal investments, loans for the construction of primary and secondary dwellings, bridge loans, and permanent mortgages.

Many of the prospective customers in this and related segments are not self-employed. Thus, they cannot easily minimize their personal income by taking it in the unrealized form of business wealth appreciation. They are therefore targets for offerings in the area of tax-advantaged financial planning.

Market Strategy
To be productive, any market strategy must be based on an assessment of the market opportunities. The wealth and size characteristics of Segment 1 3 1 1 clearly indicate significant opportunities.

The financial service firm should consider appointing a market segment manager who would be responsible for exploiting Segment 1 3 1 1 and its related segments. The manager and his subordinates should be asked to prepare a business plan for penetrating these segments. The plan should stipulate minimum increases in the firm's market share and revenue dollars. The market segment manager should be given the responsibility for developing an incentive compensation package to stimulate market penetration for specific products and services.

Direct mail marketing methods may be most productive if a two-stage design is utilized. Stage 1 would be used to qualify, by a promotional-type mail survey, the prospects in Segments 1 3 1 1 and its related segments in terms of (1) occupation/type of business, (2) interest in products, and (3) promotional sensitivity parameters based on an estimate of the size and dates of their major financial events. Prospects would be given a menu for the purpose of self-designating their current/potential use of various offerings. Forecast critical peaks and valleys in their cash flow would also be determined during this stage. (Forecast cash flow situations are invaluable to the financial service firm in its marketing of both credit and investment products.) Upon returning this information, each prospect can be categorized and assigned to a manager. In addition, during this second stage, the firm can time its messages to the prospect/customer's estimated financial situation and can note any changes in the prospect/customer's situation.

Each prospect/customer can be monitored by using this two-stage approach. A computerized dossier for each respondent can be developed and continually updated. Single-stage direct marketing is often based on an understanding of the aggregate potential of the affluent market, but it does not relate to differences in the need situations of individuals. Multiple-stage direct marketing is based on empathy for such differences.

Continued direct promotion and interaction by mail with customers are important in cases where the affluent household never develops the usage/wealth characteristics needed to support truly personalized service delivery. This is especially true of less affluent members of the 1 3 1 1 segment and related segments. Conversely, some of the younger members of these segments will mature to the highest levels of wealth and financial service use. Two-stage marketing is essential in these situations. Monitoring via this process enables the marketer to allocate human resources more effectively to selected customers and prospects.

PENETRATION AND WEALTH CHARACTERISTICS

Marketers will find it valuable to determine the relationship between the wealth within block groups and their firm's market penetration. Correlation analysis can be used in such cases. In the example shown in Table 6, separate correlation coefficients have been computed between the per-

TABLE 6
Pro Forma Relationships: The Firm's Market Penetration and Neighborhood Wealth and Income Characteristics

| | | Correlation Coefficients* | |
Penetrated Block Groups	Account Type	Percent of Households with Assets of $1 Million or More	Percent of Households with Income of $100,000 or More
81.1%	ATM	.57	.58
75.3	CDs	.34	.30
78.5	NOW	.64	.64
13.6	Discount brokerage	.13	.14
8.2	Financial consulting	.21	.21
11.4	Investment management	.10	.05
61.4	Money market	.59	.57
40.8	Overdraft	.41	.48
51.8	Private banking	.59	.58
47.3	IRA	.36	.35
12.4	Revocable trust	.30	.26
71.8	Safe deposit	.65	.59
13.4	Custody of securities	.29	.32
32.0	Small business loans	.44	.51

* Correlation coefficients are indices of the relationship between variables. A coefficient of 1.0 indicates a perfect positive relationship between variables. A correlation of 0 indicates that the variables are completely independent of each other.

centage of households within each block group that have assets of $1 million or more and the corresponding percentage of households within each block group that are current customers for each of the firm's 14 service categories. A second set of correlation coefficients has been computed between the firm's market penetration and the percentage of households within each block group with incomes of $100,000 or more.

Only block groups with nonzero levels of market penetration have been included in these computations. A correlation coefficient is an index of the relationship between two variables: a correlation coefficient of 1.0 means a perfect positive relationship, while a correlation coefficient of 0.0 means that the two variables have no relationship. Finally, a negative correlation coefficient means that the two variables are negatively correlated. Correlation coefficients are useful in assessing the firm's marketing efforts.

The firm has at least one household NOW account patron in 78.5 percent of the affluent block groups. In sharp contrast, the firm's discount brokerage services are being used in only 13.6 percent of these block groups. Trust-related services also have a low penetration level—for example, investment management, 11.4 percent; revocable trusts, 12.4 percent; and custody of securities, 13.4 percent. Often, such low penetration can be partially explained by the fact that trust customers use their lawyer's office as their mailing addresses. However, these results suggest that the firm may not be aggressively cross-selling many of its current customers.

These penetration figures show that in a significant number of block groups in the market area, not even one household patronizes particular offerings of the firm. For example, in approximately 25 percent of these block groups, not one household has a CD relationship with the firm. In addition, the correlation between the wealth characteristics of neighborhoods and the percentage of CD patrons is not very strong ($r = .34$). This would suggest that the firm's CD patrons are not distributed in perfect harmony with the level of wealth of neighborhoods. Thus, one may question whether its marketing resources are properly matched with its market opportunities.

The correlations between the firm's penetration at the block group level and high income or net worth are in general fairly high. However, that penetration cannot be fully explained by either measure of affluence. For example, the correlation coefficient between the firm's private banking penetration and the percentage of households in corresponding block groups is .59. This means that less than 36 percent (or $.59^2$) of the variation in block group wealth can be explained by the firm's penetration or, looked at in another way, that about 64 percent of the variation in block group wealth cannot be explained by the firm's penetration. This lack of relationship is somewhat of an underestimate in the context of the firm's market performance. Also, these relationships exclude all block groups with zero penetration. Yet in relation to the other services considered, private banking has one of the highest penetration levels.

While the firm has achieved significant penetration of the more affluent block groups, the variations in the penetration of its offerings are very high even among these block groups.

The lack of consistency between market opportunity and penetration is also reflected in the relationship between block group income characteristics and patronage. Logic would dictate that the firm allocate its marketing resources by marginal analysis. In other words, it should attempt to deploy its market resources in areas where they are likely to yield the greatest return and to gain its greatest penetration in the block groups that have the greatest level of affluence.

The firm's market strategy would indicate that it understands, in general terms, where the affluent reside within its trade area. However, the results of this analysis indicate that it is unable to distinguish among levels of wealth within the affluent market in general. This geodemographic analysis should be very useful as the firm targets its prospects and reallocates its marketing resources.

PENETRATION BY MARKET SEGMENT

The affluent block groups within a trade area can be categorized by constructing a multidimensional segmentation model. This model classifies each affluent block group within the trade area into financial service segments. The demographic/socioeconomic dimensions and codes for the affluent market segmentation matrix are given in Table 1.

Each affluent block group in the trade area can be categorized into a specific cell of the segmentation matrix. The dimensions of this matrix consist of:

D_1 Three levels of concentration of wage and salary income (high, medium, low).

D_2 Three levels of concentration of householders 65 years of age and over (high, medium, low).

D_3 Three levels of concentration of executive, manager, administrator concentration (high, medium, low).

D_4 Three levels of concentration of households with assets of $1 million or more (high, medium, low).

These dimensions have been shown to be correlates of financial service use. By categorizing each affluent block group, the firm will be able to determine where it has and has not penetrated significantly. This method also provides a "shorthand" indication of where market opportunities exist.

The penetration levels for the firm in the context of each cell of the ($3 \times 3 \times 3 \times 3$) segmentation matrix for each of the 14 affluent products and services are important performance indicators.

INDEX